Praise for Tobin Hart's

the FOUR VIRTUES

"This luminous book reflects the highest state of realized humanity. To read it is to be guided forward into discovering the basis for our finest selves. Rarely has there been a book of such exquisite wisdom, such potent truth about the nature and practice of virtue. (I will send it to all my friends who are in political office!)"

—**Jean Houston**, author of *The Wizard of Us*

"We seem to be at a point in human history when mystical unitive understanding, which was once the esoteric experienc of a few, is becoming present in a growing number of people. There is a new awakening to the potential of spiritual growth and the flowering of human society that it can bring. In this beautifully written book, Tobin Hart illuminates that path, skillfully applying his scholarship, experience, and insights to provide a vivid roadmap for the spiritual seeker."

—**Peter Laurence, EdD**,
director of Education as Transformation Project
at Wellesley College

"A work of wide learning and deep reflection, *The Four Virtues* eloquently teaches what is most important to learn: the art of living a meaningful life."

—**Pir Zia Inayat-Khan, PhD**, spiritual leader of
Sufi Order International and author of *Aracen Chivalry*

"Into this historic time of excessive change, fragmentation, speed, and deep spiritual hunger, Tobin Hart meets us and invites us to come through the thicket and stop—to see who we are and where we are now as a human species. He leads us on a simple footpath to a summit where he shares his vision of transformation out of a lifetime of experience as teacher and healer. Step by step, he then guides us into a clearing where he tells us stories that interweave insight and wisdom from sources Eastern and Western, psychological and spiritual, scientific and religious, ancient and modern, along with practical ways for tapping into the current of our own deepest inner natures where we may find a new way. This remarkable book is a treasured gift for teachers, therapists, counselors, and all those who wish to grow the soul."

—**Carolyn Toben**, author of *Recovering a Sense of the Sacred*

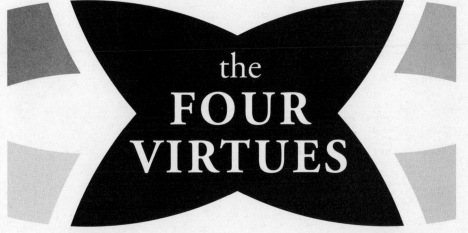

the
FOUR
VIRTUES

Presence

Heart

Wisdom

Creation

the FOUR VIRTUES

Tobin Hart, PhD

ATRIA PAPERBACK
New York London Toronto Sydney New Delhi

BEYOND WORDS
Hillsboro, Oregon

W

ATRIA PAPERBACK
A Division of Simon & Schuster, Inc.
1230 Avenue of the Americas
New York, NY 10020

BEYOND WORDS
20827 N.W. Cornell Road, Suite 500
Hillsboro, Oregon 97124-9808
503-531-8700 / 503-531-8773 fax
www.beyondword.com

Copyright © 2014 by Tobin Hart

All rights reserved, including the right to reproduce this book or portions thereof in any form whatsoever without prior written permission. For information address Atria Books/ Beyond Words Subsidiary Rights Department, 1230 Avenue of the Americas, New York, NY 10020.

Managing editor: Lindsay S. Brown
Editors: Sylvia Spratt, Emily Han
Copyeditor: Henry Covey
Proofreader: Jade Chan
Design: Devon Smith
Composition: William H. Brunson Typography Services

First Atria Paperback/Beyond Words trade paperback edition February 2014

ATRIA PAPERBACK and colophon are trademarks of Simon & Schuster, Inc. Beyond Words Publishing is an imprint of Simon & Schuster, Inc., and the Beyond Words logo is a registered trademark of Beyond Words Publishing, Inc.

For more information about special discounts for bulk purchases, please contact Simon & Schuster Special Sales at 1-866-506-1949 or business@simonandschuster.com.

The Simon & Schuster Speakers Bureau can bring authors to your live event. For more information or to book an event, contact the Simon & Schuster Speakers Bureau at 1-866-248-3049 or visit our website at www.simonspeakers.com.

Manufactured in the United States of America

10 9 8 7 6 5 4 3 2 1

Library of Congress Cataloging-in-Publication Date:

Hart, Tobin.
      The four virtues : presence, heart, wisdom, creation / Tobin Hart, PhD. — First Atria paperback/Beyond Words trade paperback edition.
          pages   cm
      Includes bibliographical references.
      1. Spirituality.   2. Spiritual life.   3. Virtues.   I. Title.
      BL624.H335   2014
      179'.9—dc23
                                                                    2013032941

ISBN 978-1-58270-447-0
ISBN 978-1-4767-3460-6 (ebook)

The corporate mission of Beyond Words Publishing, Inc.: *Inspire to Integrity*

Contents

PART IV: CREATION

17. Will and Willingness   255
18. Originality   273
19. Imagining   291
20. Calling   307

    Last Words   325
    Acknowledgments   329
    Index: Quizzes and Practices   331
    Notes   333

For Maia and Haley

PREFACE

Finally, I had just finished college. It had taken me four schools, but it was now done. Having made it through all those years from kindergarten on, I was presumably ready for the world. After all, that's what schooling is for: preparation for life. I thought, "I should know my way by now." I had packed up my stuff and taken it to my retired father's empty house, as he was spending the winter someplace warmer. The previous spring we had spread my mother's ashes at the beach after her long bout with cancer.

There I was, alone in this house, with no clue of what to do next. There was really no extraordinary tragedy I had suffered, no heroic act I could rest on. There was no military draft threatening to take me to a far-off land, and I was not really tied to anything, anyone, or anywhere. I had all the advantage and freedom that anyone should have. I had a fresh degree in hand, and yet I felt more lost than ever. I suppose the pain I felt was an amalgam of the grief, anxiety, and despair that seemed to have been building up inside me for as long as I could remember, and it had now materialized into a heavy boulder of a thing that felt like it was crushing me.

One afternoon a strange impulse welled up in me, not to go on some great journey or enlist in some noble or at least risky campaign but the overwhelming urge to repot houseplants. I don't think that I had ever watered a houseplant before, much less repotted them. Nevertheless, I found myself spontaneously doting over these green bits of life, carefully separating the small baby shoots from their parent plants into separate pots. With its tether cut and in its own pot, each shoot now had a new life. In the mornings, when the cold March air had warmed just enough, I would take them out for a stroll, placing them carefully in the sun on the front porch. Later in the day, as the sun and temperature fell, I would be sure to drop whatever I was doing wherever I was and bring them back inside to safety.

In the midst of my dark night, some green life called to me to nurture and be nurtured in this simple act. Something was moving. But the pain was not moving away; in fact, it only seemed to be growing darker and deeper.

A few days later I was walking through the house when a book seemed to jump out at me from its shelf. It was a book I thought I might have seen before. I then recalled that years before, I had been sitting on the sofa in our old house and my mother was trying to share this book with me. A young teenager at the time, I was already too difficult to be around to have any of it, so our strained conversation lasted a couple of minutes at best. But now, these many years later, and in this desperate moment, I was ready for something—anything—and this book seemed to be offered. This was an extraordinarily odd book to have in my very mainstream parents' house, as it was about karma, the Eastern law of cause and effect. But even odder was that the book was *Edgar Cayce's Story of Karma*, written by perhaps the most famous psychic of the twentieth century. Sitting on that same sofa with my houseplants nearby, I opened to a random page and began to read. I had only read a few lines when the words suddenly pierced my longing like an arrow to the heart. It didn't give me answers, exactly, but it stirred and opened something within me. I didn't know whether things actually worked that way—that the consequences of our choices are somehow carried over from lifetime to lifetime, that life is about learning, that relationships in some way endure—but the ideas acted like an electrical current applied to my insides, jolting something awake and offering up a broader view. Of course, I was primed for something, and a great number of other ideas might also have hit the mark then, but those ideas were what did it in that moment.

Two things struck me like lightning illuminating a landscape. The first was that I was responsible for my life. Welcome to emerging adulthood! Sure, things happen, the world turns, grace falls or it doesn't, but in some way I knew that it was up to me at a level I hadn't realized. I guess the message had been there all along: actions have consequences. But this was on a whole different level. It was relationship to and the quality of my love, joy, knowing, integrity, and even my suffering that was suddenly in my lap. I wasn't prepared for the thought of that much responsibility—with no one or nothing to blame. It didn't minimize circumstances past or present we don't have control of; it just changed the relationship with them.

This insight was both liberating and terrifying. "Wow. It's up to me," followed almost instantly by, "Yikes! What do I do now?" There seemed to be a gulf between that level of radical responsibility and my capacity to create or handle my life. For example, how could I make really wise choices or open my heart fully and in the right direction? How could I even notice what might be important to pay attention to and what might be less so? It felt like asking the dog to mow the lawn; however game I was, I just didn't seem to have what I needed to make this work.

But I could clearly see—feel, really—where the epicenter of this process lay. And this was the second part of my little epiphany. It occurred to me that I had been looking in the wrong direction and too much at the surface of things. The direction was first inward, inside me, and in some mysterious way, it opened up to a bigger world I had been hungry for all along. What I realized was that while all the possibility and mystery of the world lay in front of me, it took certain capacities—certain ways of knowing and being—to really meet it, receive it, and bring it within reach. In time I came to see that this inner attention didn't further my selfishness or narcissism, so far as I could tell. Paradoxically, it had just the opposite effect of opening up the world and my connection to it.

It was also clear that I wasn't exactly *making* this happen, and this seemed key. It was more like I was getting out of my own way. Like my little plants that knew how to grow or a wound that knows how to heal, there was a current flowing, some mystery at work under the surface by whatever name. The effort seemed to be a living balance of will and willingness, intention and surrender, holding tight and letting go.

Within a matter of days, things started moving inside and out for me. Quite remarkably and out of the blue, a job, graduate school, strange and helpful people, and what turned out to be a life landed in my lap in what seemed like a miraculous turn of fortune. There were still plenty of struggles, but now there was a sense of aliveness, depth, and a hint of direction. Questions I had held for nearly my whole life started to point the way. How do we find our own way? What is this life about? That's what I knew I had to pursue. I have remained a student of those big questions and mostly remain surprised by where they have led. As the philosopher Martin Buber said, "All journeys have secret destinations of which the traveler is unaware."[1]

On one cool, brilliantly clear fall day about two years later, something happened that seemed to follow the trail of my questions. My friend Art had been initiating me into hiking the High Peaks of the ancient and still-wild Adirondack Mountains in upstate New York. Our route this day was to head up Gothics Mountain. The trail was several miles of a climb mostly through dense forest without much of a view. I had gotten past the enthusiastic first phase of hiking ("This is great. What a beautiful day!") and moved predictably into the "whine zone" ("I'm tired. This is no fun. How much farther? Can't we think of something better to do?") Eventually, I settled into a steady rhythm that served as a kind of walking meditation. My eyes had been focused mostly down on the trail in front of me for miles, watching as each foot found its next move over and over again. After several hours, we approached the final ascent, made our way up the last steep rock face, and summited—and then something suddenly popped. As I walked into that lapis sky and saw the stunning view all around, feeling the sun on my face, the crisp air filling my lungs, I was ecstatic. With tears rolling down my cheeks, I started spontaneously singing a song—*that song*: "The hills are alive . . ." from *The Sound of Music*. I was so overwhelmed that I didn't know what else to do. My friend must have thought I was nuts. I couldn't describe what was happening; it was too big, and I had no words. Somehow it felt like coming home in the most profound sense I could imagine. And then *I* disappeared. Peace and the energy of creation were all that was left. Oneness, perfection, unity—no words were enough. An hour and a half later, I awoke on the top of the mountain, feeling more alive than I had ever felt.

That moment has been an enduring touchstone for me. Whatever else it has done, I think that the most important thing this secret destination revealed was that the inside and the outside, the one and the many, are somehow one and the same. This paradox didn't make sense through the lenses of logic or physics, but there it was. The question that arose and that has stuck with me all this time is, How does this get brought down to earth? That is, How, in the middle of our very human lives, do we find our way into that deep connection and communion?

It has been more than thirty years since I repotted those houseplants and made that climb. One of my daughters (the "expensive one," as she describes herself) has just graduated from college. My other daughter (the just-as-expensive one, I fear) has just started. While they are both immersed in all that new beginnings can bring, I can see that they are a little worried about next steps. Both of them are in better shape than I was at the time; this is not hard to see. But after an entire lifetime of schooling, do they have what they need to pursue a meaningful life? Aside from some professional skill or training—which is hardly a guarantee of a job these days, much less a lifetime of fulfillment—have they learned how to thrive, to tap their genius and joy? I know they have had some important teachers in and outside of school—people and situations that cut deeply into what matters or that open up new ways of seeing. And I know they have picked up pieces from peers, family, religion, sports, and those many life lessons that shape us in youth. But it is hard to see that they have what they need to find their way into the depths. The same can be said of the students I've taught at various levels, my clients in therapy, and many of us, for that matter, at whatever age—eighteen or eighty—with or without the luxury of plenty of schooling and especially in the face of today's realities. How *do* we find our way and help others find theirs?

At this unprecedented moment in history, we have for the first time access to the secrets from across the wisdom traditions, from the great souls around the globe, and from the human sciences. Brought together, this incredible body of knowledge and wisdom helps us recognize characteristics of humanity at its best. When brought together, these insights—Eastern and Western, psychological and spiritual, scientific and religious, ancient and modern—form a matrix for growing our humanity and finding our way.

In the pages that follow, we will explore four living virtues that lead toward deep connection and communion with the world and with ourselves. We can think of these as powers, capacities, or cardinal directions. Drawn from across traditions and time, from neuroscience to ancient wisdom, they help us build, balance, and integrate our psychological and spiritual life on earth.

These are not beliefs or commandments or anything of that sort. Instead, these are dynamic human qualities that appear essential for a life of flourishing, fulfillment, and integrity. In order to tap the depths of our humanity, we have to embody these powers. In other words, these four virtues can only be grown from the inside out and then enacted in our interaction with the world. These have become inner arts and inner technologies for me, as they have for others throughout time and tradition. Although they never guarantee it, they make it possible to get out of our own way and, in doing so, bring our deepest life within reach. In the smallest and the largest ways, I have come to see how these enduring virtues have brought my own heart and wisdom into life and helped me recognize beauty, rekindle awe, and find my own voice.

They help open the aperture of consciousness so that we may meet the world deeply from a profound place within. That's what this is all about: meeting the world, deep to deep.

INTRODUCTION

It's not that we want to sleep our lives away.
It's that it requires a certain amount of energy,
certain capacities for taking the world into our consciousness,
certain real powers of body and soul to be a match for reality.

—M. C. Richards

Reality these days can be intense. Stress is implicated in the top four causes of death in the United States.[1] Global climate, economic, environmental, and political change wreak all sorts of havoc and constantly require new adaptations. Global population has just topped seven billion; thirty years ago, we were at three billion.[2] The gap between the haves and the have-nots grows wider; today and every day 870 million people don't have enough to eat,[3] and unthinkable violence reaches across the globe and even into our neighborhood schools.

In many ways, the reality we all face is increasingly complex and not always obvious. For example, the effect of technology goes all the way down from the global network to our social networks to our neural nets. Technology is shaping us inside and out, from our lifestyles to the functioning of our brains. Alongside the unprecedented potential inherent in this information age, we also can find ourselves deluged with surround-sound violence and sexuality, sucked downstream by materialism and marketing, pushed along with hurried schedules and instant communication as we live as electronic nodes on an information superhighway.

The US military has an acronym for this intensity we're in the midst of: "VUCA," which stands for volatility, uncertainty, complexity, and ambiguity. In the face of all this, it may be hard to avoid becoming dizzy or numb, drugged or distracted, angry or quietly desperate. Suicide and homicide are the second and third leading cause of teen deaths. According to the National Institute of Mental Health, half of the adult population will have a diagnosable mental disorder over the course of their lifetimes. *Half*. In any given year, one-quarter of the US population is diagnosed with one or more psychiatric disorders. Thirty-five million Americans have severe depression, and twenty million have an anxiety disorder. By 2020 depression is predicted to be the second most common health problem in the world.[4]

Even among those of us who are doing OK, there often remains a hunger for something more. We're on the search for something—money, romance, car keys, chocolate—but also for something that stirs deeper down. Some of us have been searching for

- a secret that would unlock understanding;
- the element we belong to;
- an opening into a bigger world; or
- something we can put ourselves on the line for.

Deep down we search for *our* life, one packed with meaning and fulfillment, substance and satisfaction, love and liberty.

So in the midst of this growing complexity and intensity, how can we be a match for this reality? How do we lead the *really* Good Life? How do we find our way and help others find theirs?

Maybe what is most remarkable is that we actually know something about this.

We know that what is essential is not merely more computing or purchasing power, more facts to be memorized, or simply something to believe in. Instead, the essentials are inner virtues or capacities that are activated—switched on and embodied. These inner powers open consciousness and thus enable us to contact and understand the world. The world opens and is revealed to us to the extent that we can open and receive it. This is a kind of physics of the unfolding mind.

The process of opening to the world requires both the psychological and spiritual; when viewed together, these can often seem odd and paradoxical. The psychological develops our will, and the spiritual asks us to be willing. The psychological strengthens our sense of self, and the spiritual asks us to be selfless. The former helps us differentiate and individuate, and the latter invites us to lose our self-separateness. We'll see in the following chapters just how the virtues work together and that without their integration we can have trouble getting out of our own way.

In the end, what is clear is that the most ancient and enduring depictions of the life well-lived—the *Beautiful*, the *Good*, and the *True*—are dependent largely on the quality of our consciousness, the inner life. For example, goodness moves always and only through the center of our hearts. As Antoine de Saint-Exupéry's Little Prince knew, "One sees clearly only with the heart. Anything that is essential is invisible to the eyes."[5] Truth—revealed, discovered, and constructed—has to do with seeing from a greater height or seeing into the heart of something, which was Thomas Aquinas's definition of wisdom. Beauty emerges through an opening within us. As naturalist John Muir understood, "The rivers flow not past, but through us."[6] As we grow inward, we open consciousness to our deepest nature, our dearest neighbor, and to the mystery of this existence.

This approach is not about adopting certain beliefs or morals or naming the divine in one thing as opposed to another. Regardless of the particular origin story or theological debates on the nature of the divine, the underlying virtues or capacities and qualities are surprisingly universal, crossing and blending religious, cultural, and intellectual lines.

Thanks largely to those wise explorers both ancient and modern whose extraordinary lives have become signposts, certain qualities for living the deep life are recognizable across time and culture. For example, in *Hamlet* Shakespeare reminds us of the centrality of authenticity through Polonius's famous line, "To thine own self be true"; Nelson Mandela's life reminds us of virtuous qualities like perseverance, integrity, and hope; Emerson and Thoreau speak about communion, especially with nature. From Gandhi to Goethe, Helen Keller to Jiddu Krishnamurti, Einstein to Meister Eckhart, and Mohammad to Merton, the list goes ever on. Inevitably, these broad principles are realized in the unique particularities of an individual's life and circumstance. Integrated, they bring the puzzle pieces together into a unified whole.

Matrix

In what follows, enduring insights from various traditions, along with contemporary knowledge from the sciences, are distinguished, unpacked, and then brought together to form a kind of matrix—capacities essential for developing the inner life. The word *matrix* itself describes just how this energy lives within us. In Latin, the word means "pregnant animal." The matrix is "the place or medium where or through which something is developed"—a *womb*.[7] We are this womb. Meister Eckhart, the fourteenth-century Dominican sage, noted that we are indeed pregnant, and that our progeny is nothing less than everything. He said, "We are meant to be mothers of God."[8] Our very purpose here is to somehow birth divinity through our humanity. We make this happen by bringing these powers together within us and taking them into the world. The implications are as extraordinary now as they were heretical for Eckhart then.

This matrix extends out in four cardinal directions. The fourfold theme emerges across traditions and time: the four compass points, the four seasons, the four rivers flowing from the Garden of Eden in Genesis, and the four elements in nature, to name a few. Each direction will be used here to represent an overarching virtue: Presence, Heart, Wisdom, and Creation.

These four virtues and directions have been invoked by other names throughout history—names that may enrich our understanding of just how central and universal these capacities are. From the ancient Greeks to contemporary thinkers, the good life is often characterized as *beautiful*, *good*, and *true*. To these three is added the capacity of *Voice*—tied with the fourth cardinal direction of Creation. Why this addition? Creation is the energy moving through all things and is embodied personally in our ability to find our own voice, imagine new possibilities, take action, and create our own life as we will it to be. As we will see, Creation is essential in balancing the other three directions and in bringing the power of presence, heart, and wisdom into the world through us.

All directions reflect a portion of us and a potion—a medicine—for us. In some traditions, the words *medicine* and *power* are used interchangeably. These directions are powers that can be used for knowing and navigating in the world. But they also have the remarkable capacity to not only enrich us—the "I"—but also to enrich the "we" and the world at large. An act of compassion or creativity, for example, sends ripples not only through us as individuals but also simultaneously through the world.

As we move through each of these four cardinal directions—presence, heart, wisdom, and creation—we will distinguish and develop sixteen specific identifiable qualities (four qualities within each of the four virtues), or ways of being, that can be activated and grown from the inside out. The point of the journey ahead is to help us recognize, activate, and refine these essential virtues within us so that we may bring them into the world. As German writer Johann Wolfgang von Goethe said, "To locate yourself in the infinite, you must distinguish and then combine."[9]

Throughout this book, we'll explore these capacities through principles and practices that help bring these ideas to life within and between us. The practices are easy to try yourself and can also be used collaboratively. They are simple and easily modified and are there mostly to help us get out of our own way.

Alongside these practices, which are located at the end of most chapters, you will also find a simple self-scoring quiz for each of these sixteen qualities. There is also a quiz at the end of this introduction that will give you a sense of the relative strength of each of your four cardinal directions. These practices and quizzes will help clarify strengths and point toward trailheads for growth. If you do choose to take the quizzes, be sure not to take any results too seriously; they are designed to help reflect on the themes of this text, not to put you in a box. In addition, the website www.thefourvirtues.com provides further resources and support that you may find useful.

In many ways this book is modular in that you can jump into any section and that section will stand on its own. However, in its entirety, the book follows a developmental progression in which each virtue builds on the preceding one. Each chapter will help you notice these essential virtues and their specific qualities within you and in those around you. It will help clarify what they mean and how they manifest and remind us what they can do for us. Finally, the book offers ways to grow and develop these capacities through understanding, inspiration, and practice. One of the main reasons in presenting this material together as a matrix is the importance of balance and integration. When these four virtues are out of balance (lots of compassion but less discernment, for example), we may find ourselves spending energy in ways that may drain us rather than sustain us. Recognizing strengths as well as qualities that are less well developed will serve as resources and signposts as we find our way.

This work may be used individually or within a group or class and in both psychological and spiritual contexts. Activating and refining our human potentials for presence, heart, wisdom, and creation can be thought of as a kind of curricula for the inner life, no matter your creed, race, age, gender, or orientation of any sort.

In part 1, we will explore how the ancient and enduring notion of the *Beautiful* is tied to the virtue of presence. Russian novelist Fyodor Dostoevsky made a dramatic claim in his book *The Idiot*: "Beauty will save the world." Beauty is not just about mere ornamentation but it also represents an art and science of quality. The inner arts we speak of throughout this book do not give us beauty but instead enable a shift and opening of consciousness to perceive beauty. Of course, a pretty face or a beautiful sunset has some inherent quality, but we recognize and resonate with the world depending on the ability to open to it. We don't merely want to see beauty; we want to become part of it.

Developing presence involves radical *openness*, refining the *senses*, and *focusing* and steadying the *witnessing* mind so that we have it rather than it having us, such as when anxiety or addiction controls our lives. Presence provides both a kind of

mental hygiene, or steadying, as well as transcendence, or moving beyond current limits. We'll examine how these capacities are
relevant in the process of great science and in the arts as well as in
the quality and depth of daily life. To be present is to be awake
in the here and now, and while it is natural, it doesn't happen
automatically; it requires certain energy, certain "real powers of
body and soul." We'll see how the *Beautiful* and presence might
just save the world.

Part 2 explores the heart. There are many moral commandments suggesting the path to goodness, but great souls throughout
time show us that mature virtue—the *good*—arises not simply
from adhering to a script but from an interior capacity. The heart
provides the opening for a life informed by compassion and passion. The heart is recognized by the warmth generated in a loving
hug as well as the sizzle of passionate desire. The heart provides
that energy source for the *good*, a fundamental and universal ethic
for engaging the world. To love or to have heart is the great turn
recognized throughout all the great traditions as both the goal
and the path of a life well lived. Good comes as we move beyond
mere self-interest and feel into the hearts of others, as well as when
we tap deeply into our hearts to find courage. This is about right
action that stands on the foundation of care and understanding.
It is supported by realization of interdependence and, with it,
responsibility. We'll strive to locate the rightful place of desire,
which is so often confusing in life. *Empathy, compassion, feeling,*
and *belonging* are the main qualities—the powers and the medicines—grown from the inside out.

Part 3 dives into wisdom—the *true*. We don't exactly have
wisdom as if it were something to possess. Instead, one acts wisely
or not. Where love offers warmth, wisdom brings light. This is
the search for what rings true, the quest for insight over illusion.
Wisdom works to unlock our unique genius and deeply tap our

sources of *guidance*. Further, we will explore the ability to see beyond what is given into new *possibility*, *discernment* at the crossroad of decisions, and the development of *clarity* over confusion.

There is a natural overflowing abundance of the world, a creative force that pushes weeds to crack through concrete, the child that draws, paints, and plays. The primary element of the universe may just be that creative energy, that overflowing abundance that makes things grow and go. Our humble human counterpart is our own ability to create (the trailhead for part 4). Creation is not restricted to the artist but instead is about how we bring ourselves authentically into the world both through our doing and being. This final step brings the inner life into full contact with the outer world and, in so doing, enacts it. It cannot be done otherwise.

We live between forest and garden, between the wild, untamed, and uncertain on one hand and the known, cultivated, and predictable on the other. We need both of these—the garden is our safe home base, and the forest stimulates and challenges us at the edge of our understanding. The force of creation lives between forest and garden and invites us into adventure. So this compass point is about finding a way to bring forth our aliveness—our own ideas, visions, voice, and being—into the world. It develops the strength and clarity of *voice*—creative, authentic expression in whatever form. When we find our own voice, we have a channel life can flow through. This involves developing the power of *will*, the energy that moves, manifests, and makes things happen, and recognizing the *willingness* to allow those currents to move through us. It requires the power of *imagination*, celebrates difference and *originality*, and brings us to the knee of service and even *calling*, where our deep gladness meets the world's great need.

In the end, these four essential virtues do not give us wisdom; they give us the perspective to act wisely (or not). They do not give us beauty but instead enable the shift in attention and appreciation that opens consciousness to perceive beauty. They do not make us good, but they help us find the ground for compassionate action. They do not give us creativity, but they help us imagine and use our own. Like a compass, the four directions are not the path itself; instead they help us orient ourselves so that we may find our way.

Drawn from the scattered brotherhood and sisterhood of wise souls, the wisdom traditions, and contemporary science, these are the inner arts and inner technologies essential to place a claim on the meaningful life, helping us find our way. This work serves as a *field guide* to the inner life, enabling us to recognize and unlock extraordinary potential for integrity and love, genius and joy, and to bring the best of our humanity into the world.

❖   ❖   ❖   ❖

This first quiz is a simple way to reflect on the balance between the four cardinal directions. There are ten sets of four words below. Rank the words in each row on a scale of 1–4 (where 1 describes you the least and 4 describes you the most). Although it may be challenging, try to give each word a separate rank (1, 2, 3, or 4). For those items that seem impossible to rank, you may have ties.

QUIZ

Example: joy: 4 (*most like me*); friendship: 2; awe: 1 (*least like me*); freedom: 3

a.	sensitivity	empathy	guidance	doing
b.	in tune	understanding	discerning	mastering

c.	focused	compassionate	knowledgeable	originality
d.	silence	warmth	light	voice
e.	sensations	feelings	thoughts	service
f.	beauty	goodness	truth	creating
g.	appreciating	caring	clarity	imagination
h.	openness	intimate	objective	adventure
i.	aware	belonging	questioning	risking
j.	awe	love	wisdom	expression

For each vertical column, add the ten numbers and write the total below. For each column the total will be a number between 10 and 40. Your totals will provide a rough sense of the relative strength of each direction as you see it.

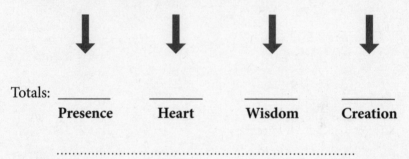

Totals: _____   _____   _____   _____

Presence   **Heart**   **Wisdom**   **Creation**

....

Throughout the book, the quizzes that follow (sixteen in total; four within each virtue) will provide a swift way to assess your own capacities. A low score on a quiz may point toward a direction for growth. A high score may reflect that your capacity for empathy or imagination, for example, is a great strength, something to affirm and own. Also, we know from experience that at times we can rely on a particular strength too much, neglecting our other assets. Our great compassion, for example, may be in need of the balance of wise discernment so that we are not overwhelmed or taken advantage of. While these capacities may be universal, the way they live in each of us is unique; we have to find our own way.

The chapters and quizzes that follow will help bring precision and depth of understanding to the nature of presence, heart, wisdom, and creation. In so doing, these virtues become easier to see, grow, and bring together within us.

Presence

Heart

Wisdom

Creation

PART I

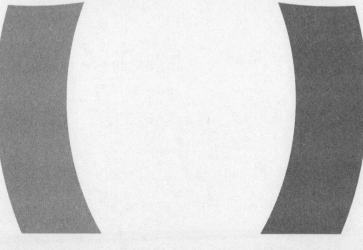

1

THE BEAUTIFUL

Beauty will save the world.

—Fyodor Dostoevsky

"In our family, there was no clear line between religion and fly fishing."[1] And so the story begins in Norman Maclean's gorgeous and poignant family memoir, *A River Runs Through It*. The story centers around Paul, Norman's irreverent, loveable, and ultimately tragic brother who became a good storyteller himself, both at home and at work as a newspaper reporter. Paul was also a serious gambler, having gotten behind in the big stud poker game in nearby Hot Springs. But most significantly, he was a truly great fly fisherman. Maclean described numinous scenes in which his brother casts for trout in Montana's Big Blackfoot River. "He is my brother and an artist and when a four-and-a-half ounce rod is in his hand he is a major artist."[2] Norman and his father, a Presbyterian minister, find themselves transfixed as they watch him. Even strangers and passersby are caught in awe as they're hooked by his artistry, his sheer beauty.

Later in the story, when his father asks for some information about his brother, Norman replies, "'All I really know is that he was a fine fisherman.' 'You know more than that,' my father said, 'He was beautiful.' 'Yes' I said. He was beautiful.'"[3] This is surely not what most men in rural Montana in the 1940s would say to or about one another. And yet they both knew that what they saw and what they felt was beauty.

The *beautiful* somehow embodies transcendence and complete immanence all at once. It shows us the reach and the depth of possibility and perfection and does so in the immediacy of an act or an art that is greater than the sum of its parts.

It is not simply the surface that makes the *beautiful*. Sometimes we mistake the shell for the nut. Instead, beauty reflects some underlying quality that is revealed when form and perception meet and open to one another. Take the beauty in works of art as an example. As psychiatrist Roberto Assagioli said, "There is much more than mere aesthetic value; they constitute living forces, almost living entities, embodying a power that has suggestive and creative effects."[4] Michelangelo's *David* comes immediately to mind. We recognize it, we talk of it, yet it remains difficult to define; we might call it *quality*. We live according to an intuitive sense of its meaning. When we are awake to it, we recognize it by its resonance within us.

Beauty is not just reserved for the artist creating a sculpture but takes endless forms—a perfect pitch in baseball, a meal prepared with special attention to detail, a perfect sunset, the deep peace of an infant asleep in loving arms. We hunger for it and are nourished by it, not just in creating art but also through giving our attention to the way the lawn is mowed or the rod is cast.

Philosopher Alfred North Whitehead went so far as to say that "the teleology of the universe is directed to the production of Beauty."[5] Even the supposed cold aloofness of science has beauty at its roots. Robert Augros and George Stanciu, in *The New Story of Science*, wrote that "all of the most eminent physicists of the twentieth century agree that beauty is the primary standard for scientific truth."[6] French mathematician and theoretical physicist Henri Poincaré understood the role of beauty in science in this way: "[The scientist] studies it because he takes pleasure in it; and he takes pleasure in it because it is beautiful. If nature were not beautiful, it would not be worth knowing and life would not be worth living."[7]

Beauty provides a doorway, gateway, or bridge inviting us from one state to another, enabling us to expand our everyday realities and respond to something that is both greater than ourselves and intimately part of us. By entering that doorway and opening into that communion, we are brought closer to the experience of the union between our inner and outer worlds, between the visible and the invisible. When not hanging out with lions and witches through the wardrobe, C. S. Lewis said it this way: "We do not want merely to see beauty . . . We want something else that can hardly be put into words—to be united with the beauty we see, to pass into it, to receive it into ourselves, to bathe in it, to become part of it."[8]

Simply beholding beauty can be transformative. A bouquet of flowers brightens a day, time in nature seems to feed us, gorgeous surroundings or a stunning meal opens our senses, moods, and more. Beauty can even serve as medicine.

My friend Jane had been a victim of childhood abuse, had a mentally ill mother, and as an adult struggled with eating disorders, addiction, and depression. Yet she had pulled herself up, held herself together, and was successful in many respects that we would recognize—college degrees, meaningful work. But finally, after all those years and all the effort to make life work and to keep the wounds of the past wrapped, she unraveled. She was prepared to kill herself and fell headlong into a very dark night.

There was nowhere else to turn. She was admitted to a psychiatric hospital, having no clue about where the bottom lay on this very steep descent. The hospital kept her safe for a while. She received talk therapy, was started on medication, participated in group time, and had a place to sleep and food to eat, but there was one thing more. And this, she said, is what made the difference.

Each afternoon Jane discovered that a projector was set up on a table in one of the meeting rooms. Beautiful pictures—mainly scenes from nature—were projected on a screen. Nothing was said about them. There wasn't even an announcement made that this was happening; it was just an opportunity to sit and watch.

It was these images—and only these images—that she claims saved her life. Somehow the depth of beauty sends a "ping" into our own depths, a message of wholeness and possibility. In and of itself, beauty is nourishment and a necessity. It serves, as it did for Jane, as medicine and mirror.

Beauty may indeed exist outside the knower, like a great work of art or a magnificent tree, but it is comprehended or covered over, enacted or ignored by the human mind and heart. A key to beauty is that we cocreate it through the nature of our presence. Stripped of her defenses, Jane was just wide open and available to these images. As we open awareness—our feelings, thoughts, sensations, and energy—to something or someone, we can see what's beneath the surface. As we dive in, the world unfolds before us and within us. Like a great naturalist, we begin to see more richness, more depth, more subtlety, and, ultimately, more beauty. Expanding perception in this way may be a step through the wardrobe into an even deeper and richer world. William Blake, English poet and mystic, told us, "If the doors of perception were cleansed, everything would appear to man as it is, infinite. For man has closed himself up, till he sees all things thro' narrow chinks of his cavern."[9]

Maybe each individual's perception is in accordance with the degree to which he or she is alive and awake. In this way, the *beautiful* is codependent with presence. The *beautiful* does not reveal itself *except* by both the investment of our attention and openness or willingness to receive the other.

I remember dropping one of my daughters off at swim practice one afternoon. The indoor pool facility was next to a small lake. A former student who was visiting rode along so that we might squeeze in a little more time to talk. We went for a short walk along the lake, which I sometimes did when waiting for swim practice to end. I had been mentioning something about longing to live on a beautiful lake and must have implied that this one was not as beautiful as I would hope for. She hesitated in our walk and said, "You know, right now this is the most beautiful lake I have ever seen."

I knew that she had seen many lakes that we both knew were more gorgeous than this one, with nicer shorelines, clearer water, and greater expanses. But I could see that she was dead serious. She was open to beholding the beauty in front of her in this moment. I suddenly wondered what I had been shutting out through some judgment, how I had been filtering beauty out rather than taking it in, how I had put this lake in a category rather than making contact with it in this moment.

I have not passed by that lake since without seeing it in a new light. Sure, I know there is more beautiful water out there, but most days I can see that it *is* beautiful. Beauty reveals itself to the extent that we open to it. How *do* we open to it?

Presence

Musician Warren Zevon led a full life. He wrote and performed songs with depth and irreverence, and he did it his way. His dark humor, political commentary, and keen irony came through all his work. If you don't recognize his name you might recognize such sacred ballads as "Werewolves of London." *Rolling Stone* magazine placed Zevon alongside Neil Young, Jackson Brown, and Bruce Springsteen as one of the most important artists of the 1970s. He wrestled with alcoholism, collaborated with a host of some of the most famous musicians and authors, retreated from and renewed his career several times, was a frequent guest band leader on the *David Letterman Show*, and won two posthumous Grammy awards for his album *The Wind*. A great creative talent to be sure, we wouldn't say that he was a great role model. He wouldn't have, either. His 1991 solo album was entitled *Mr. Bad Example*. At age fifty-five, he was diagnosed with inoperable lung cancer and elected not to pursue any treatment, fearing it might interfere with his musical abilities. He spent much of his remaining time working on a final album, joined by guest musicians, including Bruce Springsteen, Ry Cooder, and Tom Petty. In his last year of life, he was the sole guest on an hour-long Letterman show. On this evening, as he was nearing his own end, having lived this extraordinary life, Letterman asked if he had any insight or advice to give about living. His response: "Enjoy every sandwich."[10]

What?

Have you ever eaten a meal and realized that you really hadn't tasted any of it? Have you ever talked with someone and realized that they weren't listening to you or maybe you to them? Have you simply operated on autopilot, without really being where you are or in what you were doing? Zevon's hard-won revelation and his advice about the meaningful life is precisely about being in the middle of what we're doing; it's about being present. To be awake in the middle of this moment, or a sandwich, helps bring it and us to life—the taste of the food, the blue of the sky, the richness of the person we're speaking with, or even the tension in our own shoulders, rooted in some concern that is hidden just out of awareness. Without presence, we just go through the motions, unaware and unawake, without much flavor, feeling, or color. Nutritionists know that it is not merely what we eat but especially what our bodies absorb that determines how much nourishment the food provides. In the same way, it is not just what we do but how rich the experience is that really nourishes our lives. Remarkably, simply being present to our surroundings awakens and reveals a world right under our noses, including our sandwiches. Presence is about being awake in life.

Here is another way to speak of it: presence opens knowing. The sacred texts of the world's wisdom traditions are often depicted as *living words*, alive on the page. But these living words, while right in front of us, are not always so easy to comprehend. Their mysterious meaning is somehow encrypted and compressed. This is why so many traditions invite us to return to the words again and again in order to see what light might be revealed this time around.

Similarly, the "text" that is the person or situation in front of us, as well as the world as a whole, are living words, too, awaiting expansion in order to be more fully understood, more fully tasted, more nourishing. Their richness, beauty, and dimensionality already exist here and now but must be decompressed to be realized. To gain access to the mysteries and reveal the meaning, whether it's learning a secular text or knowing one's neighbor, we have to break the code.

So how do we break it? The symbol and the surface will disclose itself only to the degree that we open to it. The instruction to return to the words is an invitation to enter into relationship with the symbols and signs and allow ourselves to both open to them and be further opened *by* them. This is like a two-headed key opening a series of locks that lead simultaneously into ourselves and into the other, the data, the sandwich. The code is broken, the words come alive, and the world is opened to us only through a corresponding opening of consciousness within us, a kind of *reciprocal revelation*. This highlights that *what* we know is bound to *how* we know. And this *how* has a lot to do with presence— *knowledge by presence*.

While we come into the world wide open, we learn to modulate our awareness as we grow. Over time, this can even put us in a kind of suspended animation where things don't fully register, where we find ourselves just going through the motions like some machine.

Early one morning in a Washington, DC, Metro station, a middle-aged man was playing his violin. During the forty-five minutes he played, about eleven hundred people passed by. Only six people stopped during that time, and about twenty threw money into his open violin case as they walked by, keeping their normal paces. He didn't do too badly; he collected thirty-two dollars. The person who paid most attention was a three-year-old boy, his mother towing him along. The boy seemed absorbed, but the mother finally tugged on him, hard, to move him along. All the while the boy kept his head turned, fixed on the violinist. The same scene played out with several other children.

Who was the subway violinist? Joshua Bell, one of the most talented musicians in the world, playing one of the most intricate pieces ever written on a violin worth three-and-a-half million dollars. Two days before, he had played a sold-out concert in Boston, with tickets averaging one hundred dollars. *The Washington Post* organized this subway concert as part of a social experiment.[11] The results beg some questions: What are we missing? How can we stay awake to beauty in the middle of living day to day?

Psychologist Rollo May suggested that "the deeper aspects of awareness are activated to the extent that the person is committed to the encounter."[12] This takes engagement, even commitment, like when we are really willing to listen to another person deeply or give time and attention to this moment or this work in order to woo the world to reveal itself. May went on to say that this engagement must be followed by an openness or receptivity, "holding [oneself] alive to hear what being may speak."[13]

Although it can sound pretty simple, staying present is not automatic or easy. And these days there are tremendous forces working against presence. We are invited to pop a pill if we hurt in any way. We are offered endless distractions to keep us buzzing inside and out, and the seductiveness of such distractions will only increase as competition and technology vie for more of our attention by streaming more stimulation to ever more sophisticated devices. It looks like even our brains are changing in response to the technology, reinforcing a capacity for distraction rather than depth.[14]

It can be difficult to keep balance, staying awake and aware in the midst of all these tugs on our attention. If aliens were trying to control the population without us catching on, I think maybe this is just how they would do it: Keep the flashy stimulation coming, appeal to our lower desires for pleasure and power, give us plenty of products to modulate our sensation, and keep us wanting more. Don't get me wrong; I like my devices and distractions as much as the next person, but too much of certain stimulation narrows and numbs and can lead to addictions—more violence, more buzz, more stuff—in a way that is manipulated by marketing rather than the drive toward growth. Like an addict, our awareness becomes myopic. Because our awareness is a foundation for action, our choices risk being driven not by wakefulness, choice, and growth but instead by habit, manipulation, and reaction. The more primitive parts of the brain are stimulated by this flash, violence, and sex that evoke a kind of immediate instinctual desire to grab what we want or retaliate for some slight.

In this age of overwhelming opportunities for indulgence, the greater the stream of distraction, the greater the need for balance and awareness of both our own well-being and the world around us. The good news is that there already exists tried-and-true inner technology to cultivate greater balance and wakefulness that may even end up modifying the very structure of one's brain.

Silence

Silence is vital to the inner art and technology of presence. As we quiet ourselves inwardly—focusing on the breath, witnessing our thoughts, finding ourselves absorbed in nature, or unwinding on a walk—the chattering mind starts to recede and our experience somehow becomes more spacious. Through this process, we are brought nearer to the heart of a vibrant stillness that is so essential for a balanced life, especially in the din of today's world around us and the buzz of our thoughts inside us.

Silence and stillness give us a chance to recalibrate body and mind and recover, as T. S. Eliot called it, the "still point of the turning world."[15] Silence involves resting, pausing, and listening to an inner rhythm. Fast food and fast lives invite us to push through, but we know the value of renewal in a moment's pause, a deep breath, a little nap, a gentle hug, a cup of tea.

Neurobiology offers its own kind of explanation for the value of silence and stillness. The "rest principle" implies that an actively used neurological connection will become "stronger" if it is allowed to "rest" briefly.[16] One possibility is that silence and stillness of mind may enable intentional "resting" and thereby engender a follow-up "quickening" or deepening of certain neurological processes. This is the breakthrough stage of the creative process, the *Aha!* or *Eureka!* moment that comes in the middle of a shower or good walk, when there is a shift in consciousness, a clearing in our minds, and an access to some fresh intelligence.

Silence also provides access to the depths. In Persian poetry, the poet often refers to themselves by name at the end of the poem as a sort of signature. In five hundred odes, Rumi, the sixteenth-century Persian poet who, remarkably, happened to be the bestselling poet of the twentieth century, concludes with the word *khamush*—silence. In silence, in emptiness, in stillness, we open to some deep place and become its conduit.

In silence, we sense more subtle levels of being. In silence, we notice what has always been there but has never been attended to: feeling, sound, thought, habit. In silence, we are still enough to hear the beat of the heart and the pulse of our passions more clearly. And in silence, there is room to listen to the voice of the other.

Especially in this new millennium, being present and awake takes certain energy, certain capacities to quiet the chattering mind, tune in to the intelligence of the senses, witness the worlds within and without, and open to beauty. The following four chapters of part 1 explore these powers of presence and just how they can grow within us.

2

SENSING

I have ceased to question stars and books:
I have begun to listen to the teachings my blood whispers to me.

—Herman Hesse

In the movie *Wings of Desire*, Peter Falk plays an angel who has fallen to earth and taken a human form. In one scene, we find him in chilly, gray, still-divided Berlin, standing in front of an open-air snack bar with a cigarette in his hand, a little sketchpad, and a steaming cup of coffee. He takes a sip from his coffee and begins to draw. An angel in a dark coat approaches and stands in front of him. Falk senses his presence, much to the angel's surprise (since angels are invisible to humans). Falk begins to speak to the angel, trying to convince him to fall to earth so he can experience the sensual world for himself.

I can't see ya, but I know you're here. I can feel you. I wish I could see your face, just look into your eyes and tell ya' how good it is to be here, just to touch something. See, that's cold [Falk touches the counter]; that feels good. To smoke, have coffee, and if you do them together, it's fantastic. You can draw, you know. You take a pencil, and you make a dark line and make a light line, and together it's a good line. Or when your hands are cold you rub 'em together. See, that's good; that feels good.[1]

This capacity to sense and to feel brings life alive, and earth is the ultimate experiential learning center. While we may have a concept or idea of "hot," we really get it when we taste coffee or dip into a hot bath. Guilt is only an idea until we feel it and it becomes a mirror. Belonging is a nice concept, and when we feel the love of homecoming, it becomes medicine. A thunderstorm is a big idea until it shakes our bones and becomes awe. This life seems to be designed for us to experience it. Yet at times we have been taught that our sensitivity is too much ("You're being too sensitive.") and that our senses are too primitive to be reliably trusted ("Stop being so irrational.").

The senses and the body have fallen into a kind of disrepute and mistrust at the hands of various thinkers at various times. Plato and Augustine, two of the most influential figures in Western thought, saw the body largely as an obstacle to spiritual life rather than a gateway. Senses have often come to be considered inferior to rational thought, mathematics, detached science, and the authority of authorities. The result of such disembodied consciousness leads to a kind of alienation from our own bodies and what the senses connect us to: the world around us.

While the senses and the body in general have gotten a bad rap, they are our most natural instruments for knowing the world directly and intimately. The senses have a special place as matter and spirit joined in human life. Like the superpowers possessed by the ancient gods or our comic superheroes, we could even imagine that the human senses are like divine powers. They are the sacramental instruments we've been given. Every sound, taste, and touch is an invitation to be conscious here and now.[2]

The unique potential of being human is that we are both matter and something less tangible. Through the smell of a rose, the sun on our face, or the feeling in our gut, we utilize these "divine powers" and help the cosmos unfold itself right in our midst— actually, in some extraordinary way, right through us.

Through Us

The senses offer a kind of immediate cognition or intuition. Our bodies know things before our minds register them. Sometimes we have a "gut sense" or another felt reaction to someone or something. Neuroscience researcher Candace Pert forced a dramatic revision in the understanding of how we know. She discovered that neuropeptides and their neural receptors, which are tied to thinking and perception and were thought to exist only in the brain, are also found in the gut. This was so significant because we now had evidence that our guts seemed capable of "thinking," too; that is, they seemed to have the apparatus to perceive and digest something other than food. Pert concluded, "I can no longer make a strong distinction between the brain and the body."[3] Rather than a vehicle that the brain rides around on, the body seems to be an integral component in complex knowing.

In a clever study, University of Iowa scientists asked participants to play a card game involving four decks of cards—two blue and the other two red. In this study, each card either won the participants money or cost them money. The goal was to turn over cards one at a time from any deck to maximize winnings. The red cards offered some high rewards and high costs. But the participants didn't know that the game was set up so that they could only win by turning over cards from the blue deck.

How long did it take for the players to figure this out? Participants in this study caught on after they'd turned over about fifty cards. Although they couldn't say why, they knew they preferred the blue deck.

However, there was another aspect of the experiment. The researchers had hooked participants up to measure their galvanic skin response (GSR) in the palms of their hands. (The more stress we experience, the more we sweat, increasing the electrical conductivity of the skin, which registers a higher GSR.) Interestingly, the participants started to generate a stress response to the red cards by the tenth card. Their actions also correspondingly started to favor the blue decks at about that same time. But remember, they didn't have an idea or a hunch that any of this was happening until the fiftieth card, and it took eighty cards before the participants formed a clear theory about it.[4,5] Their bodies knew before their brains made sense of it.

We often assume that thought generates feelings, but ideas, emotions, and sensations work in a more integrated and bidirectional fashion. A thought might indeed lead to a feeling and "felt sense," but at the same time, a physical reaction may lead to a thought. For example, in the Iowa study, the chain of experience goes like this: physiological reaction (increase in sweat response), felt sense (a vague hunch or gut sense), an emotion ("I feel more comfortable with blue cards."), an idea or concept ("It's the blue cards!").

Staying "in" our bodies gives us a profound source of information about the world. Listening to those gut feelings, incorporating our hunches, feeling our way into the question, and thinking it through combine to enrich our knowing. Our thinking is actually a more sensory, body-infused, and integrated process than it has been made out to be.

This sophisticated sensory-emotional system has been mistakenly pushed to the sideline, seen as merely secondary to, largely separate from, and simply controlled by the more elevated thought process, or what neuroscientist Antonio Damasio has referred to as Descartes's error: I think therefore I am.[6] The result has been a loss of attention to the sensitivity and integration of the emotional-sensory-bodily world and instead a tendency to "live in our heads." The cultivation of sensitivity to our body begins to help us close the gap between the body-based system and our conscious awareness, reintegrating thought, feeling, and sensation.

Essentially, thought is an embodied experience; that is, there is a continuous thinking-feeling process or flow transacting with the environment and tied to the body's monitoring of its own states. Whether we're writing a paper or talking with a lover or painting a picture, we feel how our thinking is going. We sense when it's blocked. We feel when it moves forward and how it moves.[7]

The developmental possibility here involves recognizing our sensory and emotional worlds as an integrated part of a sophisticated guidance system. As part of this intelligence, sensations and feelings can signal danger or desire, direct our calling, and confirm a deepening coherence. Once we're present to our sensations it is easier to use the built-in feedback loop that lets us stay aware of when we need some exercise, when we are filled up, when we need a break. In a culture weighed down with obesity, stress, addiction, depression, and more, attending to our sensations becomes critical in assuming responsibility for our health and well-being.

Psychologist Eugene Gendlin wondered what really made psychotherapy work. He knew that sometimes it did work, providing the kind of breakthroughs it promises, but it seemed that just as often it didn't seem to do much. Through his research on psychotherapy, he uncovered a key ingredient to the process of change: Individuals who achieved significant insight and growth had a bodily "felt sense" of the issues at hand. While they may have also had intellectual insight, change was catalyzed at the level of sensation. He discovered that he could even predict before they entered therapy who was likely to benefit from it. He noticed that successful clients had a manner of speech that included particular pauses throughout their speaking, as if they were feeling into themselves and drawing some sense out from the body to form their words. He developed a method he called *focusing* that involves a kind of contemplative approach that helps us feel within and integrate thought, feeling, and felt sense.[8]

At its most essential, the work is to find that felt sense of things as it lives in the body and find the right focal length, the right distance at the right moment from what we're experiencing—not so close that it feels like it overwhelms us and not so far that we can hardly recognize it. The practice basically involves experiencing and naming it, and in so doing, transforming it. In any moment we can ask ourselves to briefly pause, tune inward, and notice what's going on in our bodies. Is there a particular area you are drawn to? What does it feel like and look like? What is its texture and tone, shape and color, sound and movement? This kind of inward-directed awareness helps bring us in touch with those inner sensations. As it comes more clearly into view, try to capture the experience of the overall sensations in a word or phrase. (Is this jumpy, stuck, dense, or something else?) You might then name this overall experience "abandonment," for example, or whatever seems to really capture it. If it doesn't come clear you might try having an imagined dialogue with it in one way or another, perhaps through journaling: "What are you? What is your name?" The more precise we are in naming what is going on, the more likely it is to shift. This process of experiencing and naming integrates sensation and thought not only in our lived experiences but also at levels of brain and body for a more whole-brained and whole-bodied knowing.[9] The result of this awareness is more integrated, embodied, and ultimately richer consciousness—a front edge of human capacity.

Coming to Our Senses

A wine connoisseur, a music aficionado, a mechanic whose ear is tuned to the subtle sounds of an engine—these all represent ways in which awareness in the form of sensory perception can open outwardly, bringing more depth and richness to life. Individuals who live close to the land may develop keen observational skills, and great naturalists like Charles Darwin and John Muir noticed subtleties that others may miss. Such fine-honed sensitivity helps us recognize the potential of the senses. Sometimes a change in one sense reveals untapped possibility.

At two years old, Ben Underwood had his eyes surgically removed due to cancer. Yet as a teenager, he played foosball and skated deftly through his neighborhood, avoiding cars and trash cans. He seems to be able to navigate through his life as if he has eyes. He discovered for himself that by making clicking sounds with his mouth and listening to how the sound bounces back to him he could "see" where objects are. This echolocation technique is basically the same mechanism that dolphins and bats use so effectively.

The backstory to Ben's incredible ability is his mother. When Ben announced after surgery that he couldn't see, his mother immediately reminded him that he could hear and touch and taste and basically can do anything through his other senses. He didn't know that he wasn't supposed to navigate like a dolphin or bat, so he just figured out how to do it himself. Like Ben, when we tap into our inner capacities, the world opens up.

Not only can our senses be opened in unusual ways but also to unexpected depth. Sensitivity involves not just looking *at* things but also *into* them. Pierre Teilhard de Chardin, the Jesuit sage and world-class paleontologist, had a glimpse into this depth as a child: "I was certainly no more than six or seven when I began to feel myself drawn to matter—or more exactly by something that 'shone' in the heart of matter."[10] He sensed something below the surface, something that was subtle and somehow more complete than what his eyes first took in. For Teilhard de Chardin, this was the impetus for an entire lifetime in pursuit of both the spiritual and the scientific as he tried to understand these multiple dimensions of reality. When we open that deeply and directly, our relationship with the world changes.

Jacques Lusseyran was a teenage leader of the French Resistance in World War II and a survivor of the Buchenwald death camp. As a boy of seven, he was permanently blinded in an accident. After several months of total blindness he suddenly discovered a new way to see—he learned to see *light*.

> I realized that I was looking in the wrong way. . . . I was looking too far off, and too much on the surface of things. . . . I began to look more closely, not at things but at a world closer to myself, looking from an inner place to one further within. . . . I was aware of a radiance emanating from a place I knew nothing about . . . But radiance was there, or, to put it more precisely, light.[11]

He explained that his perception, his light, was directly impacted by his attitude. "[T]here were times when the light faded . . . It happened every time I was afraid. . . . [Fear] made me blind."[12] Anger and impatience had the same effects, as did jealousy and growing anxious to win at all costs; they threw everything into confusion. Jacques explained,

> I could no longer afford to be jealous or unfriendly, because, as soon as I was, a bandage came down over my eyes. . . . Armed with such a tool, why should I need a moral code?. . . . I had only to look at the bright signal which taught me how to live.[13]

These extraordinary descriptions betray our own human potential and hint at the secret for opening perception. As Jacques said, he somehow learned "to look from an inner place to one further within." Growing and opening the inner life in order for us to more fully take in the world is an essential part of coming to our senses.

In addition to the expanded sensory capacity like Ben's hearing or Jacques's light, we also discover that senses don't necessarily exist so distinctly and segregated from one another. There is a curious sensory "disorder" called synesthesia. The word means merged, or multiple, senses. Someone might take a bite of food and see geometric shapes in her mind that in some way correspond to the flavors. While hearing Mozart or the Beatles, a synesthete may see colored balls float in front of him. It has been described as a neurological artifact, a mutant throwback to when senses may have been less distinct from one another, merged instead of specialized. But diagnosed synesthetes are hardly Neanderthals. They generally have above average intelligence and also describe their "disorder" as extremely enriching. Several studies have even suggested greater creativity among synethetes.[14]

Instead of being a throwback, synesthesia may represent a reminder of our potential—the multisensory human. The

French philosopher Maurice Merleau-Ponty said that we are naturally synesthetic, but culture has shifted "the center of gravity of experience, so that we have unlearned how to see, hear, and generally speaking, feel, in order to deduce [what we sense]"[15]—that is, education and culture not only teach *what* we are supposed to know but especially *how* we know. Early in life, we become conditioned as to how to talk about (and thus experience) our senses as fairly distinct from one another. We are taught to describe a meal by its taste and music by its sound. But senses may not be so distinct.

During moments of expanded awareness, nearly everyone can have synesthetic experiences, and young children seem to have them often. Some of our great thinkers seemed to know in this multisensory way, pointing to a possible source of their powerful metaphors or unique ways of both taking in and representing the world. "I heard flowers that sounded, and saw notes that shone," wrote eighteenth-century philosopher Saint-Martin.[16] Synesthetic impressions occur not only in perceiving outwardly a magnificent tree or the song of a bird but also inwardly as with the birth of an idea. Mozart described his process of composing in this way:

> I can see the whole of it [musical composition] at a single glance in my mind, as if it were a beautiful painting . . . in which way I do not hear it in my imagination at all as a succession . . . but all at once.[17]

Like the artist or poet, cognitive neuroscience is coming to understand that the "key to robust perception is the combination and integration of multiple sources of sensory information."[18]

We can dismantle the fences of our own perception by moving inward, paying close attention, and inviting our awareness to open through unexpected questions: "What shape does that sound have?" or "Draw what that song feels like in your body," or "Does that idea have a sound, a taste, a shape, a movement, a color?"

The front edge of human development includes becoming more fully multisensory beings, reawakening the delicate sensitivity of all our ways of knowing and, in so doing, returning to the body as a legitimate source of knowing. Perception becomes more robust, our metaphors more meaty, and our contact with the world more intimate and enriched.

Nature-Deficit Disorder

One of the places where our senses seem easily activated is in nature. Nature can serve as wonder for the mind and nourishment for the body. There is something about nature that resonates with us deeply and directly. "Nature is on the inside," said French artist Paul Cézanne. "Quality, light, color, depth, which are there before us, are there only because they awaken an echo in our body and because the body welcomes them."[19] In this sense, we are not just on the earth; we are of it. Even our name, *human*, speaks to our origin, as the word has origins in the Latin *humus*, which means "earth."

As if to convince us that our relationship with nature is very special, moments of ecstasy are most frequently reported as being "triggered" by nature.[20] For example, at age eleven, my friend Debbie was alone on her swing set. As she described to me, "I was looking up at the sky, just watching. I don't know how it happened, but all of a sudden it all opened up to me. I don't know how to say it, but I felt that everything was perfect and connected. I can't say I was thinking anything; it's like there was no room even to think. It felt like my chest could just burst open and fly into a million pieces. It felt like I could explode and be the sun and the clouds." Powerful moments like these can shape the course of an entire lifetime and help underscore a profound and sacred connection.

When he was eleven, cultural historian and Catholic priest Thomas Berry's awareness opened in some inexplicable way and formed a center point for his entire life. His family was having a home built at the edge of a small town. Downhill from the house was a small creek and across the creek a meadow. Berry recalled,

> It was early afternoon in late May when I first wandered down the incline, crossed the creek, and looked out over the scene.
>
> The field was covered with white lilies rising above the thick grass. A magic moment, this experience gave to my life something that seems to explain my thinking at a more profound level than almost any other experience I can remember. It was not only the lilies. It was the singing of crickets and the woodlands in the distance and the clouds in a clear sky. It was not something conscious that happened just then. I went on about my life as any young person might do. . . . As the years passed, this moment returns to me and whenever I think about my basic life attitude and the whole trend of my mind and the causes to which I have given my efforts, I seem to come back to this moment and the impact it has had on my feeling for what is real and worthwhile in life.
>
> This early experience, it seems, has become normative for me throughout the entire range of my thinking. Whatever preserves and enhances this meadow in the natural cycles of its transformation is good: whatever opposes this meadow or negates it is not good. My life orientation is that simple. It is also that pervasive. It applies in economics and political orientation as well as in education and religion.[21]

For Berry, as for so many others, this deep resonance with the natural world activated not only what was beautiful but also, as is the case when we go deep enough, what is good and true, shaping his entire worldview. This is how beauty can save the world; it awakens us to what is sacred. And through this intimate communion, we realize we are joined and thus responsible.

However, we have to wonder whether we are growing further away from the natural world, not closer to it. When we do not recognize and treat the natural world as sacred, it is easy to see the effect on air and water, plants and animals. The consequences directly to humans can be a little less obvious. Author Richard Louv suggests that today young people run the risk of having something akin to nature-deficit disorder.[22] The seduction of surround-sound stimulation, excessive screen time, and the fear of litigation that may inhibit adventurous activities (read: lawsuit waiting to happen); suburban sprawl, which paves over and reconstitutes previously wild places; and overscheduled childhoods, which preclude time for quiet and for imaginative play all push us away from the nourishment nature provides and may form habits that carry into adulthood. Making opportunities for silence and stillness, pause and rest, and especially contact with nature invites an expansion of awareness that can lead to wonder, awe, and even guidance, as it did for Berry. Any sense in any moment can lead the way.

Taste and touch, scent and sight, and more are the portals through which the world finds us. Beauty reveals itself to the extent that we open and meet it from the inside out. With all our ability for abstract, complex, sophisticated thought that enables us to construct everything from technology to theology, the elemental return to sensation and the body provides the most intimate contact with the world and serves as the very ground for human existence. Enhanced integration of sensation and thought

brings a richer, grounded, and more intimate capacity for knowing and being—one that enables presence and opens beauty.

Sensing
Sensing inside and out brings intimate contact with ourselves
and the world around us.

Quiz

For each statement or word, circle the number that describes you best.
(least like me)   1   2   3   4   5   (most like me)

I "drink in" the world of nature.	1	2	3	4	5
I take time to stop, pause, rest, and find my own rhythm.	1	2	3	4	5
I am sensitive.	1	2	3	4	5
I experience (see, hear, feel, know) things that others don't seem to perceive.	1	2	3	4	5
I trust my felt sense.	1	2	3	4	5
I notice and need beauty around me.	1	2	3	4	5
I am attuned to details such as texture, temperature, tone, colors, and smells.	1	2	3	4	5
I notice little things in my environment.	1	2	3	4	5
I am aware of what my body is telling me.	1	2	3	4	5
I am comfortable in silence.	1	2	3	4	5

Add up the circled numbers.   Total: _____

10–19	20–29	30–39	40–50
A trailhead	**More is possible**	**A good ally**	**A great strength**

PRACTICES

Here and Now

What are you aware of in this moment? Take a few deep breaths and bring yourself into a comfortable and relaxed position, closing your eyes completely or partially—whichever you feel comfortable doing. Take some time. What sounds, tastes, bodily sensations, and so forth are available in the moment? Just notice how each feels. You might start outside and then move inside to those bodily sensations. Notice the subtleties of each.

Slow Food

Enjoy every sandwich. Making the intention and the effort to really look at, smell, taste, and feel our food brings us into the present moment and opens the possibility for nourishment beyond the vitamins and proteins. We might start with eating a single item, like a raisin, and give this our full attention without doing anything else. This becomes a practice in presence and pleasure when we do this regularly, daily, for every sandwich.

Mindful Walking

Bathing, brushing teeth, eating a sandwich, or most anything else can serve as a practice of staying present to our senses. While it is quite normal to be thinking ahead of what we're doing, presence is grown by being in the middle of any activity. Simply make the effort to stay present, awake, and aware of opening the door. When the task is to wash the dishes, for example, enjoy the warm dishwater and scrubbing off the remnants of a well-cooked meal, or be present during a walk, feeling the crunch of the ground underfoot, the temperature of the air, the muscles in the body as they tense and relax, the rhythm of your breath, the birdsong above, and so forth.

Like mindful walking, formal practices like tai chi or hatha yoga are designed as active meditations, which are especially useful if we have trouble stilling ourselves while sitting quietly. Like anything—washing, walking, yoga—they can be done with presence or as something to merely get through and mark off our to-do list. Without presence we take the shell and leave the nut behind.

Seeing

With paper and colored pencils or whatever you have available, take time with an object, a face, a scene, or nearly anything in which you are able to observe detail. Draw it while keeping your focus on the subtleties of how lines come together, how the light hits your object, the shading that results, other little details that you may not have noticed, and whatever else emerges for you. You might end up working on one aspect of it rather than trying to capture everything, or maybe you see something under the surface that wants to come forward. The goal of this experiment is not to be a good artist but instead to practice delicately and carefully seeing the subtleties of your object. Be sure to take time to look back at your drawing and your object when you're finished and reflect on your process.

Grounding

Invite yourself into a relaxed state. Get comfortable in your seat or on the floor and take a few deep, clearing breaths. Close your eyes if you are comfortable doing so and just settle in for a couple of minutes. Notice where you are, and gently invite your body and mind to become comfortable and feel safe. If you need to wiggle or stretch or find a better position, be sure to do so.

Now gently invite your awareness to the bottom of your feet. This may work best if your feet are flat on the floor or ground.

Notice the sensations. See if you can keep your attention there and allow your bones and flesh to soften and gently spread out and really make contact with the ground. You might imagine your feet growing out wider, longer, and perhaps sinking roots into the ground. Just notice how that feels, how you feel. Once you have a good sense of being grounded, without losing that connection, you may want to spread that awareness slowly to your legs and buttocks. Let them make contact, helping to ground you like the roots of a tree or the solid base of pyramid. Just be aware of the sensations, feelings, images, and thoughts that arise as you relax into this. Is there resistance to grounding? Is there safety here? The idea is that it is difficult to be fully embodied, whether as a tree or a person, unless we have a solid base. This helps make it safe and solid enough for us to feel and sense and experience the world more fully. Without this, it may be more difficult to gain the richness and intelligence of the body.

Other more physically active practices like exercising can serve as grounding practices as well.

Inner Listening

Find a safe and comfortable space where you won't be disturbed and settle in quietly. You may want to begin by stretching a bit, taking some deep breaths, and letting gravity just gently do its work. Eyes closed usually works best, as this helps us turn inward, which is where this work will take place. Once you've settled in slowly and gently, inwardly and silently, move through the following instructions adopted from Eugene Gendlin:

1. Pay attention inwardly and see what arrives when you ask, "What is the main thing for me right now?" or "How is my life going?" Let the answers come slowly. When some concern comes, rather than entering into it, stand back and just

acknowledge it. Wait again and see if other concerns or topics arise.

2. From among what came, select one to focus on. Sense what the whole issue feels like without going inside it. Let yourself feel it all.

3. What is the quality of this unclear felt sense? Let a word or image arise (tight, spacey, or jumpy, for example). Go back and forth between the felt sense and the word or image. Check how they resonate with each other. Is there a bodily signal that lets you know that it's a fit? Let the felt sense as well as the word change until they feel just right in capturing the quality of the felt sense.

4. Now ask yourself, "What is it about this whole issue that makes this quality?" Sense that quality word or image again. "What makes this whole problem so _____?" Be with this feeling until you sense a shift, a slight give.

5. Receive whatever comes gently and openly. Stay with it for a while; you may find other shifts, or perhaps your first shift comes later.[23]

3

FOCUSING

Squirrel!

—*Dug the dog,* Up

L inda Stone, a former Apple and Microsoft executive, addressed her audience at a Silicon Valley computer conference. A majority of the people in the crowd looked down at their laps as she was speaking rather than at her. They were working on their handheld devices, checking email, and text messaging; some were probably writing snarky comments about the speaker on Twitter or a blog, and who knows what else. She got their attention when she named a new "disorder": Continuous Partial Attention, or CPA.[1] The demanding quality of the internet and constant virtual stimulation distorts life into rapidly changing sound bites, image bites, and data bytes. This steady pull on our attention can inhibit us from being able to give anything or anyone our full, undivided attention. It may also engender a sense of constant crisis. We are always on the lookout, always ready to respond with a tap on a keypad or the swish of a finger. Our attention and our mind are here and there and everywhere, constantly interrupting itself and always on its way to somewhere else. No wonder energy drinks, coffee franchises, and anti-anxiety medications have been doing so well. In this race, the goal isn't to get somewhere; it's just to try to keep up and react.

Splintering our attention with multitasking and jumping to the next call, text message, or sales pitch has become increasingly the norm. To be sure, some situations really benefit from multitasking, and for some, it provides welcome stimulation. And there are a few advantages to functioning as live electronic nodes constantly plugged into the World Wide Web. But there are downsides, too. Like a dog whose attention is instantly captured by the squirrel bounding by, we can be taken for a fruitless run by anything and everything. Talking to people with CPA is like talking to someone at a cocktail party who is constantly on the lookout for the next, presumably better conversation. The conversation doesn't get very far before their eye catches the next more interesting mark, and they're off (the "squirrel!" reaction). The result is that continuous availability and response actually inhibits any ability to really meet others deeply and give them our undivided attention. In this sense, constantly being accessible—a node on the information superhighway—can ultimately make us profoundly inaccessible.

Out of Time

A key distinction between states of CPA, in which we are racing to keep up, and states like *flow*, where we are absorbed in the moment, is how we experience *time*. The Greeks used two different words for time: *chronos* and *kairos*. Chronos is that sequential progression of time that we recognize when we're late for a date or notice the years adding up. It's a quantity. "I'll be with you in five minutes." "They've been married for half a century." It marches on or races along, and most of the time we seem to follow along. But we know that the *experience* of time is not consistent. Time flies when we're absorbed in some activity, or maybe time drags on at a painfully dull event.

Kairos names this other kind of time. The ancient Greeks depicted Kairos as the god of the fleeting moment. This kind of time is variously represented as an opening or opportunity, a passing instant we have a chance to step into deeply, such as the birth of a child or the death of a loved one, a moment where courage or kindness is called for, or when we're grabbed by the beauty of nature, when awe transports us out of time. *Carpe diem*, Latin for "seize the day," captures both the sense of opportunity presented and the responsibility to engage it. The instant is lost if we aren't present, if we don't *present ourselves* to it. I suspect we've all had those special moments when the god of the fleeting moment visits and time seems altered.

But special moments that call us out are not simply dependent on the wheel of fortune or the whim of the Fates. It may be that every moment presents an opportunity to enter another way of being. This is an extraordinary shift in perspective from being at the whim of outer circumstances to intentionally altering time—and thus our own experience—through the quality of our attention. Sure, there are special opportunities, but any moment presents an opening to kairos. Being awake to what we are in the middle of moves us into another level of being, a deepened level of reality. Attention has the effect of sharpening colors and distinctions and revealing a hidden or overlooked world. Take a four-year-old into nature and we begin to see how natural being out of time is. Thomas Merton suggested a spiritual practice of doing the ordinary while being absorbed in it intensely and utterly.[2] Being present or mindful and entering kairos time does not take us away from action and engagement with the world but instead allows us to be fully present in our actions, whether eating a sandwich or enjoying the company of a child.

Not only for a moment but also as a general way of knowing and being, paying attention has the effect of freeing us from circumstance. I remember years back when my wife was out of the country, and I was trying to juggle my work, her work, and our two young children along with all their activities. It was to be the longest period of time that I was alone with our children. By the end of the first day, I was already tense, resentful of my wife, the kids, childless adults, and everyone and everything else. I found myself being very curt with my tender little sprouts. "Just go to sleep! Please!" Ouch. Something would have to change drastically or a miserable week would be in store for the three of us.

After putting the children to bed, out of desperation I did manage to be still for a few minutes and ask myself, "What's really important during this week? How could this go better?" I realized that my expectations for my work were unrealistic and really unnecessary during this week. I had some self-imposed and entirely unnecessary deadlines looming. I just didn't have time to keep up with everything on my agenda. I then stripped away my own expectations for getting anything done except what was absolutely necessary and decided that the priority, the direction of my focus and attention, was to just be with the children.

The next day felt so completely different that I still chuckle about it. After a dreadful start, we ended up having a glorious week. I enjoyed them so much and fell more deeply in love with them than I had thought possible. I loved being with them in this way and secretly looked forward to the next time my wife would go out of town. What felt to me like an absolute transformation was possible simply by pausing for a moment and giving attention to what I realized was most important. Giving attention reflects our priorities.

Paradoxically, freeing us from circumstance can involve moving fully into them and into the moment. Artist and author Julia Cameron described attention as a way to connect and even to survive. She wrote, "Life through grandma's eyes was a series of small miracles: the wild tiger lilies under the cottonwoods in June; the quick lizard scooting under the gray rock she admired for its satiny finish."[3] Her grandmother's life was hard—so hard that Cameron's mother exclaimed, "I don't know how she stands it." But, the author wrote, "The truth is, we all knew how she stood it. She stood it by standing knee-deep in the flow of life and paying close attention."[4]

For all the gifts we are given, perhaps we are asked to give back only one thing: our attention. Not on occasion but *always*. Can we stay awake and aware in the middle of our life? Are we in the middle of this fleeting moment or already on our way to the next and then the next? Our attention gives the cosmos its opportunity to come alive before us and within us.

Paying Attention

It's hard to stay present when a constant stream of distractions vie for our attention. These distractions come not only from outside us—the text message, the noisy neighbor—but also from within. Thoughts and worries about the past or the future, about others or ourselves seem to be desperately trying to get our attention ("Hey look at me!"). This nearly constant, restless, uncontrollable chatter has been referred to in Buddhist tradition as monkey mind. It appears to be inevitable and natural. We might lie in bed at night and have the same thoughts circle around and around, keeping us from sleep. We may replay an unsatisfying conversation or worry about something on the horizon. "Is this a good decision?" "Why did I say that?" "Can you believe she's wearing that?!" This can absorb so much of our awareness that it inhibits the capacity to give our attention fully to anything else.

However, we know that at times our minds operate in other ways as well. This internal dialogue seems to ebb and flow; in some moments the monkey mind chatter recedes and another mode surfaces. This might occur when we are entering or waking from a dream or experiencing an intuitive flash, during a good work-out or a moment of love or appreciation, when we are absorbed in an issue, or when nature, art, or beauty grabs our attention.

My friend Nancy once described a memorable morning to me. It was one of those beautiful fall days—fresh breeze, brilliant sky, vibrant colors. She was lying outside on her back in the large lawn by her rural home with her four dogs, none older than ten months, who were licking, playing, and lying with her. "I had the best morning I can remember," she said. The chatter quieted down, and with it, she was freed to be more alive and awake to the present moment. She entered kairos time.

This just happened spontaneously for Nancy as perhaps it has for you or me from time to time. But the capacity for presence can involve learning how to intentionally settle down that internal chatter and, in so doing, inviting a more spacious and gracious way of knowing.

Focus involves the ability to intentionally steady and shift attention. We know how important concentration or focus is for the world of schooling. If you've ever read some pages in a book only to realize that you have no idea what you'd just read, you know the quality of attention can easily trump the amount of time on a task. Likewise, great athletes and performers of all sorts narrow their focus in order to stay locked on the job at hand, and when they or we lose focus, the results are often easy to see:

"Argh! I missed the shot/the note/my cue!" The capacity for concentration is equally essential in becoming a good reader or an Olympic athlete.

Focus can become hard and single-pointed in order to narrow in on a target, such as working on a problem or concentrating on an activity. The function is like a camera lens zooming in and holding steady on a target. Attention can also be soft, diffused, and open to the unexpected, as when we see something without any agenda. Like adjusting the lens on a camera, we can, on one hand, step back and find a more panoramic view, taking in the whole scene and seeing what leaps out at us, as Nancy did with her furry friends. Focusing allows us to narrow in or open up, to redeploy or steady our attention, which in turn alters our overall state of mind.

William James, the father of American psychology, thought that this ability to focus attention was extraordinarily important.

> The faculty of voluntarily bringing back a wandering attention, over and over again, is the very root of judgment, character, and will. An education which should improve this faculty would be *the* education *par excellence*. But it is easier to define this ideal than to give practical direction for bringing it about.[5]

At the beginning of the twentieth century, James was apparently not aware that so many wisdom traditions had already developed tried-and-true internal technologies specifically to cultivate attention. These technologies are readily available to us today. Virtually every meditative or contemplative practice begins with intentionally shifting focus and concentrating on something— a word, an idea, the flow of thoughts and sensations, an image, or breathing.

We might, for example, simply try to bring our awareness to our breathing for several minutes and notice its natural movement—in and out. When we find our thoughts drifting, we bring our attention back to the breath (or word or image or idea). We are likely to find our attention wandering and, again, when we do, we can simply acknowledge that and bring our awareness back to the breath. In time, such a simple practice can develop the muscle of concentration. In various practices, other dimensions are sometimes added, such as an invitation to focus on compassion, but the foundation remains the same, directing and sustaining attention, which James understood to be so important.

This is pretty simple. In fact it's so simple that it may be hard to see what all the fuss around contemplative practices is actually about. But what we've discovered is that when we shift like this, there is both a physiological *state* change as well as a change in our perception and thinking. It's not unusual to hear contemplative practitioners describe themselves as more present, clear, composed, centered, and spacious thanks to their practices. These immediate state shifts also appear to have the potential to engender *trait* shifts to endure changes over time. These include a sense of less judgment toward others and ourselves and greater emotional balance or resilience.

While presence is its own reward—the taste of that sandwich or the intimacy of understanding another person—it is also extraordinarily useful for our down-to-earth existence, from health to performance and emotional balance. Awareness practices, such as meditation, have long demonstrated a direct impact on stress, from lowering blood pressure to altering brain wave activity.[6] Practices based simply on noticing or watching our inner sensations rather than resisting or getting lost in them have demonstrable effects on pain management[7] and increase the production of antibody titers to the flu vaccine (meaning simply that the immune system works better as a result of these practices in presence).[8] Neuroimaging even suggests that contemplative practice may not only change how the brain is functioning but over time may also change the very structure of the brain itself, specifically increasing cortical thickness.[9] (Thinning of the cortex is associated with brain disorders like Alzheimer's.)

Beyond its utility as a natural performance and health enhancer, the ability to focus can also help us open to joy and deep satisfaction. The state described by psychologist Mihaly Csikszentmihalyi as *flow* involves being fully absorbed in the activity at hand, whether working on a math problem, building a chair, or running rapids in a kayak. This state of mind and body is characterized by high concentration on a particular activity, the merging of action and awareness as we lose our sense of self and, along with it, our usual sense of time. This immersion is typically deeply satisfying, and the effort seems almost effortless. We and it are flowing; we're in "the zone."[10] The capacity for being absorbed is also associated with deeply satisfying, deeply beautiful experiences, including peak or mystical moments.[11] Attention opens us that deeply. Developing the capacity for focus gives us the power to direct and steady our minds intentionally, and this essentially helps us get out of our own way in order to tap both ourselves and the world at a greater depth.

In addition to that sense of locked-on concentration that occurs with flow states, attention can also take a more open presence that brings its own rewards. When we brush our teeth, eat a sandwich, or read a book, where are we? If we are present to a good meal, for example, there is nourishment beyond what is provided by the food itself. Vietnamese Buddhist monk Thich Nhat Hanh is an embodiment of someone who tries to stay awake to the immediate experience of mind and senses.[12] His intention is to bring a quality of presence and sensitivity to everything he does. When he opens a door, he is attempting to do just that and only that. When he is chewing a bite of sandwich (or whatever he eats), that's what he's trying to be present to. It requires a quality of mindfulness in order to deeply experience the immediate moment, even and especially in the simplest act or sensation. We might practice with our own next sandwich, door, walk, or anything else.

Various traditions have their own particular approaches to developing the muscle of focus, from sitting meditations and contemplative prayers to active movements such as tai chi. These include the long history of Buddhist meditation, various forms of yoga from Hindu traditions, contemplative prayer in Christianity, such as that of St. Teresa of Ávila or Thomas Merton, radical questioning through dialogue, such as that expressed by Plato or the self-inquiry of the Indian mystic Ramana Maharshi, metaphysical reflection of the Sufi tradition, or the deep pondering suggested in the Jewish Kabbalah. Some are more active and movement oriented, while other practices involve quiet stillness. One shoe doesn't fit all, and the challenge may be for each of us to find ways that work for us. In addition, various practices have different goals. Some meditation is geared toward insight, others toward creativity or enhancing compassion. But they all rely first on this ability to focus—that is, to shift and sustain attention in order to tap or open consciousness in some direction.

Like most changes we make, developing the muscle of focus may take some practice in order to move us past conditioned habits of mind so that we may stay awake in the here and now.

Focusing
The ability to intentionally steady and shift attention.

Quiz

For each statement or word, circle the number that describes you best.

(least like me)   1   2   3   4   5   (most like me)

I can maintain concentration easily.	1	2	3	4	5
I notice the thoughts and all else running through my mind	1	2	3	4	5
I am not easily distracted.	1	2	3	4	5
I am comfortable with silence.	1	2	3	4	5
I get absorbed in what I'm doing.	1	2	3	4	5
I often experience states of "flow."	1	2	3	4	5
I can easily "lock on" to a task I'm interested in.	1	2	3	4	5
I feel balanced and peaceful.	1	2	3	·4	5
I can usually quiet my mind.	1	2	3	4	5
I am present to what is going on around me.	1	2	3	4	5

Add up the circled numbers.   Total: _____

10–19	20–29	30–39	40–50
A trailhead	**More is possible**	**A good ally**	**A great strength**

....

PRACTICES

Steadying the Mind

First, take a couple of deep, clearing breaths. Next, simply bring awareness to your breath, noticing its natural movement—in and out. When you find your thoughts drifting, bring your attention back to your breath. No judgment, no worry. Just notice and bring your attention back. For some, counting along with the breath helps them keep focus (for example, counting "1, 2, 3, 4" during the inhale and 1–8 for the exhale). For others, naming or noting the distraction, like "thinking" or "hungry," for example, and then moving back to their breath is helpful. In time, such a simple practice can develop the muscle of focus that is so central to any number of activities. Five minutes is a good start. Many suggest that over time fifteen to twenty minutes or more serves as a powerful source of nourishment.

Not Doing

If our attention is somewhere else, scattered, or racing, perhaps, we may have little capacity to be present. Paradoxically, we may need to not do for a few minutes in order be more available for doing the task at hand.

Sit down and take a few deep, slow, clearing breaths. Take your time. Let your body release and relax, allowing any parts of you that need to wiggle or stretch to do so. Now feel the gentle pull of gravity and allow the chair you're sitting on and the floor beneath to support you without any effort on your part. Just let go and allow yourself to be silent and not do for a few minutes. You may want to focus only on your breathing, allowing it to flow in and out without effort. If you find yourself thinking, distracted, or working on a problem, don't fight it, don't get stuck in it. Just allow it and you to be and redirect your awareness back to your breath and to not doing.

Following this exercise, which may last from just two or three minutes to fifteen or so, notice any difference before and after "not doing." If in a group, you might share experiences with one another or reflect for a few moments in a journal, or you might say nothing and just move into your next moment.

Centering Prayer

1. Choose a sacred word or saying—that is, a word or phrase that has significance for you, like "peace," "love," or "let go," for example. Any brief word(s) that provides a touchstone for you will work.
2. Sitting comfortably and with your eyes closed, settle briefly and silently introduce the sacred word.
3. When you become aware of thoughts, return ever so gently to the word.
4. At the end of the period, remain in silence with your eyes closed for a couple of minutes.[13]

Pause

Take a rest or a pause in silence. Silence and stillness make space for gaps and pauses in a hurried and buzzing existence. Pausing in silence provides moments of rest and reorganization for our minds and bodies and helps us tune in to our natural rhythms. This may be for twenty seconds or a few minutes. It serves as sort of a micro-nap, helping us to refresh and reorient.

4

WITNESSING

Our thoughts first possess us. Later, if we have good heads,
we come to possess them.

—Ralph Waldo Emerson

Where are you right now? What are you aware of in this instant? What thoughts, feelings, sensations rise to the surface of awareness? If you were able to notice something, then some part of you was doing the noticing and something was being noticed.

Bill was a dark-haired good-looking teen living with his mother in a small town. He often had a girlfriend, was barely getting by in school, and seemed to be partying a great deal. Usually this meant drinking and hanging out. From what I could gather, at his mother's insistence and some prompting from the police, he came to the clinic where I was working as a therapist. Apparently the police had come to know him quite well in recent months. His face and his fists seemed to be in the middle of nearly every disturbance involving teens. His violent tendencies were getting serious and frighteningly regular; he was getting into fights almost daily.

In our brief conversation, and as his mother confirmed, I learned that his father was dying in a hospital a half hour away, but Bill refused to see him. His father had been violent toward Bill throughout childhood, and the resentment and estrangement now seemed like an impossible gulf to cross.

As we sat in my office, I started to wonder about something. "Can I ask you a question?" I asked.

Bill paused and, with a mix of suspicion, irritation, and defiance, his arms defensively across his chest, said, "Yeah."

"What percentage of your time are you angry?" I asked.

I was genuinely curious. He was wearing anger on his sleeve. It was obvious from his furrowed brow and his clenched fists. As soon as he heard the question, I watched him become very still, his face relaxed, and it seemed that he was really taking this question to heart. It took a good half minute of silence before he finished his search inside. He suddenly refocused his eyes and announced, "Ninety percent."

"May I ask you another question?" I asked.

"Sure," he said.

"What about the other ten percent?"

"I'm drunk," he said without hesitation.

We didn't say much more that day, and while his answers surprised me, I learned later that they had shocked him. In this moment of looking within, he saw himself as two dimensional—angry or drunk. This was not the image he had of himself, and it did not sit well with him. During an unexpected visit with me a few weeks later, he came in to tell me that this simple look within provided a revelation that helped him begin to get control of his life and face his anger rather than just being angry. He told me he'd gone to see his father, and while he did not forgive him, he'd made a reconnection before his father died. He could still be angry with him, but he felt as much pity and loss as anything.

And while he was fully capable of being angry, the daily fighting subsided dramatically. His shift was really pretty remarkable, and we really hadn't done anything. He had just witnessed and reflected on his consciousness.

When we're angry, hurt, or caught in any strong emotion, it can feel all-consuming. We're just a bundle of emotion ready to explode or wither. Witnessing what's going on gives us a little distance between us and the sensation, thought, or feeling so that we have a chance to play and work with it without being overwhelmed. Witnessing can develop life-long powers of reflection and introspection. This capacity does not require years of meditative or intellectual practice. As it was for Bill, it can be tapped and explored immediately. It is a capacity that even young children possess.

Once at the end of a week of school, one of my daughters, then in elementary school, was dredging out the week's papers from her book bag. I noticed a very low score on a spelling quiz I knew she had prepared for. When I asked what had happened with the quiz, she explained that her class had been doing math just before the teacher gave the spelling quiz. She said, "I still had my math head on."

In her own way and her own words, she demonstrated a capacity for noticing and reflecting on her state of consciousness. Had she been given a few moments of silent pause, witnessing, and shifting, she, in Emerson's words, could have come to possess her thoughts rather than having them drive her. In this case, just a few moments to shift out of her "math head" may have made a difference. Observing ourselves gives us greater power to choose our state of mind.

"I" and "Me"

Let's make a distinction between "I" and "me." The "me" represents the contents of our consciousness—the thoughts, feelings, and sensations that rise and fall throughout our waking lives. The "I" is that part of us that watches, witnesses, and observes the contents.

Witnessing develops as we just notice inwardly without getting lost in the content. This enables a type of "detachment," as Meister Eckhart called it, from thoughts, feelings, and sensations that flow though our minds and bodies.[1] This allows us to observe the inner reactions rather than simply being captured by them. Such arms-length distance enables us to recognize and therefore potentially interrupt habitual patterns of thinking and impulsivity, freeing the mind to notice unexpected insights. For example, instead of just seething with anger or throbbing with desire, witnessing may allow a little more space from the feeling. We might still *have* our anger or desire but also *notice* it. "Look at me being angry; what's that about?" or "I really want that; what's that about?" rather than simply being overcome and thus lost to the anger or desire.

This not only develops the potential for emotional regulation and impulse control but it also develops interior "muscles" of reflection leading to metacognition—an ability to notice and reflect upon patterns of thought and reaction. Through this witnessing or watching, what occurs is "a mindful reflection that includes in the reflection on a question the asker of the question and the process of asking itself."[2] This process "begin[s] to sense and interrupt automatic patterns of conditioned thinking, sensation and behavior."[3]

Without engaging the observing mind, we tend to either get seduced by our reactions as they run away with us or try to push them away because they make us uncomfortable. But the inner technology of the observing mind opens us to see in fresh ways. In addition, as we simply and honestly observe and tolerate our own reactions, we may also gain a tolerance for others that is so

essential for understanding multiple points of view. This is a profound moral outcome of a simple practice of presence.

A simple question posed in a moment of relaxed pause can
activate the capacity for witnessing presence. "Where am I now?"
we might ask ourselves. Are you thinking about the day ahead?
Rehashing some past experience? Caught in an emotional hangover about a situation with a friend or family member? How
much of you is in your body? In your head? Floating outside you?
Stuck in an internal nook? Just watch for a few moments, noticing
where you are and how this is without getting lost in the content
of thoughts, feelings, and sensations.

Once again, there is often a tendency to either let a thought
or a feeling capture us or try to avoid it by pushing it away. Witnessing involves neither. The practice is just to notice without
judgment, to be curious without clinging.

"Where am I now?" might become internalized as a kind of
personal check-in perhaps every time we're about to eat, every
time we hear a phone ring, or just whenever we think of it. This
invites a simple yet powerful practice of developing the muscle of
self-awareness, of *the witness*.

As mentioned, practices like these are traditionally designed
not only for short-term *state* shifts—getting ready for that spelling test or calming the anger—but also as a way to cultivate more
generalized long-term *traits*, such as detachment or compassion.
Witnessing appears to help us return from and modulate a state
of arousal and therefore may be valuable for balance and bounce
(resilience). During stress, the HPA axis (hypothalmus, pituitary,
adrenal) coordinates the nervous system response that gets us
ready for fight or flight in part by increasing levels of cortisol.
But in an age of constant stimulation designed to grab our attention, shock, or arouse us, not to mention the accelerated pace of
our days, we may not return to an optimal baseline state. The

hyperarousal of the HPA axis and elevated levels of cortisol have been related to obesity, memory deficiency,[4] and even the neurobiology of suicide.[5] The good news is that contemplation, like the simple witnessing practice above, reduces the level of cortisol during non-stressful events, increases response during stress, and quickens the return to baseline levels.[6]

Someone once asked the Dalai Lama, "What's the most important thing you do?" I imagined that this exiled religious and political leader who had regular meetings with the world's political, religious, and scientific elite had some important things to do on the world stage. But his answer was, "I watch my mind. It's the most important thing I do."

As we look within, witnessing the flow of consciousness, we are developing capacity and sensitivity in the primary instrument we use to investigate the world: our minds. This heightened inner awareness helps us notice, regulate, refine, and receive. The body becomes a resonance chamber as we learn to listen to it; our interiority feels more spacious, allowing us to take in more of the world and tolerate more of ourselves.

Who am I?

Across time and tradition, we hear ideas of heaven and earth, spirit and matter, formless and form, and so forth as ways of grappling with the mystery of our own existence, of what we see and what we don't see. When it comes to our nature as humans, there is a related distinction between, as Islam claims, the greater self and the lesser self. That lesser self—what we often refer to as the ego—is that part of us that we most often identify as "me." The other part of the story is that there is this big self, true nature, spiritual self, higher self, and so forth. Much of Western psychology has had a harder time getting its arms around the idea of a big self, mistaking the ego for our whole being.

The old story goes like this: being all we can be means that we are somehow to regain awareness of our true nature, our divinity, or, if you prefer, our larger capacities for love and wisdom, virtue and value, in order to connect heaven and earth through our consciousness or awareness. The primary impediment, problem, error, sin, ignorance, or challenge we are to overcome is that we don't realize that we're not merely that small self. We tend to overidentify with the limited sense of self with all its parts and get caught up in its drama and trauma (all that "me" stuff). The liberation that is the goal of spiritual life comes through the recognition of what and who we are: that bigger self and, in some views, no self at all. Every major tradition, in one way or another, has recognized this same notion of our separateness and our oneness: "The Kingdom of heaven is within you." "Atman and Brahman are one." "Those who know themselves know the Lord." Even if we don't accept the idea of a spiritual self—Christ consciousness, Buddha nature, and so forth—we can still recognize in very down-to-earth terms that some folks really seem to live large. I don't mean with lots of possessions or publicity but instead lots of character, courage, creativity, and compassion. They are the Gandhis and Kings, Picassos and Teresas, and those local heroes who just seem to have a quiet source of character or wisdom or authenticity that is not hard to recognize. Maybe we even recognize our own larger nature in moments when we've spoken up against some injustice or stepped up in offering some kindness or woken up to some understanding. We sense a deep potential inside and wonder how to live it out. According to this story, as a species we've been underestimating ourselves. We're more than we realize we are.

In a script that would have been rejected by Hollywood as too unbelievable, Nelson Mandela was inaugurated as the president of South Africa in 1994 after a lifetime under apartheid and twenty-seven years in prison. During his imprisonment he had had some time to think about human nature. For that momentous inaugural speech, he decided to speak about living large.

> Our greatest fear is not that we are inadequate, but that we are powerful beyond measure. It is our light, not our darkness, that frightens us. We ask ourselves, Who am I to be brilliant, gorgeous, handsome, talented and fabulous? Actually, who are you not to be? You are a child of God. Your playing small does not serve the world. There is nothing enlightened about shrinking so that other people won't feel insecure around you. We were born to make manifest the glory of God within us. It is not just in some; it is in everyone. And, as we let our own light shine, we consciously give other people permission to do the same. As we are liberated from our fear, our presence automatically liberates others.[7]

How are we supposed to realize this larger nature? Just having the idea doesn't seem to get us there and may even catapult us into a narcissistic delusion without genuine realization ("I'm great!" as opposed to "I'm great, and so are we all."). The capacity to witness is one tool that helps us see more, including more of who we are. As soon as we witness, we experience another aspect of ourselves. By watching the contents of consciousness, we can gain a little distance from them, freeing us from overidentification with the limited self, that major impediment to realization. Every time you actually witness something you dis-identify with it to a degree. This expands our view to include the witness itself.

The ancient injunction "To be in the world but not of it" is one of those instructions that can seem befuddling. I'll sidestep the religious interpretation and focus on the experience for a moment. For me, the *lived experience* of this paradoxical instruction is revealed through the practice of witnessing. Through the gifts of our senses, feelings, and thoughts, we are invited to fully experience life—the sweetness of an orange, the bitterness of betrayal, the juiciness of passion. The great souls seem to really invest in the lives they're leading. They find the beautiful thing that's worth putting themselves on the line for and they throw their hearts and souls into it, along the way suffering all the joys and those slings and arrows of outrageous fortune. The result is a life really lived. As American author and philosopher Henry David Thoreau wrote, "I wanted to live deep and suck out all the marrow of life . . . to put to rout all that was not life . . . and not, when I came to die, discover that I had not lived."[8]

That's the "in the world part," but what about "not being of it"? To be able to witness our experience helps us avoid getting fixated, stuck in some small corner of life, seduced by and lost to power, possessions, pornography, or whatever. It permits us to explore those experiences without so easily allowing them to swallow us. This allows part of us to recognize a larger picture, to rest not in the inevitable ups and downs of a life, tied to success or failure, but instead to rest in the center of a larger view—in it up to our necks but not over our heads. This is the power of witnessing.

Witnessing
Watching our own thoughts, feelings,
and sensations without getting lost in them.

Quiz

For each statement or word, circle the number that describes you best.

(least like me)   1   2   3   4   5   (most like me)

In most any moment, I can easily answer
the question, "Where am I now?"   1   2   3   4   5

I notice the thoughts and all else running
through my mind.   1   2   3   4   5

I find myself watching my own behavior,
thoughts, or feelings.   1   2   3   4   5

I know the difference between my own
thoughts and feelings and those of
people around me.   1   2   3   4   5

I notice my own patterns of thinking,
feeling, or doing.   1   2   3   4   5

I am curious about what I'm feeling while
I'm in the middle of feeling it.   1   2   3   4   5

I can step into or back from my feelings.   1   2   3   4   5

I recognize and experience more to me
than my ego.   1   2   3   4   5

I am self-aware.   1   2   3   4   5

There is some space between the part of
me that experiences thoughts, feelings,
and sensations and the sensations,
thoughts, and feelings themselves.   1   2   3   4   5

Add up the circled numbers.   Total: _____

10–19	20–29	30–39	40–50
A trailhead	**More is possible**	**A good ally**	**A great strength**

PRACTICES

Where Are You Now?

Take a few moments and just relax. Take a few deep breaths. Close your eyes if you are comfortable doing so, and tune in to where you are right in this moment. Where are you now? Are you thinking about the day ahead? Rehashing some past experience? Caught in an emotional hangover about a situation with a friend or family member? How much of you is in your body? In your head? Floating outside you? Do you feel out in front of you? Stuck in a painful nook? Does an answer emerge about where you are on the path of your life? Just be aware for a few moments, noticing where you are and how that feels.

Like many of these exercises, this could be extended into a daily activity. "Where am I now?" might become internalized as a kind of personal check-in, inviting self-awareness. We might find particular reminders to check in, like anytime we hear a phone ring or when we walk or take a sip of something or when we brush our teeth.

Just Watch

Gently settle into a comfortable but alert position. Take several deep, clearing breaths. Now just feel your breath come in and out naturally without trying to force it or move it in any way. As you settle in more deeply, just watch what arises in your mind. Notice all the thoughts, feelings, images, and sensations that come to you without judgment, without grasping on to them or pushing any away. You might imagine each thought and sensation rising like bubbles from the bottom of a lake. Just witness them and let them pass by on their way to the surface, where they gently burst and disappear. Come back to the breath, just noticing. If you find yourself grabbing on to one idea or tryinig to judge another one, just come back to your breathing and let the ideas and judgments go. Be assured that anything of importance won't be lost by just watching and allowing them to float to the surface. An attitude of curiosity and non-judgment are often helpful. This practice of mindful watching is often taken up as a daily practice lasting several minutes or more.

Body Scan

Move yourself into a relaxed state, taking some deep breaths, getting comfortable in your seat, and closing your eyes. Settle in for a couple of minutes. Just notice where you are and invite your body and mind to rest and become comfortable.

Once you're settled, bring your attention to the bottom of your feet and establish a gentle and solid grounding. You may need to spend some time here just letting your awareness settle down and connect with the earth. Then, starting at the bottom of your feet, use your attention to slowly scan every part of your body all the way up to the tip of your head. Notice what comes into awareness—tightness, color, space, numbness, pain, pleasure, tautness, softness, sound, images, and so forth. Just be aware of what each area, from front to back, side to side, is like and note it in your mind. Just bring an attitude of curiosity as you take notice and move through.

Once you've scanned the length of your body, which may take several minutes, think about what you discovered. Is there a place you are drawn to or repelled from? A part that feels numb or tight or seems to catch your attention? As a second part of the exercise you might notice which area of your body seems to call to you. Bring your focus back to it, and just through watching, get a clearer or more detailed sense of all you can about that area, including what sensations, images, feelings, or associations arise. Once you have a clearer take on it, ask yourself what this means or what this area needs. Perhaps you can enter a dialogue with this area: "What are you about?" "What do you need?" and again, see what arises. You may then try to provide in your imagination some form of what this is calling for in this moment.

5

OPENING

To see a world in a grain of sand
And a heaven in a wildflower
Hold infinity in the palm of your hand
And eternity in an hour.

—William Blake

What is it about extraordinary individuals that make them so unique? Certainly talent helps a bit. Opportunity or timing makes a difference, as do hard work and motivation. But there is another aspect that seems important for a great many individuals who have made a difference. It is not positive thinking or devotion, not a work ethic or a moral imperative, although each of these may be of value as well. It has to do with a particular attitude toward the world or at least some part of it.

A chemist and physicist by training, Marie Curie was the first person to win two Nobel prizes, the first woman to have a professorship at the University of Paris, and personally instrumental in the use of radioactive isotopes in treating cancers. She is perhaps most associated with coining the term "radioactivity." Her diligent work ethic, sharp mind, and good timing certainly contributed to her achievements, but note another quality she names.

I am among those who think that science has great beauty. A scientist in his laboratory is not only a technician: he is also a child placed before natural phenomena which impress him like a fairy tale. We should not allow it to be believed that all scientific progress can be reduced to mechanisms, machines, gearings, even though such machinery has its own beauty.[1]

Fellow Nobel laureate Barbara McClintock made remarkable discoveries in genetics that took years to unravel. When asked about her scientific process, she said, "You have to have a feeling for the organism. . . . You have to have an openness to let it come to you."[2] The organisms she worked with were not monkeys or mice you could imagine some kind of responsive relationship with; instead, she worked with corn. The key to her astounding and extremely advanced understanding of genetics was, as she described, "the openness to let it come to you." She claimed that this attitude of openness and sensitivity, or "feeling for the organism," in her words, was the primary instrument of discovery.

For both of these great scientists, as it is for so many other great souls, an attitude of radical *openness* is described as the key to everything, from perceiving beauty to scientific discovery. This is really quite an extraordinary instruction we often miss along the path of learned maturity and control. Openness allows us to see past our preconceptions and knowledge, our fears and pride. Openness invites an expansion of consciousness that allows us to see beyond where we are to where we might be.

In Zen, this attitude or way of seeing is called "beginner's mind." It means being open to the world, appreciating and meeting it with fresh eyes—just watching it (and ourselves) without preset expectations or categories. In the same vein, the Bible tells us that one enters the kingdom of heaven only by becoming like a child: "And calling to him a child, he put him in the midst of them and said, 'Truly, I say to you, unless you turn and become like children, you will never enter the kingdom of heaven.'"[3]

When we hear the peals of delight from a child who has just seen a hummingbird up close or witness a child's sheer awe during a huge thunderstorm, we have a sense of the wonder of the world when seen through beginner's eyes. And like children, wise souls often discover that everyday encounters—a bird's song, a cup of tea, a loving hug, even a corn plant and a grain of sand—become extraordinary when we fall deeply into them and simultaneously into that place life flows from. This moves us from living in front of things to living *with* them. Religionist Abraham Heschel says it is precisely awe and wonder, which come from this radical openness, that enable us to see a larger world: "Awe enables us to perceive in the world intimations of the divine, to sense in small things the beginning of infinite significance . . . to feel the rush of the passing of the stillness of the eternal."[4]

Nice Personality

Psychology has spent considerable energy trying to describe human personality, or what makes you different from or similar to the person sitting next to you. One approach has been to look at various *traits*, those enduring patterns of thought, action, and feeling that seem to characterize you, me, or a neighbor. Currently, the most widely recognized mapping of these traits uses five dimensions to describe personality, or "The Big Five." The one relevant for this discussion is "Openness to Experience." While it is always incomplete to lump individuals into categories, the trait approach does capture some patterns of personality we may recognize.

Individuals who register high in Openness are typically described as tending to be intellectually curious and open to their feelings and those of others. They may be sensitive to beauty and are often willing to try new things. The trait is made up of clusters or aggregates, and we should note that exceptions and variations exist. You might be open to new cultures or ideas, for example, but not have much interest in art. One might have openness in the areas of aesthetics, fantasy, feelings, actions, ideas, and values.

Open individuals tend to be actively curious, interested in, and receptive to a variety of ideas and experiences. In fact, they are described as needing diverse, varied experiences and tend to seek them out, although they still may enjoy particular routines and rhythms and familiarity and consistency in some areas. They are more likely to be creative and divergent thinkers and can be characterized by their nontraditional attitudes, their rich emotional lives, and flexibility in both action and thought. They have a more fluid and permeable structure of consciousness. They can tolerate subtlety and ambiguity more readily. Openness is not to be confused with self-disclosure or gullibility. On the contrary, it appears that people who are open to new experiences or ideas may be particularly thoughtful or reflective toward the ideas they encounter. The bottom line is that whether through intellectual inquiry, art, action, or other means, there is a sense that open individuals are looking to expand their experience of the world and themselves.

The contrast to openness may be recognized as narrow-mindedness. Whether in beliefs or behaviors, there may be a tendency toward the familiar and conventional instead of the novel or divergent, toward the straightforward or obvious over the ambiguous and subtle, toward shutting off rather than opening up. There appears to be less flexibility of mind, thus greater resistance to change.

While traits are qualities that tend to endure over time, they are not necessarily rigidly fixed. Change does happen; we grow.

My friend Julie had been depressed and guarded her whole life. She struggled with frequent thoughts of suicide, had lost a marriage, and had spent most of her life in gray despair, closed off from new experiences. She was surviving but not really living. It's a cliché, but a death sentence brought her to life. At age fifty-five, she was diagnosed with an advanced form of cancer with little hope of recovery. After the diagnosis, her attitude changed radically. She started to open up to life. She wanted to be near her grandchildren and rented a small house a short distance away to do so. Her sullen, dark isolation transformed into engagement, curiosity, and appreciation. She wanted to plant things in her garden, to visit with loved ones. She and her ex-husband became caring friends again. While once bitter toward life, she now wanted to taste all of it. She asked her ex-husband and the rest of her family to come from across the country for a visit. Their conversations were animated and eager, open and honest. The resistance to life that had defined her was now gone. Although near the end she was very weak, she insisted on doing anything and everything she could. She wanted to cut up the fruit for the fruit salad just because she enjoyed doing it. At the smell of morning coffee brewing, her face betrayed almost an ecstasy, and she had to taste some even though she could not really swallow any longer. Being around Julie had been a chore, but now her company was easy and joyful, despite her declining health.

A bottle of champagne was kept chilled in the refrigerator. Julie asked that upon her death her family would toast her passing. As that moment approached, the family gathered around her bed and waited as her breath seemed to disappear. At one point, one member of the group suggested it was time to open the champagne. With the faintest smirk on her face, Julie whispered, "Not yet!" They were able to laugh together, and it wasn't too much longer in the afternoon before she whispered, "It's time."

They got the bottle and poured the glasses. As they toasted her, one of the family members touched a few drops on her lips with their fingers; she smiled for the last time, and then she was gone. Left in her wake was a passing well done, from a deadened and narrowed life to a vibrant and open death.

Sometimes, as it was for Julie, powerful moments—facing death or birth, trauma or challenge, a peak experience or sudden realization, or even a good laugh—can pop us open. But we don't have to wait for something to happen to us to practice this art of opening. We can intentionally move toward it and, in doing so, move toward beauty.

So much of our energies can be spent building our nests, accumulating those beliefs, possessions, degrees, habits, attitudes, careers, and friends that will make us feel safe. Throughout our lives, one of the things we work toward is a sense of comfort and security. Feeling safe and secure can help us risk opening to something new. Sometimes it's easier to consider a new idea if we're secure in our own. When we really feel safe, welcomed, and appreciated, it is easier to open ourselves.

But there is another side: our nicely feathered nests of familiar ideas, habits, and comforts can become a closed system—safe and familiar but closed and stiff. One of the qualities of a system, whether a cellular one or a social one, is its homeostatic mechanism, or the tendency to stay in balance and reject or fight off change. In a closed system, something new is a threat to the status quo. Societies and individuals protect the gates and reject what doesn't fit or sit well. When it comes to the inner life, sometimes we can get a little stale, closed, completed, and complacent, and sometimes this appears self-satisfied or just stiff and stodgy.

The general fear is that if we open our gates, we'll be overrun and overwhelmed in some way. But here's the dilemma: unless we find moments to open a bit, we end up living clamped down inside some tight shell, bouncing off the walls. We are left, in the words of William Blake, "seeing through the narrow chinks in our cavern" rather than seeing the world more fully.[5] Opening brings our choice and our will to the center of life. When we open, we don't lose the essential capacity to be vigilant, prudent, or discerning. Instead, we now have control of our defenses rather than allowing them to control us. The defensiveness maintained by the old territorial brain relaxes a bit and allows the cerebral cortex—the part of us that really thinks—to come online. We have flexibility of response rather than just fixed reaction. This is the potential of the open mind.

Various traditions have found ways to shake things up, opening and recalibrating our minds and hearts. For example, education, especially the liberal arts, is supposed to broaden one's perspective and deepen the ability to think critically and creativity, to open our minds. Done well and deeply, it may indeed open us to the *good*, the *true*, and the *beautiful*. Australian aboriginals go on a walkabout, some Native American tribes have sweat lodges, and various shamanic cultures make use of hallucinogenic plants, fasting, and musical ceremony to shake lose the doors of perception. Even travel, especially arduous or unfamiliar travel that takes us out of our comfort zones in one way or another, can shake our moorings lose. Extremes like fasting or isolation (theologian and mystic Teresa of Ávila), or sacrifice and service (Mother Teresa), the unloading of a confession, an act of forgiveness, or a powerful ceremony—all have a long history as a process of purgation in which we cleanse ourselves or our souls. The presumed result is disorientation followed by a fresh way of seeing or being, a recalibration of the system that is us. Altered states of consciousness can lead to altered traits of consciousness. A metaphorical whack on the side of one's mind or a periodic spring cleaning helps shake things up a bit and lets us see what's worth holding on to and what it's time to let go of.

Basically, the practice of opening is a process of consolidation and purgation. Breathing in and breathing out. Holding on and letting go. Leaves drop so new growth can occur. Even at the neurobiological level we go through stages of neurological pruning—a spring cleaning of sorts that makes us available for another level of learning and integration. Without this we tend to remain filled and closed.

Many years ago in Japan, it was the tradition among Buddhist monks to travel from monastery to monastery, seeking the teaching of the masters. As was the custom, the master would serve his guest tea and they would talk. One young monk was a particularly outstanding student. In fact, he was so exceptional, he had made a bit of a career out of showing up lesser masters with his skill and tremendous intelligence.

One day he called at a very famous monastery attached to one of the most sacred temples in all Japan. The master there was old and most wise. The young man begged an audience with the master in hopes of being accepted as his pupil, to live and study with the great man. The young man, whose reputation had preceded him, was ushered into the master's chambers immediately. This was most unusual, and the young monk was greatly flattered.

The young man told the master of his journeys, the teachings he had heard, and the monks he had "bested" in his search for truth. It was a most impressive tale. The master listened intently and acknowledged the young monk many times for his wit and intelligence.

A teapot and cups were brought in, and the master began pouring tea for them both. The young man addressed the master. "I wish to remain here and study with you, for I sense that here, unlike with the others, there is much you have to offer me—"

All of a sudden, the young monk cried out in pain and alarm, jumping up from his place on the floor, shaking his robes and dancing about. The scalding hot tea had spilled all over his lap.

The master sat calmly and continued pouring tea, which was overflowing the student's small cup and spilling out over the table and onto the straw-matted floor where the young man had been sitting.

"What are you doing?!" the young monk demanded. "I have been burned! Stop pouring! The cup is overflowing!"

"Go away from me, young man," the master said, "I have nothing to teach you. Your cup is too full . . . overflowing with all that you know and all that you think you don't know. Come back to me when your cup is empty and you are ready to receive what I have to give."[6]

Openness gives us a chance to empty the mind of prejudgment and pride.

Experiments with opening aren't always triggered by some big event or exotic journey. In the space of facing a friend or nemesis, in pondering an idea we honor or abhor, at the well of our grief or some feast of the senses, there is a chance to practice the art of opening, maybe just a millimeter more than before. That's all. We don't even really do anything in opening; just the opposite, really. We simply make a choice to relax those mechanisms of mind and of muscle that keep us held in and held back. We can stay focused and sensitive and bear witness to our own internal world and let our awareness drop just a little further, lingering just a little longer to see what's there. We might push just a little deeper into a conversation or try something outside our comfort zone, striking up a conversation with a stranger, breaking routine, risking adventure. There is risk, vulnerability, and fear of the unknown and the unexpected, but this is where the edge of beauty and presence lives.

Inside the Gates

Through our capacities to witness and pay attention to our senses, it's not too hard to notice the places, people, or situations we recoil from or are closed off to. But one of the slipperier places to bring an attitude of openness and non-judgment is ourselves. Most everyone I know has a well-developed inner critic, a voice inside that at times takes on the role of tormenter. It is a threat from the inside, and consequently, we tighten down and close up in order to defend ourselves. This seems like an impossible situation to overcome, since the enemy is somehow already within our gates. But openness makes room for this, too.

I remember the first course I took in my doctoral studies. I hadn't been accepted into the program but was allowed to enroll in a class. There was some added pressure beyond acclimating to a new environment and trying to get a good grade. Just a couple of months before, my family and I had packed up all we owned and left good jobs in a town we enjoyed to move to a new state so that I could try to enroll in this doctoral program that I thought was a perfect fit. Fortunately, we had found worthwhile work and a place to live, but we had a big investment in my getting into this program.

Normally, a prudent person might apply first and see what happens before making a move like this. But it just didn't happen that way. This had to work out. So beyond whatever learning I might gain in the course, I wanted to be sure to impress the two instructors involved in selecting the handful of people for next year's incoming class. At the very least, I didn't want to make a fool out of myself.

So there I was on the third or fourth day of class. Things have been going all right; so far, I thought I'd said a couple of coherent things during class discussion and didn't seem to be alienating my peers or the instructors. My internal image managers were in full gear, making sure I didn't do something stupid. We were in the middle of some unfathomable experiential exercise in which each of us was asked to physically act out something we're fairly good at. The first thing that came to mind was that I was a pretty good basketball player, so I acted out shooting foul shots. Although I felt foolish, I pretended to dribble the ball on the floor, take a clear sight at the imaginary basket, take a deep breath, and make sure I followed through with my shot. OK, I looked ridiculous, but everybody else did, too. So far, so good.

And then it happened. After a few minutes of shooting imaginary baskets, one of the professors, Jack Wideman, walked over, stood in front of me, and watched silently for a moment. Jack was probably six foot three with dramatic, out-of-control eyebrows, and a deep, deliberate, and imposing voice. He said in my general direction, "Ah, I see something."

All I could think is that I'm doomed. He had caught me, exposed me as some imposter who really didn't belong and certainly would never get into a doctoral program. My mind raced, my temperature shot up, and face turned scarlet. I stopped my imaginary foul shooting.

"Don't stop," he says.

Dang, I thought, *I shouldn't have stopped!* I went on, more self-conscious and clumsier than before, but I had to continue as he stood there, arms folded over his chest, eyebrows bushing out.

Then he said it again. "I see something."

I'm dead. I know it, I thought. What seemed like a very long silence soaked up all the oxygen around me. *What did he see?! Put me out of my misery. Tell me!*

More time passed, and I had to keep shooting. I was now sweating like I was running up and down the imaginary court. Then he said it: "I see your inner critic."

What? I thought.

"I see your inner critic. It's pretty busy," he said.

I had no idea what to do, so I kept shooting imaginary balls toward the imaginary basket. He said that I could stop if I wanted to.

What an idiot I am. I should have known to stop! I thought.

He then said, "You know, I think we should start an inner critic support group."

What in the world is he talking about?!

"Yeah," Jack went on, "We should start a support group for them. They seem so desperate that they can't get our attention except by criticizing us. Let's get them all together so they can maybe meet in a circle, and they can offer each other a little support."

I froze but in a different way than I had when my inner critic had me by the throat. This monster, who seemed to live in my head or as a knot in my gut and criticize everything, who seemed to have a style oddly reminiscent of my father's (go figure), was actually weak and needing attention. For someone like me who had a very active inner critic, this was a revelation. Instead of *believing* this monstrous voice as it criticized my actions and my very being, bringing doubt and fear with it, I could actually see it as a scared little part that could be worked with. Maybe it even had something to offer, some quality control or cautionary words, but it was no monster.

What Jack's brilliant remark did was open up a new possibility. Even the inner critic can sit at the table (maybe the kids' table) rather than biting my head off. As this tolerance for myself opened, it made more room to tolerate others. There was less judgment to project onto others and more room to open to them. Carl Jung must have had some understanding of his inner critic when he wrote, "Acceptance of one's self is the essence of the moral problem and the acid test of one's whole outlook on life."[7] Self-acceptance is one of the best predictors of life satisfaction, so we should practice it whenever we get the chance.

Sensitivity, focus, witnessing, and openness provide the foundation and tools for growing presence, which moves through the center of silence to welcome the *beautiful*, right here and now. This sets the stage for the *good*, the *true*, and more, as we shall see.

Openness
Openness allows us to see past our preconceptions and knowledge, our fears, and our pride to see in new ways.

Quiz

For each statement or word, circle the number that describes you best.

(least like me)   1   2   3   4   5   (most like me)

	1	2	3	4	5
I am curious.	1	2	3	4	5
I am open to new experiences.	1	2	3	4	5
I like to try new things (such as food, ideas, and places).	1	2	3	4	5
I often feel a sense of wonder	1	2	3	4	5
I am not defensive.	1	2	3	4	5
I am open-minded.	1	2	3	4	5
I am open-hearted	1	2	3	4	5
I often have "beginner's mind."	1	2	3	4	5
I want to expand my world.	1	2	3	4	5
I am receptive.	1	2	3	4	5

Add up the circled numbers.   Total: _____

10–19	20–29	30–39	40–50
A trailhead	**More is possible**	**A good ally**	**A great strength**

....

PRACTICES

Beholding

When noticing your senses, concentrating your attention, and witnessing the contents, try to bring an attitude of curiosity and openness to the practice. As anything arises or as you direct your attention toward a word or phrase or a feeling or the moment in front of you, just gently open to what arises, like a curious child. At each step, invite yourself to open further. You don't need to do anything with what you notice. Beginner's mind doesn't judge or manipulate; it just beholds as our experience unfolds, opening ourselves gently as the world opens to us.

Something New

Sometimes just changing the routine helps us open to see in new ways. We often navigate through the day on autopilot. This is just fine some of the time, but being present and awake in what we're doing brings more richness and vitality. Simple acts such as going home a different way than you usually do, speaking to someone you would not ordinarily speak to, asking someone you know a question about themselves that you would not ordinarily ask, giving someone a compliment that you might not usually do, telling someone something about you, reading a new book—almost anything can shake up the routine and bring us into the moment a bit more. Challenge yourself to think of even more ways to shake things up.

Walkabout

Walkabout near where you live with no other intent than taking in your surroundings. What do you notice about the world around you when you've finished? Reflect upon and then describe how you typically meet the world (defensively, open-hearted, racing past, or in another way). What is it like for you? What has this done for you in the past? Where did you learn this? Is there a change you would like to make to your style? What would it look and feel like? Perhaps there is an image, metaphor, or model of what it would be like. How might you make it happen? Do you have concerns or doubts about a change like this? How might you address them? What will you do?

Capturing a Moment

Write a haiku about a moment in your day. A haiku is a Japanese poem of seventeen syllables (in three lines of five, seven, and five) intended to capture a moment. Most haikus (a) are acute observations of nature, (b) use simple language and present objects rather than describe them, (c) often contain an object, time, and place, (d) blend in and embody a sense of stillness or harmony, and (e) often present a new discovery or insight in the third line. For example:

> Butterfly awaits
> As it calls for another
> A fountain of hues.[8]

Journaling

A personal journal can be a powerful tool for reflecting, questioning, and dialoguing with various aspects of yourself. Most people agree that the key to journaling is to free write—that is, to write in a stream of consciousness. Whether starting with questions or instead noticing how you're feeling or what's on your mind in the moment, the key is to keep writing without worrying about editing or your audience and just see what arises. Visual journaling—drawing, painting, doodling, making collages, and so forth—can also be a powerful way to get the juices flowing or as a complement to writing itself.

You might just sit quietly for a few moments and see what arises, and then start to write from your flow of consciousness and keep writing until you feel that you have brought something out. Try to capture where you are. You might then read and reflect on what you've just written, and then see whether there is more to be written or if there is a kernel of an idea in one sentence or even one word that calls for more. Continue to free write for another several minutes and then review your progress again.

Inner Critic

Invite yourself into a relaxed, comfortable state of mind. Take a few deep breaths, relax, close your eyes, and settle in for a minute or two.

Next, imagine yourself in a place where you might think and work creatively. Can you find a word or an image that captures the positive sense of this creative flow? Maybe your scene is in front of a computer where you write, in a conversation with someone, or just lying in bed. It's whatever and wherever speaks to you. Imagine the scene, the sounds you notice, the objects that surround you, the temperature—whatever makes up the feeling you have in this space.

Imagine that a guest arrives. You show them what you're working on and talk with them about your ideas. They don't seem to be as pleased about these ideas as you are. Imagine what they say, how they say it, and what their tone and body language tell you. Give the guest a name if they don't have one already.

Begin to write in their voice. Become this inner critic. While they may be a real person, we're now working with them as if they have become part of us (they have, after all). How does the critic view you and your work? Allow the critic to be honest and allow yourself to write whatever they say. You might be surprised. Ask the critic what they want from you. What do they think they're doing for you? What are they afraid of? What does your critic need from you? Notice under what circumstances your critic comes forward. Notice what your reaction is. What's the pattern here?

Now respond to your critic in writing. You may want to let them know that while you have some respect for their opinion, it's time for them find a more constructive role. Perhaps you'll ask them to back off but still remain a quality-control specialist if they have a useful point of view. Tell them what you would like from them, what you would like to hear from them, and what new role they can play. In a written dialogue, negotiate an agreement between the two of you. Be creative and find a way for both parties to agree. Seal the deal.

If your critic slips out of their new role or you get a bit too much lip from them, kindly but firmly tell them to step back while calling forth the scene you established at the beginning of the exercise. This can serve as a reminder, a talisman, or a touchstone, helping you to break the cycle of the destructive inner critic.

Presence

Heart

Wisdom

Creation

PART II

6

THE GOOD

And, in the end, the love you take is equal to the love you make.

—John Lennon and Paul McCartney

Some time ago I worked with a mature graduate student. He was a successful college English teacher who had come back to school for some studies in psychology. He also had a ministry. He independently ministered to death row inmates near his home in the Deep South. The men he encountered had committed horrific crimes. There was really no doubt about their guilt. My friend would spend time with them each week. He saw his work as bearing witness to their lives. In time, they came to understand that he wasn't selling anything—religion, judgment, not even forgiveness; he was just there to be present and meet them where they were. While he offered them the generosity of his careful listening, he was also curious. Who were they? How could these horrors have happened? They weren't going anywhere, and he dropped any agenda other than to be there with them.

In these small private moments, a human being poured out, accompanied by a shattered life's tale usually filled with regret for having already spent this one life so carelessly. My friend made no excuses, and in time he stopped trying to find an explanation for their actions; it no longer seemed to matter. But he said that something else shone right through. He could see not only their humanness but also their divinity. He had trouble finding words to convey the world that opened up in front of him. What he understood was both tangible and ephemeral. He would say that these people were God's children, too. He made it clear that he wasn't saying this because it was what was expected of him or his ministry; instead, he experienced it firsthand. The love he felt for them shocked him. As they were heard, as they were given the space to meet, they seemed to move toward their tender selves where some light still glimmered, however faint. Through the way he looked, he came to see them in a new light, and that light shone on them as well. In recognizing beauty and goodness in every face, he—and we—lift others into the highest self. This is the physics of love. Antoine de Saint-Exupéry's *The Little Prince* reminds us of the secret to this kind of knowing: "One sees clearly only with the heart. Anything that is essential is invisible to the eyes."[1]

The heart is widely regarded as both the goal and a path to our highest possibility. The Indian poet Rabindranath Tagore described love as "freedom: it gives us that fullness of existence which saves us from paying with our soul for objects that are immensely cheap."[2] He tells us that the most important aspects of life are revealed only through the heart and without it our lives are chained to pursuits of little value. Sixteen hundred years ago, Augustine, who generally had plenty to say about how life should be lived, summed it all up this way: "Love, and do what you will."[3] It's that central, that important.

The heart is about relationship, about meeting—communication, community, and communion. We could think of meeting as a way of knowing. But this kind of knowing is different than, say, knowing how to spell a word or that the capital of Kansas is Topeka (I had to look it up to be sure). Something special is happening in the knowing that comes from the heart, as poets, sages, lovers, and mystics have been trying to tell us for a long time.

While modern conceptions generally locate "knowing" in the head, various traditions often identify the most essential knowing with the heart. For example, the Chinese word *xin* is often translated as "mind" but includes both mind and heart.[4] Heart-knowing is recognized as the eye of the Tao in Chinese philosophy. Plato called it the eye of the soul, and the power of the heart is identified as the southerly direction on some Native American tribes' use of the medicine wheel.[5]

The great souls have shown us what the wisdom of an integrated heart can look like. Jesus's love and Buddha's compassion, for example, speak of radical, relational, and sometimes seemingly irrational intelligence—the logic of the heart. As a way of knowing, love opens the world only through a corresponding opening within us.

While the intellect tends to *hold*, categorize, cut, and re-form the world, heart knowing tends to *behold* it. When we see a stunning piece of art or a beautiful natural vista, we may be captured by it for a moment without thought. We just seem to be in a kind of frequency lock as we behold what it has to offer. The gap between us shrinks. This opens to a sense of appreciation, curiosity, even awe. The mysterious but oft-reported grandparent-love phenomenon seems to be of this ilk. While parents often describe remarkable bonding and I'll-do-anything-for-you caring and sacrifice, grandparents often report being surprised by the quality of the love they feel for their grandchildren that is in some way different than what they'd experienced with their own children. The difference has something to do with appreciating and beholding this child without so much worry about judgment, discipline, or whether they get to school on time. The love of a grandparent often feels unconditional, freer, and less psychologically complex than a parent's love. Often grandparents may be able to just enjoy children for who they are. And maybe this shows us a particular quality of love that may be possible even if we're not grandparents.

This goal and this path of heart has something to do with trying to maintain that openness and freshness throughout our daily lives. Sometimes this means slowing down and taking time out just to appreciate the moment at hand, like a young child lost in the passing clouds. There is no way to force this. It's like trying to push a limp noodle; it just does not respond to force in the way we would hope. But we can develop graciousness toward welcoming it, just like the death row minister or the grandparent. There is no judgment, no discrimination from the heart—just an opportunity for connecting.

Seeing through the eye of the heart is essential not only in human relationships but in science as well. Recall that this intimate knowing provided a portal into another world for Nobel laureate in genetics Barbara McClintock, who described a less detached empiricism, one in which she gained "a feeling for the organism."[6] With this feeling and openness, the other is no longer separate, and the gap between us shrinks as we become participants, not just bystanders. We get in sync, in tune, in harmony and arrive at understanding. (The word "understanding" literally means to stand under or among.)

When we stretch past our self-separateness and self-interest to truly meet the other, communication can deepen to a genuine sense of communion. From the global economy to global warming, we come to understand and experience the world as interdependent, and therefore, our satisfaction and very survival depends on the quality of our relations with others and with the world. At no time in history has this been both more apparent and more urgent.

Good for Something

A heathen once came to Rabbi Hillel and said that he would convert if Hillel taught him the whole Torah while standing on one foot. Without missing a beat and apparently standing on one foot, Hillel replied, "What is hateful to you, do not do to your neighbor: that is the whole Torah while the rest is commentary; go and learn it."[7] This familiar Golden Rule is found across traditions and time as a moral touchstone for right action, for the Good. In Hinduism, for example, "This is the sum of duty: do not do to others what would cause pain if done to you."[8] Around the fifth century BCE, Confucius wrote, "Do not do to others what you do not want them to do to you."[9] The Greek philosopher Epictetus says it this way: "What you would avoid suffering yourself, seek not to impose on others."[10]

This ethic of reciprocity, as the Golden Rule is referred to, cuts deeper still in the language of Black Elk, the Native American Sioux elder whose childhood visions and wise insight helped lead his people during the North American genocide of the 1800s. Black Elk said, "All things are our relatives; what we do to everything, we do to ourselves. All is really One."[11] Black Elk described not only reciprocity but also a profound realization of unity, of indivisibility, as the source for right action. Any idea that is as universal as the Golden Rule comes out of our shared human experience, an outer expression of a kind of unfolding courtship—communication to community to communion.

However, the work of the heart isn't to make or even to follow rules, golden or otherwise, but instead to meet the world heart to heart and, from this meeting, recognize one another as relatives. Rumi pointed precisely to the epicenter of the *good*: "Out beyond ideas of wrongdoing and rightdoing there is a field. I'll meet you there."[12] Rumi's powerful heretical lines teach that goodness is most fundamentally not about rules but instead about meeting ("I'll meet you there."). It surely does seem that we need moral codes. We benefit from the rule of law, but the step in our evolution toward right action has something to do with the intelligence of the heart.

There is plenty of evidence that we have capacities for greed and violence. We don't have to look far to find selfish and monstrous acts in our history or in today's news. But there is also plenty of evidence for something else that seems quite natural. Even among young children there is mounting evidence of more loving capacities.

Our birthright seems to include natural compassion, a capacity to feel sympathy for suffering and the impulse to reach out and help others. When someone falls in front of us or an injustice occurs within our view, we often feel a push from our insides to take action and help. Apathy, fear, violence, and self-absorption can be overcome by the recognition of suffering and the action of service through an open heart. Even tiny children seem to have some kind of natural compassion built right in.

My friend Stacey was visiting her parents' home for the Thanksgiving holiday. A large group of family and friends had gathered. For several years, her marriage had been difficult, and on this day, her hope and her effort seemed to finally be exhausted. In the comfort of the family home, she let herself really grasp that the marriage was over. At one point she drifted away from the group and wandered through the large house until she landed alone in a quiet room. She suddenly found herself just letting go to all the struggle and grief of this loss, and she started to weep. She didn't think anyone could hear her until her almost-two-year-old nephew walked up to her. He simply stood there still and touched her arm. In that moment, she said, it was like a current going through her. "It simply blew me away," she said. "I have never forgotten it, and it has always stood for me as a supreme example of the healing capacity of a silent, loving presence."[13] Surely this little child didn't understand her predicament. And maybe we're making too much of it. But she had a distinct sense that he felt her pain and reached out with an innocent heart to simply make contact. We'll explore how this might work a little later on.

The inherent goodness or badness of our nature will probably remain an area of debate indefinitely, since there is plenty of evidence for both. Freud saw our fundamental nature as animal-like, sexual and aggressive, and that it needed to be tamed and contained by the rational ego. The twentieth century seems to bear that out. The Vietnam-era anti-war protest song "Get Together," popularized by the Youngbloods, recognized our options. "You can make the mountains ring/Or make the angels cry."[14] But are we naturally good or are we bad? Are we endowed with sin or goodness?

In the fourth century, there was a doctrinal debate between Augustine and a fellow from the British Isles named Pelagius, also called Morgan. Augustine made the case for original sin—that we are all born as bad seeds. Morgan, although also quite interested in sin, believed in our perfectibility; he thought that we have a natural capacity to do good and that our work in the world was about divinization, or working toward the perfection of our being. Morgan believed that we strayed from the good not because of some flawed nature but because of following a bad example. It was not because of our inherent badness but because we may be ignorant of our true nature and potential and thus have trouble drawing "upon the treasure of our soul."[15] As you might recognize, Augustine won that debate and with unsportsmanlike conduct tried, repeatedly, to have Morgan declared a heretic.

In Morgan's view, to help us make the right choices we are endowed with three faculties or capacities: *posse* (natural ability or potential to do good), *velle* (free will or choice), and *esse* (action). Like love, the *good* becomes a verb, an intention and action. The word "sin" comes from archery and means missing the mark, as when the arrow strays from the bull's-eye, implying that we are in some way living off-target from our true nature or what is possible. But the good news is that with each next shot, so to speak, redemption is possible as we bring our actions in alignment with our own true nature. This, like most things involving living beings, is a feedback loop. We recalibrate our direction through our misses, so they, too, are our grace. In this sense, it is our practicing of making moral choices that brings perfection, or at least the possibility of improvement.

Knowing and feeling are at the root of love, but there appears to be yet another part to it, as Morgan identified. When we think about how we live life each day, it may be helpful and practical to also consider love as a verb, as the *good* is something we do: "The will to extend one's self for the purpose of nurturing one's own or another's spiritual growth" is how psychiatrist M. Scott Peck defined it.[16] It can involve care and affection, but as author bell hooks said, simply giving care doesn't mean we are loving; imagine begrudging, obligatory, burdensome, resentful care.[17] This is not exactly oozing with warmth and generosity. The experience of genuine love doesn't just involve care but also things like respect, commitment, trust, knowledge, responsibility, recognition, courage, honesty, and openness. As Peck wrote, "Love is as love does."[18] To think of love as an action rather than exclusively a feeling gives us accountability and responsibility.

Maybe we are like the trinity—that is, Dorothy's trinity of the Lion, Scarecrow, and Tin Man in *The Wizard of Oz*. They each already had the capacity for what they most desired: courage, heart, intelligence. They just needed to claim it. And they did, making it theirs for all to see, precisely through their actions. Said another way, they were not just good; they were good for something. This is the challenge of the heart.

Heat

Whether our sun or a great soul, it is both light and heat that is their offering. Love gives off heat that we recognize in the warmth of caring eyes, a tender touch, and an act of kindness. Heat brings comfort, belonging, and a sense of being at home or being welcome wherever we are. Heat is the fire we gather around as it makes us comfortable enough to stick around and unbutton the coverings over our hearts. We are drawn forth when someone's warmth or caring for us is evident, when that friend or relative sees a spark in us or reaches out to us, and the coach or teacher who notices a child's effort and who, by simply saying, "Nice job today!" affirms the child's worth and maybe their very existence. These are moments when someone takes the time to hold and behold us for who we are. Especially these days when isolation and alienation are common, little gestures of kindness can be like glue that holds our lives together.

Psychologist Ira Progoff told us, "Love depends upon the capacity to reach beneath the surface of persons, to feel and touch the seed of life that is hidden there. And love becomes a power when it is capable of evoking that seed and drawing it forth from its hiding place."[19] Seeds sprout when the soil is warm enough.

We know of human resilience. Many people who have grown up in very difficult, abusive, or neglectful situations but have thrived nonetheless have nearly always had a "leg-up" person, a spiritual friend, someone who made a difference in life, who saw a spark in them, who noticed them, who offered a kind word or took genuine interest in them and, in so doing, warmed their lives.

Sometimes we can recognize a thing by its absence. The absence of the heart in any human endeavor is described as cold-hearted, without connection or resonance, no care or concern, and the result is a fundamental absence of humanity, a lack of sensitivity, and usually a destructive, mechanical, or brutal out-come. Coldhearted action is driven by things like expediency, greed, and fear rather than by the heart. Without heart, the good seems to slip away, love seems absent, and we leap into judgment. Without the heart we see an old oak tree as merely wood to be cut down and cut up. We consider cutting the top of Kentucky hill-tops off as the most sensible way to get coal to generate electricity or dropping bombs as the only way to solve certain problems. Such actions may be expedient, even necessary, but to the heart they are never good.

These days, from hearing the news or even being on the play-ground or in the boardroom, it would be easy to get the message that might makes right and the strongest ultimately win, that greed is good, that technology and celebrity are power, and that power is happiness. But the great souls of the world and the wisdom tradi-tions remind us that greatest power is not force or money or fame but the heat of love. We find our way when we turn toward this endless source, as Teilhard de Chardin said.

The day will come when, after harnessing the ether, the winds, the waves, the tides, gravitation, we shall harness for God the energies of love. And, on that day, for the second time in the history of the world, man will have discovered fire."[20]

One of Teilhard de Chardin's insights was that human evolution is inhibited by disconnection. The cold of isolation and the coldheartedness that engenders marginalization is precisely the opposite of the heat of love. He wrote, "No evolutionary future awaits anyone except in association with everyone else."[21]

Beyond heat as the warmth of caring relationships, we also know heat as passion. Young people especially often feel the pulse of passion for loves of all sorts, from new partners to new fashion. My father would take me to the Syracuse University home basketball games when I was a young boy. He had season tickets, although he would sometimes boldly sneak me through the turn-style and into the arena ticketless by the sheer momentum of the in-rushing crowd and his air of confidence. On at least one occasion when there wasn't a seat for me, I remember him telling me to sit on the end of the team bench where, momentarily, there was an extra seat. On those occasions, from the opening warm-ups dribbled to the closing buzzer, I felt like I was ready to burst open. I was so excited and alive. I both loved and hated watching. I wanted to get out there and play so badly, but at nine years old I had to confine myself to shouting and jumping up and down in my seat (or any I could find). In those days, there was a track that ran around the basketball floor in the old Manley Field House where the games where held. At halftime I would take my bursting passion behind the bleachers on the far side of the building and run as fast as I could back and forth on the track until I was out of breath or it was time for the second-half warm-ups.

Passion, from Latin *patior* means to suffer or endure—and still want more. Passion and desire (*eros* in Greek) heats and motivates.

Passion adds drama and energy to life, and it can be a powerful telltale for our longing, love, and work in the world—what we may be good for. Without some degree of passion, life can feel flat, like we are just going through the motions. We are sometimes pushed from within by our own heat, perhaps to overcome shyness and uncertainty or a social convention to approach some new love. We also know that sometimes this kind of fixation on a love of any sort can get out of hand, as heat can singe and even immolate. The challenge is to find a way to use the energy of this passion without being used up by it. We'll explore this navigation and integration as we proceed.

Our capacity for love is innate. It can expand and warm or contract and turn cold. As we'll explore in the next four chapters, the heart may be directed toward others as the understanding of empathy or move us toward action as compassion. It may be expressed as gratitude or given away as tenderness or forgiveness. It can be recognized as interdependence and also felt as the heat of passion. And it serves as the basis for community and communion, and some even see it as the force behind the front edge of human evolution.

7

COMPASSION

I slept and dreamt that life was joy
I awoke and saw that life was service.
I acted and behold, service was joy.

—Rabindranath Tagore

On a back road on the way to school one morning, my daughters and I quickly approached what appeared to be a good-sized turtle in the middle of the road. With a quick turn of the wheel and palpable relief all around, we successfully swerved to avoid it without careening into the ditch. As we arrived at school a few minutes later, my then nine-year-old became very serious and said, "Dad, will you go back and make sure the turtle gets across OK?"

I could see my five-year-old in the backseat, eyes wide with concern, repeatedly nodding her little head to reinforce the request. Although I needed to be somewhere, I said I would go back. And for the record, I did. Well, the turtle turned out to be a wadded-up old shirt. (Time to start wearing my glasses more often.) But both of the little ones felt that natural deep impulse of connection and compassion and, with it, the responsibility to help if we could.

Whether we think of this impulse in terms of Morgan's *posse* (the natural capacity and tendency to do good) or from a Buddhist perspective in which compassion is seen not as something to develop like a muscle but as an expression of our true nature, compassion seems to be our birthright. Moral codes, rules of conduct, and virtuous ideals may be helpful handholds as we navigate through life, but the goal is to free our hearts and allow them to do what they do naturally: love.

Five-year-old Hanna was walking with her mother along a city street in her home of Vancouver, British Columbia, when they came upon a man eating out of a garbage container. Hanna was confused and questioned her mother about what she had never seen or imagined before. Her mother explained what homelessness meant. Hanna recalled,

> I was very sad and felt sick about it. "Why? Why? Why?" I asked. If everybody shared what they had, would that cure homelessness? Then I started school, and one day when I was going to school, I saw another homeless person. Everything she had was in one grocery cart. Now my heart was too sad.
>
> That night before I went to bed I wished I could cure homelessness. Everybody needs a home. I love my home. My mom told me that sometimes when you worry and feel sad about things, if you do something to change the problem, your heart won't feel so sad.

That got Hanna thinking about what she might do. She began by taking empty baby food jars and coloring them red with black spots. When asked, she explained that they were Ladybug Jars. She was going to fill them with coins for the homeless. One day she took the jars to her classroom at school and explained her plan. It didn't take long before the class joined in, bringing their own compassion and coins to the surface. And soon other teachers heard of the plan and followed Hanna's lead. The local media got wind of this, and the word spread and along with it red-and-black coin-filled baby food jars. When the heart is touched, it spreads like a contagion.

Hanna was asked to be the keynote speaker at Toronto's prestigious Empire Club when she was only seven years old. In her speech, she said her hope was for everyone to have a home to sleep in and a fridge. So far Hanna's ladybugs have raised more than five hundred thousand dollars for the homeless.[1]

Hanna's compassion serves the "we" and simultaneously nourishes the individual, the "I." Compassion is self-reinforcing; it just feels good to give freely. But the heart of compassion may also be the base for the transformation of the species. Charles Darwin is known for his classic *The Origin of the Species*, which introduced the theory of natural selection to the world. *Origin* was about the biology of prehuman evolution, but the extension of some of his ideas into the fields of human sociology and politics—namely Social Darwinism—led to a kind of justification for the survival-of-the-fittest mind-set that has in part justified the hyper-competition and selfishness among modern humans. It served to reinforce our lower drives for domination rather than partnership. However, in his final work, *The Descent of Man*, Darwin wrote that, indeed, the survival of a species was driven by mutation, selection, and certain drives that enhanced an organism's likelihood of passing useful genes along, but also according to Darwin, other forces entirely, "higher agencies," as he called them, account for human development.

David Loye, a former Princeton psychology professor, discovered that while Darwin used the phrase "natural selection" only twice in his last work, he used the word "love" ninety-five times and "morality" or "moral sensitivity" ninety-two times.[2] Darwin's theory of human evolution was pointing to none other than love and compassion as the agent of human development. Mutuality, sympathy, mind, reason, consciousness, imagination, and especially love are the words Darwin used to describe this human transformation. Remarkable. Also remarkable is that while Darwin's earlier principles have come to define the foundation of fields like evolutionary biology and have provided generations of students with a social imprinting that survival of the fittest is the natural way we get ahead, his thoughts emphasizing love are rarely associated with him or human evolution. And yet, as so many have recognized through the ages, it is precisely the reclamation of the force of the heart that is needed to evolve through our current dilemmas—where greed, violence, selfishness, and domination seem to be the cultural legacy of applying only half of Darwin's ideas. We have a chance to become conscious agents in our own evolution, and for Darwin, the secret to doing so was right in our hearts and minds.

Like Darwin's *Descent*, the wisdom traditions tell us that if there is only one thing we should know, one piece of advice for us to heed about the spiritual path, it is that both the path and the goal are in our hearts. Christ's message was love; Buddha called it compassion. To have love and to offer compassion are what make us both fully human and fully divine.

In many religious traditions today, if one is to be blessed and belong, they must believe. We are asked, "Do you believe?" or "Are you a believer?" There is a long habit of separating those who believe in the "right thing" from those who don't, and we all know the past and present violence done in the name of "correct belief." Religious scholar Karen Armstrong suggests that *belief* took on a meaning of trust in God and then in the seventeenth century became its contemporary understanding as an intellectual acceptance of something, such as "I believe in ghosts," or "I believe in UFOs." But the origin of "to believe" meant to love, to prize, to hold dear, to give one's heart. So for one to believe did not imply simple adherence to a certain creed or doctrine or idea of God or a god. To say "I believe," to be a believer, was instead to make a commitment to love, to help others overcome their suffering, to engage in acts of loving-kindness. Importantly, one was to understand the central point of the faith not through holding on to an idea but only through the practice of loving commitment. As Armstrong suggests, the test for this time is not about believing things; it is about behaving differently.[3]

In It Together

There is a fundamental change in worldview that has been elbowing its way into everything from physics to business. The bottom line of this shift is captured in the prefix of the word "compassion" (*com* means "together"). We are in this life together. From melting ice caps to economic meltdowns and the melding minds of social neuroscience, we're beginning to understand the degree to which we are connected or part of a whole. We're coming to take for granted the realities of environmental systems and global economies, and at even more fundamental levels, the wild and wacky world of quantum physics, where many of our conventional assumptions about how the world operates get turned on their heads, yet it provides support and metaphor for a truly unified universe and demonstrates just how interconnected we are.

The perfect example is non-locality, the direct interaction of two objects that can be separated by any distance yet demonstrate simultaneity, showing in experiment after experiment that the objects are interconnected at a fundamental level that we can observe but not explain very well.

Quantum physicist David Bohm spoke about "the implicate" and "the explicate" as a way of making sense of the quantum world.[4] Essentially, the explicate is the material form governed by rules of space and time, while the implicate implies a "hidden," or deeper, level or system of reality. For Bohm, everything within the implicate order is interconnected, and in principle, any individual element could reveal information about every other element in the universe. Bohm saw an "unbroken wholeness of the totality of existence as an undivided flowing movement without borders."[5] He believed that this not only applied to quantum physics but was also an appropriate way to see human consciousness.

We don't have to go to the quantum level to explain this invisible and indivisible nature of reality. From biology to family therapy, many have put forward systems to help us understand the nature of this interconnection and its influence on our lives.

Anthropologist Gregory Bateson described it as the "pattern that connects."[6] Bateson fought against the reductionism of everything to matter and sought to reintroduce the mind into the understanding of the world. In Bateson's view, nothing exists on its own; relationships define an object, and in a psychological or anthropological sense, we are always a self-in-relation, defined by everything connected to us. Like Bohm, Bateson implies that there are deep structures and patterns that undergird and integrate. We are connected, like bio-electromagnetic fields overlapping in time and space with one another. Systems theorist Ervin László reprises the ancient Hindu Akashic field, where we have potential access to all information through a kind of frequency lock.[7] Like the atmosphere or biosphere that we share, Teilhard de Chardin used the term "noosphere" in 1922 to describe a kind of emerging global consciousness.[8] The Greek root *nous* means "mind"; thus Teilhard de Chardin was describing the shared space where our minds interconnect. This space grows more complex and aware as our social interconnection moves, in Teilhard de Chardin's view, toward greater consciousness and more integration—what he called the Omega Point. In some ways, the internet is providing a technological underpinning for one kind of shared global consciousness.

Biologist Rupert Sheldrake demonstrated connections of this sort in some surprising ways.[9] Sometimes our dogs, he showed, know when we're coming home.[10] Not by clock time or sunlight or cues from the environment such as the noise of a bus route, but from some connection that exists between us. Regardless of how random our return schedule is, before we arrive, the dog gets off the forbidden sofa and moves into position to greet us at the door with its tail wagging. Such claims are not without controversy, of course, but his evidence appears legitimate and compelling. Sheldrake explained this and related phenomena by the concept of morphic fields and morphic resonance—that is, some kind of energy field that connects us through a kind of resonant frequency. This should not be so utterly surprising, as we already have other invisible, well-established fields, such as gravitation and electromagnetism, and at least on the quantum level the demonstrations of interconnection are largely taken as fact.

Psychologically and socially, we exist between autonomy and connection, between independence and interdependence. From the Renaissance to the apex of Modernism, the Western world has emphasized the self, individuality, agency, free will, and the like. This has unleashed incredible creativity and heroic accomplishment as well as greed and selfishness. But this emerging worldview that emphasizes our lives together provides metaphors and recognition that reinforce inherent connections with one another, the world, and ourselves.

The realization experienced by so many of our great models was that we don't just interact but interconnect and interdepend and thus are inter-responsible. This is a fundamental change in worldview that has profound implications for our assumptions about living. This may serve as a conceptual guide that provides an alternative to things like social Darwinism and ultimately helps balance the power of autonomy with the power of interconnection. Organizational development expert Peter Senge recognized it this way:

> Connectedness is the defining feature of the new worldview, connectedness as an organizing principle of the universe, connectedness between the "outer world" of manifest phenomena and the "inner world" of lived experience, and, ultimately, connectedness among people and between humans and the larger world. While philosophers and spiritual teachers have long spoken about connectedness, a scientific worldview of connectedness could have sweeping influence in "shifting the whole" given the role of science and technology in the modern world.[11]

The great sages and saints recognize that we are in this together. As Black Elk told us,

> I was standing on the highest mountain of them all and round about beneath me was the whole hoop of the world. For I was seeing in a sacred manner the shapes of all things in the spirit. And the shape of all shapes as they must live together as one being. And I saw that it was holy.[12]

When have you seen in a sacred manner? What is it that you have seen? What engenders this kind of seeing? Bohm, Bateson, and Black Elk all implored us to peer into the deeper structures and patterns that undergird and integrate our lives, and we do so, especially through the heart.

Compassion in Action

Compassion, whether embodied through an act of generosity, kindness, care, or forgiveness, is a gift freely given. A true gift, one with no strings attached, has power and medicine for everyone involved. Mother Teresa understood this as the heart of service.

> To me, God and service are one and the same. Compassion is the joy of sharing. It's doing the small things for the love of each other—just a smile, or carrying a bucket of water, or showing some simple kindness. . . . The fruit of love is service, which is compassion in action.[13]

When service is seen in instrumental ways, as something one does to "be good" or earn a place in heaven, then its power is diluted. No longer is there the joy that Mother Teresa named. Rather than being comprehended as a moral issue or a way of doing good, service may be best understood as a "way of knowing" the world directly; it is a chance to come in close and assume responsibility for something or someone, if only for a moment.[14] The result can be monumental. This capacity is our birthright, once again evident and able to be activated even in small children, reminding us just how natural this loving heart is.

When a dove got out of its cage in her classroom, Megan, an elementary school teacher, gave seven-year-old Kendrick, an extremely disruptive and uninterested student, the responsibility to capture, hold, and care for the dove before placing it back in the cage. Megan related what happened.

> When another student came up to my desk and tried to help, he politely told him it was his job, and he could finish it on his own. He had rarely spoken politely to adults before that moment, much less to his classmates. For the first time, I saw

a loving and caring side of him. Before that incident, when I had tried to hug him, he would freeze up, as if he didn't know what to do. Now we can't get him to stop giving us hugs. At the end of the following day, he approached me and said that he wanted to come back to school the next day. Before that he would often and only say, "I hate school."

Kendrick's school performance suddenly made dramatic improvement. One day, when asked to describe his favorite teacher, he wrote, "Mrs. Partain I like." I was amazed to have gotten that much structure, since most days I just received a conglomeration of letters copied at random. Often I could not even read them. Now he had not only written words that were not displayed on the word list, but had organized them into a phrase to answer the question. A few weeks later, he read his first book. I was so proud of him that I started crying as he was reading to me.[15]

This event actually began with Megan herself being given an assignment in her graduate class: to first bring to mind a current student who is disconnected, maybe a student who is your least favorite or most disruptive. It was not hard for Megan to pick Kendrick. The task then was to simply make contact with no other intention than trying to get to know this student. Megan's willingness to listen with her heart and take action—in this case, to ask Kendrick for help—was just the opening that made the difference in both their hearts. Our work sometimes may just be to help others find ways to express their compassion.

We know the world differently when we serve it. A teacher serves a child, a child cares for a dove, and this becomes power and medicine that serves the heart of the world. With compassion in action, it does not matter what the act is or its scale—giving a sandwich or a prayer for a homeless person, caring for a hurt creature, or building a school for hundreds of children. Gratitude and appreciation, forgiveness and generosity, kindness and care— the challenge is to allow ourselves to be touched and find a way to let this stream through us and through the world. All expressions of love are maximal.

Compassion
The sympathy and desire to reach out and help another.

Quiz

For each statement or word, circle the number that describes you best.

(least like me)   1   2   3   4   5   (most like me)

I take time to show appreciation to those around me.	1	2	3	4	5
I give freely and easily to others.	1	2	3	4	5
I don't hold on to grudges and hurts.	1	2	3	4	5
I am tolerant and patient toward my own limitations and mistakes.	1	2	3	4	5
I stay heart-centered through my day.	1	2	3	4	5
I accept others without judgment.	1	2	3	4	5
I am loving and kind toward others.	1	2	3	4	5
I am kind and nurturing to myself.	1	2	3	4	5
I serve my community.	1	2	3	4	5
I feel compassion toward others often.	1	2	3	4	5

Add up the circled numbers.   Total: _____

10–19	20–29	30–39	40–50
A trailhead	**More is possible**	**A good ally**	**A great strength**

....

PRACTICES

Living Kindness

What if our practice for this day, or perhaps several days, was simply to lead with kindness, in the first words upon greeting someone, the expression on our faces, our body language, and, most significantly, the underlying attitude and intention in our hearts and minds? Give it a try. At the end of the day or days, reflect upon the experience. How were you feeling? How did others respond? What surprised you? What gets in the way of kindness?

Loving-Kindness

The following is a form of the classic loving-kindness meditation, or metta, from Buddhist practice:

Sitting comfortably, assume a relaxed and upright position. Take a few deep breaths and allow your body to relax and settle in. See if certain phrases emerge from your heart that express what you wish most deeply for yourself, not just for today but in an enduring way. Find phrases that are big enough and general enough that you can ultimately wish them for all of life, such as, "May I live in health and harmony. May I be fulfilled. May I find my way." While in a contemplative state, gently repeat these phrases over and over again and have your mind rest in the phrases. Whenever you find your attention has wandered, don't worry; just see if you can gently let go and begin again.

Next, call to mind someone you care about. Visualize them and say their name to yourself. Get a feeling for their presence, and then direct the phrases of loving-kindness to them. "May they live in health and harmony. May they be fulfilled. May they find their way." Use whatever phrases seem best to you.

Next, call to mind someone you know who's having a difficult time right now. They've experienced a loss, a painful feeling, or a difficult situation. If someone like that comes to mind, imagine them sitting in front of you. Say their name. Get a feeling for their presence and offer the phrases of loving-kindness to them.

Think of someone who plays some role in your life, some function that you don't know very well, whom you don't have a particular feeling for or against. Imagine them sitting in front of you, and offer these same phrases of loving-kindness to them.

When we aim the heart in this way, we're opening to connecting, extending our caring in all directions, boundlessly, infinitely. Ultimately, we open in this way to all beings everywhere. "May all beings live in health and harmony. May all beings be fulfilled. May all beings find their way." When you feel ready, open your eyes and see if you can bring this energy with you throughout the day.

Prayer of the Loving Gaze

The instructions are as simple as it gets: Look on everything with love. That's it. Whether a family member or stranger, a tree, or your lunch, simply bring a loving gaze and feeling to all you encounter. Over the course of several minutes or a whole day, we may find our intention and attention drifting, so gently remind yourself to bring back the attitude of a loving gaze that is key.

Gently Listening

This can easily be done with a group seated together. Divide the group in two and pair each person with a partner. Have partners sit facing one another. The group leader briefly explains the necessity of trust and confidentiality, that what will be said will be kept respectfully between the partners. The task is just to listen deeply and take in what the other is saying as fully as possible. There is no need to respond with words to the speaker; just listen deeply to the other. Once that is agreed upon, invite everyone to settle into relaxed silence. Take a few moments to really fall deeply and gently inward. Upon the ring of the bell or whatever signal you use, each person will take turns speaking to their partner from the heart for two minutes or more about one of the following:

- A time when you were gentle to yourself
- A time that was difficult for you
- A time when you felt loved

Gently hold the space for one another without speaking a response. Thank one another. You might want to talk about what that was like with one another or even try another round.

Thanks

In many traditions, there is frequent emphasis on gratitude, on noting and naming what we are thankful for. This is usually taken up as a devotional practice. Whether in a blessing before a meal, a prayer at bedtime, a daily journaling activity, or a deep feeling of appreciation for a loved one or a lovely day, there is something about thankfulness that seems to bring forth a desirable quality of mind. This can help settle our hunger and allow us to humble our ambition and appreciate the gifts we're given. The power is not in merely saying the words; simply going through the motions usually does little.

Take a few deep breaths and settle into your seat. As you relax, bring your attention to the area of your chest—that place inside where you have experienced the feelings of love, care, or appreciation. Bring to mind and heart something or someone you genuinely feel appreciation for. Take a quiet moment to really bring them to view, to bring them to your heart. What feeling do they evoke? Do your best to really feel some of that right now and hold on to that for several moments. If distractions arise, just bring your awareness back to the area of your heart. Now simply radiate your appreciation, gratitude, or love in some way, sending that energy to them through your heart.

Alternatively, you could keep a gratitude journal. Simply note the things you have been grateful for over the course of a day. When done earnestly, many describe that throughout the day they find themselves looking for things to be grateful for. They have attuned themselves to gratitude.

8

EMPATHIZING

All real living is meeting.

—Martin Buber

Most of us notice that when we really pay attention and are open to the person in front of us, we come closer to understanding their experience. This is simple enough, although it can be easily forgotten when we are caught up in agendas and the hurry of daily activity. But when we really meet another, we begin to *feel into* another's world, which is the meaning of the word "empathize." When this occurs, understanding grows into that sense of, "Oh, this is who you are. I didn't really see you before." The person in front of us begins to take on new dimensions, like a cardboard cutout coming to three-dimensional life. They have depth and substance, meaning and complexity, value and beauty, beyond what we had seen previously. And often our own fantasies of who we thought the other person was or who we wanted them to be are revealed as the individual steps into existence outside the gravity of our projections. In this way, empathy and understanding provide a powerful experience of both self and other.

Because of the profound importance of this kind of meeting, empathy has been described as the basis of moral development[1] and even the trait that makes us most human.[2] We realize our humanity and our divinity through the quality of our meetings. As theologian Martin Buber told us, "All real living is meeting."[3] Our lives are lived at the intersection of you and me. And when we really meet and understand others, it becomes much more difficult to perpetrate violence against them. This is the root of a living morality.

Linking

There is a natural tendency to synchronize, to link up with others. Fireflies flash in unison by the thousands. Women who live together regularly have their menstrual cycles sync up. In 1665 Christiaan Huygens observed that his two pendulum clocks would swing in unison when they were hanging on the same support. Remarkably, this same phenomenon takes place on the level of planets, protons, and persons, essentially on every level of the cosmos. Synchrony—ordered behavior through time— occurs everywhere, from the quantum level to the herd mentality of stock traders.[4,5]

The kind of linking in empathy is not only about rhythm but also about frequency. When two violins are located in the same room and a string is plucked on the first one, the string tuned to the same frequency on the second violin will vibrate, thus sounding the note. In the field of acoustics, this is called sympathetic resonance. Lovers, parents, close friends, a good therapist and their patient, or a child and their puppy can recognize a kind of emotional resonance as we "feel into" the other or pick up their "vibes" or get "in sync" with them. Through this resonance, we have the capacity to know the other with profound immediacy and directness and, in so doing, come in touch with their pain, anger, or joy very quickly.

Neuroscience has been uncovering a bit of the hardwiring for this linking between mammals. Brain structures called mirror neurons are capable of responding instantaneously to the emotions or actions of another person in such a way that the brain of someone witnessing another person is activated as if they were the person they were seeing. This neurobiological phenomenon was first identified in macaque monkeys.[6] A monkey was hooked up to electroencephalogram (EEG) measuring brain electrical activity. Researchers recorded patterns of brain activity when the monkey peeled a banana. What surprised the researchers was that when another monkey or a person peeled a banana in front of the wired-up monkey, the same areas of the brain were activated as if the hooked-up monkey were peeling it himself. It wasn't just that he was seeing it; it was as if he were doing it. This led to the identification of mirror neurons, constellations of brain tissue that mirror or resonate with another person's (or monkey's) brain and may be a component of empathy. This "neurological looping" demonstrates a kind of very real brain-to-brain connection and helps open the budding field of social neuroscience.

Just like two singers finding the right pitch, when we successfully link up with someone, we harmonize in some way. This linking or looping also happens with the athletic team, the loving couple, a mother and child—even with those who have had a rough start in life.

In response to rising levels of aggression in schoolchildren, Mary Gordon, president of the Roots of Empathy program, has taken the unlikely step of bringing babies and mothers into public school classrooms in various countries around the globe.[7] The program introduces a mother and her new baby to a classroom for twenty-seven visits over a school year. An instructor from the program accompanies them and coaches the students to observe the baby's development and label the baby's feelings throughout the visit ("What do you think the baby is feeling?"). The instructor also invites students to notice and reflect upon their own feelings and one another's feelings along the way ("What are you thinking?").

Mary relayed the story of Darren: "Darren was the oldest child I ever saw in a Roots of Empathy class. He was in grade 8 and had been held back twice. He was two years older than everyone else and was already starting to grow a beard." Mary knew his story. "His mother had been murdered in front of his eyes when he was four years old, and [he] had lived in a succession of foster homes ever since. Darren looked menacing because he wanted us to know he was tough; his head was shaved except for a ponytail at the top and he had a tattoo on the back of his head."

The instructor of the Roots of Empathy program was explaining to the class about the differences in temperament that day. She invited the young mother who was visiting the class with Evan, her six-month-old baby, to share her thoughts about her son's temperament. Joining in the discussion, the mother told the class how Evan liked to face outward when he was in the Snugli and didn't want to cuddle into her and how she would have preferred to have a more cuddly baby. As the class ended, the mother asked if anyone wanted to try on the Snugli, which was green and trimmed with pink brocade. To everyone's surprise, Darren offered to try it on, and as the other students scrambled to get ready for lunch, he strapped it on. Then he asked if he could put Evan in. The mother was a little apprehensive but then handed him her baby. Darren then put Evan in the Snugli, facing toward his chest. Instantly and to his mother's surprise, Evan snuggled right in. Darren gently took him to a quiet corner and rocked back and forth with the baby in his arms for several minutes as the jaws of those looking on dropped, amazed by Darren's tenderness. Finally, Darren went back to where the mother and the instructor were waiting and asked, "If nobody has ever loved you, do you think you could still be a good father?"[8]

When systems link, whether within us or between us, such as with Darren and baby Evan, we find harmony. When we fail to harmonize and integrate, living systems, from individuals to families and countries, tend to move toward either chaos or rigidity.[9]

Tuning In

Improving empathy means learning how to better tune in to both one another and to ourselves. An example is paying close attention to what another person does or says: *I noticed that she rocked back on her chair when I asked her that question; I wonder if that means that I've hit a nerve and she is trying to back away from answering.* Or we might take note of the particular words used or notice how they are spoken, such as the subtle inflection in someone's voice that betrays some sarcasm or skepticism. For example, think of all the tonal variations and thus meanings in a sentence like, "Are we there yet?" and you get a sense of how easily meaning changes with little shifts in tone. Or we might pick up the subtle changes in pupil dilation or facial muscles. Researcher Paul Ekman has helped demonstrate that the forty-three muscles of the face are basically neurologically hardwired to the emotional system, and he has been using his research to train airline security screeners, among many others, to read faces in this way.[10] Universal across cultures, a fleeting frown or smile may betray the feeling underneath, and if we pay attention, we may learn to read these cues accurately.

We know from experience that much of our communication is beneath the surface of the words. Knowing what to look for and carefully observing may help uncover the submerged meaning and thus allow us to understand the other. It is easy enough to practice paying attention to the subtle cues of another person, imagine what that means based on our own experience, and then check our accuracy with a question when it seems reasonable and appropriate, such as, "Am I feeling [X, Y, Z]?" The goal is to fine-tune our observations and then reflect back with as much precision as possible through our words, metaphors, or images to see how well we are tracking—that is, the degree to which we perceive the other accurately or project our own experience onto them.

Practicing taking another's point of view is a powerful move that stretches toward the other. Recall the Roots of Empathy instructor's questions to the children: "What do you think the baby is feeling?" and "What are you feeling?" Being able to turn our attention to the feelings of others and ourselves opens the gates for contact and self-awareness.

But there is more to empathy than this. In addition to careful observation and deduction, there is a process of direct and visceral resonance at work. In this deep empathy, the body serves as a kind of resonance chamber through which we pick up the "vibes" of the other and then make some sense of the experience.

We become part of a system that includes you or me and the other(s) in this kind of resonant field. Because we are linked together, we are able to make use of information in this system not only by observation of the other but by gaining awareness of our own reactions. For example, we may notice tightness in the gut or a feeling or impulse to act or say something. Psychologist Carl Rogers described his own spontaneous reactions in this way: "When I can relax and be close to the transcendental core of me, then I may behave in strange and impulsive ways in the relationship, ways in which I can not justify rationally, which have nothing to do with my rational thought processes." But, he realized, "These strange behaviors turn out to be right, in some odd way."[11]

Deep empathy is quite direct and can touch such depths as to transcend our sense of separateness. I remember something like this happening spontaneously in my first psychotherapy internship, when I would experience an unusual connection with some clients. I lost a sense of time, light in the room changed, background sounds retreated, and the boundaries between us seemed to collapse. I recall a sense of the client and myself being in a kind of luminous egg. Later, I experienced the deep connection as an exchange, like spiral waves flowing back and forth. Later still, there was somewhat less awareness of the sensations themselves and instead a sense of "just knowing." Beyond the depth of understanding that this seemed to provide to the therapy (after all, this was the point), I realized that these connections were deeply nourishing for me. At that time, these were the moments when I felt most human, most intimate with the world. These moments of knowing provided a profound feeling of communion.

Rogers described his own experience of some special, even mystical-sounding moments of empathy in his work as a therapist: "It seems that my inner spirit has reached out and touched the inner spirit of the other. Our relationship transcends itself and becomes part of something larger."[12] This is not a technique; it is the result of an openness to really meet the other deeply. In such experiences, the gap between self and other shrinks, and we enter into shared space. Martin Buber called this space where we come together "the between,"[13] philosopher Martin Heidegger spoke of this as a "clearing,"[14] and Nobel Peace Prize nominee Thich Nhat Hanh calls it "interbeing."[15]

Empaths

If we lack the capacity for empathic connection, we may find ourselves socially isolated, unable to connect easily with those around us. On the other end of the continuum are those who have plenty of empathic sensitivity to others—empaths. They have highly permeable emotional boundaries or in some way link up easily with others. Deep empathy is a powerful tool for knowing and navigating the world, one that can sometimes be overwhelming and confusing.

Some of us have such permeable emotional boundaries that we end up feeling confused or tugged by the feelings or thoughts of others or just plain overwhelmed by the deluge of feelings that wash over us. If you're highly empathically sensitive, you may instantly recognize what I mean.

My sixteen-year-old friend Sarah once described a surprisingly typical circumstance of being a kind of psychic sponge. "I'm an empath, and I hate school. I walk around and people walk in and out of classes, and I get everything from them—their anger, frustration, even happiness or joy. But it's no fun. I'm not a big fan of crowds . . . but I'm working on turning the empathy on and off."

Another friend, June, who said she was extremely sensitive to the "vibes" of others, dealt with this sense of being overwhelmed in her own way. Looking back on her youth, she said, "I became a loner. I didn't understand why at the time. I was naturally tuning in to so many things, and I didn't know what I was tuning in to or what to do with it, and I became a very moody child. I don't know why I picked up all different people's feelings, but I did. Plenty of times I would be down and I didn't understand why, and I then I'd realize I was picking up other people's moods. My escape was sleep. I would sleep long hours to keep away from all those feelings. I didn't know what else to do."

A psychotherapist might have reasonably diagnosed June as depressed. It is hard to say how many individuals withdraw like June in order to compensate for their empathic sensitivity. Some turn to alcohol or drugs to try to decrease this sensitivity, creating merely a numbing distraction rather than an effective boundary. Along with moodiness, withdrawal, and feeling overwhelmed, some try to manage their sensitivity by creating a kind of barbed perimeter around themselves by adopting a hostile personality or even aggressive behavior. The tough kid or acerbic adult may be trying to fight against boundary violations of all sorts. Without knowledge of what's happening, sensitive individuals may grow up coping in unsatisfying ways. But this doesn't have to be the case. For someone who is highly empathic, refining and modulating this deep way of knowing involves several keys:

1. *Noticing.* "Where am I now?" Staying mindful of our own feelings and reactions, our bodies, and our thoughts helps us stay aware and awake to what is happening within and between us, providing us with an early-warning system before we're overrun.

2. *Distinguishing.* What's ours and what isn't? This helps us get a little space between us and our feelings. This can be hard to do, since feelings seem to run together and take on a life of their own, but by pausing to ask the question in some form ("Is this mine?") we immediately bring our witnessing mind to the question, and this gives us a little space to work in.

3. *Naming.* Expressing the feeling in some way also gives us a little distance from it and brings precision to our understanding. "What am I feeling? Where am I feeling it in my body? What does this look, feel, taste, move, and sound like?" We might do this with ourselves, write it down, or talk it out with someone. Sometimes we need more than words to express

our feelings. This is why expressive therapies use things like movement, art, sound, and interactivity when trying to help capture the inner experience. For example, it's hard to know what is going on with a friend of mine until she starts to dance; another brings his inner experience to the surface through drawing.

4. *Getting physical.* Because emotions are experienced not only in thought but also in the body, some physical action—a walk or run, a good scream or cry, beating a drum or just taking a drink of water—can be helpful to discharge and recalibrate our systems. In many ways, what we're attempting to do is to modulate and manage emotional arousal. The work is to keep our hearts open without overstimulating and thus overwhelming our emotional system. A daily discharge or clearing of this energy serves to rebalance the system and prevent emotional baggage from accumulating.

5. *Housekeeping.* Things get stuck to the inside of our emotional resonance chambers because we may have "sticky spots." Like a rough spot on the inside of a cooking pot, sticky spots tend to form where there is friction. We may have particular sensitivity to anger, for example. Perhaps this developed as a first-alert protective mechanism because someone in life posed a threat when angry and we thus became attuned to the emotional frequency of anger in general. With a little distance and some reflection, we may begin to notice the patterns of our emotional sensitivity, recognizing where we tend to get hooked, how we react, and what our typical reactions tend to mean. Recognizing this gives us a chance to unwind our habits. Ultimately, this allows us the freedom to be able to use this magnificent system of knowing without being used up by it. Empathic capacity is a birthright for nearly all of us. But it is the integration and balance of this incredible

relational, resonant system that allows us to know so directly without being overwhelmed. With awareness and a bit of practice, we can grow and refine this way of knowing.

A Communion of Subjects

It's self-evident that empathy helps us understand and connect with one another, but what may not always be so clear is that an empathic style of knowing also helps us understand the world in general.

This more immediate and direct style of knowing flies in the face of the common way we are trained to know through contemporary education, which tends to invite us to put things in objective categories, separating and measuring them in one way or another, rather than making direct contact. However, the radical separation between observer and observed is artificial, a cognitive repression of the awareness of interconnection. I am not speaking of the valuable arm's-length perspective that the intellect can provide; instead, I refer to the inflation, distortion, and institutionalization of objectivism, which reduces the world to a collection of objects.

The root meaning of the word "objective" is "standing against" or "apart from." Educator Parker Palmer described the consequence of this stance.

> It puts us in an adversary relationship with each other and our world. We seek knowledge in order to resist chaos, to rearrange reality, or to alter the constructions others have made. We value knowledge that enables us to coerce the world into meeting our needs—no matter how much violence we must do. Thus our knowledge of the atom has brought us into opposition to the ecology of earth, to the welfare of society, to the

survival of the human species itself. Objective knowledge has
unwittingly fulfilled its root meaning: it has made us adversar-
ies of ourselves.[16]

With the distance between knower and known maintained
and without recognition of their interplay, we remain separate
from the world. The objectification of the other, including the
natural world (environment and body), contributes to difficulties
in relationships and limits the experience from which to make
ethical choices. At the beginning of the twentieth century, William James recognized that "materialism and objectivism" tend to
lead human beings to see their world as alien. And "the difference
between living against a background of foreignness [as in, treating the world as alien] and one of intimacy means the difference
between a general habit of wariness and one of trust."[17] The result
of this habitual wariness and distance is anxiety, depersonaliza-
tion, alienation, and narcissism—the psychological epidemics in
the world today.

Objectivism is an insufficient ground to fashion character
or human values on. Such objectivist knowing tends to invite
self-separateness in which we never experience the other or the
other's subjectivity. Whereas empathy invites contact and partici-
pation, objectivity creates distance. The other remains an "it" for
our distant examination and utilitarian manipulation or an object
to either possess or defend ourselves against. The capacity for
differentiation of self from other is a basic capacity of the mind,
but its overemphasis fragments us from ourselves and the world.

On the other hand, an empathic style of knowing tends
toward, in the words of Thomas Berry, seeing the world as a communion of subjects rather than merely a collection of objects.[18]
I am reminded of the death row minister who saw those he met
transform into human beings, of Barbara McClintock's "feel-

ing for the organism" and "openness to let it come to you"[19] that enabled her to see deeply into the inner workings of genetics, and of Thomas Berry's "magic moment" while overlooking a field of lilies that opened an understanding of our intimate connection with all of nature and all that is.

The move is very simple. It takes place when we lead with curiosity instead of judgment, when we make contact instead of categories, when we appreciate, when we open to the encounter rather than defend against it, when we don't try to get anything but simply meet what is before us.

Empathy allows us to begin to see from multiple points of view rather than just defend our own. This is the essential complement to critical reasoning. To get to know the other, take up their position, and see through their eyes, whether a person or a plant, engages the empathic heart as a legitimate source of knowledge. Without it, the world remains merely a collection of objects.

Empathizing

Empathizing allows us to feel into another person or even the planet and understand them. Refining this capacity is essential for meeting the world directly.

Quiz

For each statement or word, circle the number that describes you best.
(least like me)   1   2   3   4   5   (most like me)

I seem to pick up other's vibes.		1 2 3 4 5
I connect easily to those around me.		1 2 3 4 5
I can regulate my personal boundaries.		1 2 3 4 5
I usually understand others deeply.		1 2 3 4 5

I feel other's feelings directly.	1	2	3	4	5
I experience all things as interconnected.	1	2	3	4	5
I connect easily with animals or other parts of nature.	1	2	3	4	5
I can see another's point of view.	1	2	3	4	5
I'm empathic.	1	2	3	4	5
I meet the world directly.	1	2	3	4	5

Add up the circled numbers.   Total: _____

10–19	20–29	30–39	40–50
A trailhead	**More is possible**	**A good ally**	**A great strength**

....

PRACTICES

Linking Up

In a group setting, pair up with a partner and face each other in an attentive posture. Take a few moments to relax your minds and become more present. With an attitude simply of curiosity and appreciation, see if you can meet the other. You are asked to be open to the encounter, both to meet and to be met.

It is important not to probe or invade the other in any way. Instead, just meet in that space between you (what Martin Buber called "the between"). The process will involve opening your eyes periodically to catch a glimpse or brief view of your partner. Then close them again and repeat as it seems right, as staring at each other is often too intense. Do this in silence and simply notice what arises in your awareness.

After a few minutes, stop and take some time to share what you noticed in whatever way this came to you—feelings, vague impressions, images, or hunches related to the person or the meeting. It is not unusual for there to be a sense of intimacy and connection among many, although not everyone feels this way. Did any insights, feelings, sensations, or questions that arise? Check out the accuracy of your impressions. In addition, process what the experience of meeting in this way was like for each of you, noticing when and how you were open or how you might tend to hold back. How this is similar or different to what you do in other situations?

Points of View

Recall the Roots of Empathy instructor's questions to the children: "What do you think the baby is feeling?" and "What are you feeling?" Being able to intentionally turn our attention to others' feelings as well as our own opens the gates for contact and self-awareness. Being able to compare our perceptions with others allows us to open the possibility of multiple points of view. "Oh, yeah, now that you mention it, I did feel that. I just didn't think anything of it until you said something about it. I need to trust that more." Or "I never thought of seeing it that way." These simple questions—"What are you feeling? What do you think they are feeling?"—begin to expand empathic capacity. In addition, sharing our perceptions of others directly with them allows us to get some direct feedback on the accuracy of our emotional reading. "Are you feeling betrayed?" or "I would feel betrayed if it were me. How about you?" The response allows us to refine our accuracy. Simply reflecting back what someone has said, felt, or meant is a way to check out the accuracy of our perceptions and reveal our projections. We might try this gently as an intentional practice with those we encounter throughout the day. In addition, using an imaginative process helps open up new vistas. "How would I feel if I were the terrorist? A new mother? A crying child?"

Read My Lips

The goal here is to practice noticing the face and the body's subtle cues. While this is a natural skill for most, it is also one that can be developed. There are a variety of ways to do this, but the basic idea is to simply observe faces (and other body language as well) and try to identify the feelings that seem predominant. You might simply take photos from a magazine or observe people in a restaurant whose conversations you cannot hear. You might watch a movie or TV show with the sound off. Try to identify the feeling(s) portrayed. Sharing these with others to compare notes is a good way to gain some confirmation and see a greater range of possible feelings. You might also "listen" to someone with your ears covered and ask them to speak in a low enough voice so you can't hear them. Again, try to identify the feelings without knowing what the content is. Notice how your own face and body want to respond to them. There are many variations on this practice, but the bottom line is to observe body expression without verbal content, identify the feelings present, and compare notes to check for accuracy.

Finding the Beat

Empathy involves getting in sync or in tune with someone or with the world around us. Literally sharing a rhythm, as in, tapping hands on a desk or a drum to follow a particular beat together, walking in unison, dancing with a partner, or mirroring another's body, face, pace, or tone are all ways to sync up with one another. Practice following along. We might start with following one person's lead rhythm that they clap or tap, beginning with a simple pattern and adding more complex rhythms once everyone seems to get it. We might take turns leading, as this requires sensitivity both on the part of the leader and the rest of the ensemble. Drumming groups are often powerful ways to help folks get in sync with one another and with themselves. Ask yourself if there other ways you might play with following someone else's lead. For example, while standing and facing a partner, put your hands so that your palms face one another's without actually touching. Have one person lead by moving their hands while the partner tries to follow. The task is to get in sync with one another. Take turns in each role.

9

FEELING

Let yourself be silently drawn
By the stronger pull
Of what you really love.

—Rumi

Have you ever had a dream that seemed both real and important? I had been wondering about joy, curious about what it's really about, and how I could have more in my own life. One night, as if in answer to my query, I had a dream that I could not have expected less. It centered on a young girl who had apparently developed a terminal illness. In spite of this, she appeared quite well but was going to be euthanized so that she didn't have to suffer. My heart ached more than I thought I could stand as I watched this scene unfold. Thoughts screamed through my mind: *What more life might she have to live? What will she miss? She's fine! She's not ready yet!* I watched in agony as she was placed in the seat of a large convertible. Sand began to fill the car and swallow her up. Someone said, "She has already had four pills," but the girl was still conscious as the sand steadily engulfed her body until her head disappeared and she was buried alive.

Dreams are funny things. They're messages in symbols, arti-
facts of indigestion, a tap in the cosmic internet. They're hard
to understand sometimes, but like all things, dreams provide an
opportunity for us to look for meaning. Feelings seem the most
natural place to start. The sheer agony of watching this girl buried alive apparently to escape the pain of her condition (a very
human condition—we're all terminal, after all) was at the center
of this dream for me. I was stunned at how intense the feelings
were and how they absolutely broke my heart. I had a dream
hangover the next day, and it took another night's sleep to quell
the ache. How could this be an answer to my question about the
nature of joy?

While happiness is often defined as the result of a pleasur-
able experience, joy lives deeper down. It is an aliveness that
manifests through the depth of the full human experience, not
the segregation or preference for certain feelings. If my dream
(or how I made sense of it) had any significance, it had to do
with joy being big enough to encompass all of it—angst and
anger, delight and despair. To protect us from certain feelings
or constrict the degree of feeling is to bury us alive, like the girl
in my dream. Suffering may be the first grace because it lets
us know we're alive, making us pay attention to each moment
because each moment is the only one where life is lived. Feelings
let us know we're really alive.

We are faced with the inevitability of suffering every day.
The Buddha's first noble truth is that suffering is part of life.
But Meister Eckhart said this about this relationship between
suffering and joy: "The swiftest steed to bear you to your goal
is suffering . . . Nothing is more gall-bitter than suffering, nothing so honey sweet as to have suffered. . . . for joy brings sorrow
and sorrow brings joy."[1] As much as we may not like it, adversity
can activate untapped potentials. As Paul wrote in his letter to

the Romans, "Suffering produces endurance, and endurance produces character, and character produces hope."[2] A difficult situation can bring out our best as we rise to the occasion and transform suffering. We find stunning examples of courage in the face of long odds. When the last marathoner crosses the finish line after a ridiculously long time, we're brought to tears, seeing this suffering as an act of heroism. It is out past the edge of our comfort zones that things get stirred up; it's out here in the wild that there is possibility for powerful growth. And when we see another suffer with illness, homelessness, or grief, it can activate compassion in us so that we reach out and offer up our hearts to them (like Hanna and her ladybug jars). We might even wonder whether compassion could exist without suffering, as suffering often enacts compassion.

But what makes the difference? What turns suffering into grace? Paradoxically, the essential action is not to step away from or sidestep suffering, which is the instinctive tendency when something hurts. Instead it has something to do with stepping *into* what is given.

We are transformed not by allowing some feelings in and keeping others at bay but by bringing into the clearing of our awareness all the elements of our selves—the dark void, the small light, the blackest dreams, and the shimmering hopes.[3] When we do so, we stop wasting time and energy discriminating against, hiding from, and fearing ourselves. The heart grows not so much by what we exclude but by what we embrace.

Rumi, the twelfth century Sufi mystic and poet, tells us no matter how bleak or bright, that we treat whatever arises in our consciousness as a guest: "Welcome and entertain all!"[4] Make a comfortable seat for them. Offer them food, maybe a little pillow or a cup of tea, and then, as Thich Nhat Hanh said, embrace them "like a mother holding her crying baby."[5]

At the Mercy of What We Cherish Least

Welcoming is easier said than done. However, the intent provides an antidote to habits of resisting and numbing the emotional world, or at least the parts of it we don't like. If we can be curious about these feelings and stop discriminating against them, we have a chance to transform them. The practice is very gentle: we welcome the guest.

Compassion implies listening *with* our hearts. We turn the focus outward, toward others. It means that we listen in order to understand, appreciate, care for, forgive, and love. Listening *to* the heart means paying attention to our own feelings and sensations. The radical graciousness toward our feelings that Rumi, Hanh, and Eckhart prescribe allows spaciousness for these emotions to settle down and stretch out a bit. Why do we need to welcome *all* these emotions? Maybe, as William James said, because "the things we cherish most are at the mercy of the things we cherish least."[6]

In a study conducted by psychologist James Pennebaker, one hundred laid-off white-collar workers were randomly placed in one of three groups.[7] The first group wrote in a journal about their deepest feelings, especially feelings related to their job loss. The second group participated in "time-management" training in which they were asked to write down a detailed daily record of their job search efforts. The third group was asked to write about trivial things. After four months Pennebaker felt that he had to call off the experiment because one "medicine" was clearly working so well that he felt irresponsible not to offer it to everyone in the study. Thirty-five percent of those who wrote about their feelings had gotten jobs. Five percent of the control group (those writing about trivial things) and none of the time-management group had secured a new job. Those who expressed and explored their struggles and sufferings were better able to move on with their lives rather than remain stuck in anger and anxiety, which seemed to be the case for the other two groups. A simple practice of welcoming feelings affects not just our insides but also our interactions with the world around us.

Once these guests are welcomed and have enough space to settle down a bit, after we take a breath, step back from the intensity, count to ten or one hundred, cry or yell, sit quietly, start to write about it, draw a picture, talk to someone who will listen, or just be mindful of what's arising in our awareness, we can get to know more about our guests, marking more subtle distinctions within the flow of experience.

- *Where do they live?* "Where is this in my body?"
- *What do they look like beyond first impressions?* Often under a feeling like anger, for example, there may be feelings of hurt.
- *What lies under their makeup?* What shape, color, voice, texture do these guests have?
- *Where are they from?* "Have I felt like this before?"
- *What are their real names?* What words or images capture this best? Our vocabulary tends to reduce to generics ("I'm mad!"), but there is a release and recognition when we bull's-eye the feeling with more specific words.
- *What characterizes the feeling?* Is it feeling jumpy, hardened, or something else?
- *What gift do they bear?* "Now that you're here, what are you trying to teach me?"

When we explore and explicate the feeling world in this way, we are essentially integrating levels of brain structure and function—limbic and cortical, emotional and intellectual—for a more whole-brained and full-bodied experience. This kind of intentional emotional exploration helps us move toward enriched understanding. "The explication releases the tension" of the feeling.[8] When we accurately label a feeling, it actually soothes limbic firing in the brain.[9] Through this practice of mature integration, we keep attuned to the feeling world and step back when we need to take stock.

Psychiatrist Dan Siegel recounts his time with Stuart, a ninety-two-year-old retired attorney whose son had brought him in for a consultation for fear that he was depressed. Siegel explained that while Stuart's cognitive properties seemed to be in great shape, he also seemed emotionally empty. Following his wife's recent bout with pneumonia, which she recovered from, he was more aloof, thus prompting the concern from his family. What was discovered was that his parents, as his wife said, "were the coldest people I had ever seen." Their lack of emotionality, including the lack of emotional mirroring so essential for full development, apparently left Stuart to rely on his cognitive powers alone. The consequence for Stuart was this emotional vacancy, remaining out of touch with those feelings, senses, and images that color our lives.

Was it possible to activate these capacities for feeling and integrate them with Stuart's well-developed intellect so that he might fill what seemed empty? Are the brain and the mind still flexible (neuroplastic) enough at ninety-two to learn to reconfigure itself (neurogenesis)? Siegel tried to find out through a series of simple exercises. For example, Siegel would make various faces— sad, fearful, excited, and so on—and ask Stuart to identify each emotion. Stuart was then asked to watch television with the sound off as an effort to engage his nonverbal perception. As he became a bit more attuned to nonverbal cues, he was directed to "just notice what emerges in your awareness," whether in recounting a scene or in the moment. Drawing, reflection, imagery, and journal writing, along with Siegel's empathic, attentive communication, helped Stuart notice and attend to that flow of nonverbal experiences that provide us with such richness and depth.[10]

Did it work? Stuart's wife was so stunned by his new capacity to relate to her feelings that she asked whether he had been given a brain transplant. Stuart reported that his life had new meaning and was actually fun.

But we don't have to wait until ninety-two to deepen our feeling of the world.

Pink and Purple Ponies

Beyond an understanding that the world of feelings is essential and our work is to welcome and try to understand it, we also benefit from balancing our feelings in some way. This includes gaining awareness of our feelings and thoughts, as well as those of others, handling emotions, directing goals, and developing healthy relationships. This kind of emotional intelligence may be as important to success and well-being as the faculty of reason.[11] The concern, whether we're nine, nineteen, or ninety-two, is to allow feelings to bring color to our lives without painting us into corners.

I remember sitting in front of the television one day with one of my daughters when she was five or six. We were watching a children's show, and at each commercial break, there was a zippy flood of sparkling stuff. My daughter, eyes growing wide, stood up, pointed at the object of desire on the TV screen, and burst out, "I want that!" The next thirty seconds, stuffed talking puppies filled the living room. Again, "I want that!" Then plastic pink and purple ponies. "I *really* want that!"

Direct marketing to children in the United States alone targets $180 billion in spending, which children like my little girl steer.[12] I do remember a stable of pink and purple plastic ponies in our house, but she didn't get everything she wanted, really. There will always be plenty more pink and purple ponies marketing wizards and others aim at some longing or desire within us. In cultures flooded with abundance and media, our desires are amplified and pulled in all sorts of directions.

Desire is natural. It's central to the emotional repertoire. Appetites—and satisfying these appetites—can bring contentment, pleasure, and relief, at least until the next desire arises. These feelings of desire are the benchmark, the sign that something here is stimulating. But we know that following certain leads can get us in trouble and usually has little to do with the *Good*. From the Greek virtue of temperance to the Buddhist goal of nonattachment, from cloistered nuns to wandering Hindu ascetics, desire is recognized as a complicated emotion. Denying desires, trying to avoid them, and cloistering ourselves from the world doesn't seem practical, especially in a global information age. The lure is all around. However, we also know that not all desires are created equal. A bit of lust may lead to a different path than passion for beauty. Following through on a desire for revenge may be quite different than an impulse to overcome injustice. Each brings a sense of natural vitality and energy, but some may bring an even deeper sense of satisfaction and meaning. In the end, some desires may have more heart, and that's where the nourishment lies.

Desire is fuel for action, for the will. But we may confuse the object of our desire, mistaking the shell for the nut. When we are either out of touch with our feelings and motivations or overwhelmed by them, we have trouble sorting out the superficial from the sustaining. Sometimes we may jump over the deeper desire and into a fix, such as drugs, entertainment, or other short-term pleasures, as a way of trying to fulfill our heart's desire.

The trouble with this is that these things never satisfy for long. We just get on the gerbil wheel to nowhere and drain our life or bank account in the process. Self-awareness and reflection help us understand where it is we are trying to get to; self-discipline allows us to keep our eyes and actions on the real prize.

It is not the felt desire that needs elimination; it's the attachment to the outcome that gets us in trouble. As author Steven Levine contended, "Freedom is the ability to have or not have what you want without it closing your heart. Freedom is not to act compulsively on all the contents of the mind, but to let the contents flow away and tune in to the unfolding."[13] The feeling of desire or passion is never the problem; it's seduction without reflection that leads us to dead ends.

If we have little room for our feelings, then our passions may burst out in ways that do not serve us or them. It's just a release valve, a premature ejaculation of energy, satisfying for a moment but ultimately not sustaining us. Rather than trying to suppress desires, instead we return to Rumi's welcome: welcome them all. But what helps us accommodate them without being overwhelmed is a spacious house. As we develop the capacity to be present and to witness, as discussed in part 1, we gain capacity to tolerate the experience without immediately having to react. Things settle down just enough so that we can understand what these guests are about. Anytime an impulse arises, we might stop, enjoy the sensation, and then pause for a moment to ask ourselves, "What's that about?" and in doing so, reflect upon our desires.

Maybe the trick is to watch passion transform into love. When the thing that we long for ends up nourishing, healing, and bringing us toward some deeper coherence and toward the mystery of communion, it may be the thing worth putting ourselves on the line for. Krishnamurti said it this way: "Find out for yourself what you really, with all your heart, love to do. . . . Then you are really efficient, without becoming brutal."[14] This requires us to align our hearts with this deeper current.

Are We Having Fun Yet?

While we can talk about welcoming all feelings in order to experience the richness of life, we know that we want some feelings more than others. To illustrate the point, which would you prefer: happiness and satisfaction or jealousy, irritability, and hostility? Happy feelings just *feel* better, and thus we spend our lives in pursuit of a holy grail of happiness in one way or another.

Historian Darrin McMahon described how the meaning of happiness has changed over time. Aristotle used the term *eudaimonia*, which is typically translated as happiness but probably means something more like well-being or flourishing, and for the ancient Greeks, happiness was tied to leading a virtuous life. For the Romans, it implied prosperity and the favor of the gods (good luck). For medieval Christians, happiness was synonymous with living in alignment with the will of God and making our way to heaven. For many today, happiness means pleasure and good feeling; since the eighteenth century it has been our right ("life, liberty, and the pursuit of . . ."), even our obligation to pursue. Many feel an expectation to feel happy and thus feel pressured to judge their experiences harshly if they're not. McMahon suggested that despite these historic changes there are some constants over time, and the most significant one is that this feeling of happiness, flourishing, and fullness is associated with the highest human capacity.[15] In this sense, good feelings let us know we're on to something. They serve as an internal barometer.

There are different ways to pursue happiness, and we could think of it as coming from at least three general approaches:

1. Positive emotion or pleasure (the pleasant life)
2. Engagement (the engaged life)
3. Meaning (the meaningful life)[16]

Sensual pleasure—the pleasant life—got a bad name from the likes of Augustine and the Puritans. As covered in the section on sensitivity in part 1, opening up those sensual portals of the body helps us receive these birthright gifts. A friend of mine who happens to be in a religious order once recounted a little epiphany to me. She had been trying (and succeeding, I'd say), to live a life of real virtue, service, and devotion. But what she discovered was that she wasn't having as much fun or joy as she'd thought she would. Her feelings told her something was off, even though she was doing all the "right" and "virtuous" things. Something shifted, however, when she overcame her sense of guilt for having pleasure (her guilt was of the "Jesus suffered and so should I" variety), and she basically gave herself permission for sensual pleasure. She took time to savor the cup of coffee in the morning and the comfort of a hot bath. She started to prepare meals with a renewed attention to the joy she felt in cooking that she had prior to her commitment to religious life but seemed to have pushed to the background with the idea that it was indulgent or unimportant, even unholy. In the end, it was the simple feeling of pleasure that balanced her life. Aristotle would have appreciated her balance, good habits, and dispositions that were the practical art and heart of virtue. Practitioners of mindfulness would likewise understand her attentiveness to simple acts as a source of emotional nourishment as they walk a middle way between indulgence and asceticism.

On the other side are accounts of those who pursue a life of pleasure or power but find hollowness and dissatisfaction in the hedonism that results. Like the race dog catching the mechanical rabbit only to find it really wasn't that tasty after all, these folks get a wake-up call when success or pleasure doesn't fulfill them. While sensual pleasure, wealth, and status are often seen as a means to happiness, by themselves these aspects define a kind of good life that is different from the "Good Life" that most of the wise souls have advocated. The often distorted and unbalanced lives of those who have achieved peaks of celebrity, wealth, and indulgence, and yet seem profoundly unhappy, give us some clue that there is more to it than this. Sure, we'd like to have what they have, but if this is the ultimate goal of our search for happiness, we're probably missing something that lives deeper down.

Taking another tack toward happiness, psychologist Mihaly Csikszentmihalyi (pronounced *cheeks-sent-me-high*) recognized that we sometimes have deeply satisfying moments in life that really "flow."[17] These states of flow are characterized by concentration and absorption on a goal-directed task. Rather than the immediate pleasure of, say, eating a piece of chocolate or watching your favorite television show, over the long haul the focused effort on challenging and goal-directed tasks leads, he claimed, to a deep sense of satisfaction. For Csikszentmihalyi, the path to happiness is primarily about engaging life in largely goal-directed pursuits rather than immediate pleasures. He points to four ways through which one is able to be a more engaged and thus "flow-filled" person:

1. Setting goals
2. Becoming immersed in the particular activity
3. Paying attention to what is happening in the moment
4. Learning to enjoy the immediate experience

We will explore these concepts further in the practices found at the end of this chapter.

Matthieu Ricard, cell biologist turned Buddhist monk, has been described as the happiest man alive, a label he wisely disavows. But such a lofty claim makes a nice sound bite and is thus hard to slough off. But how did he earn this title? He collaborated in advanced brain scanning at professor Richard Davidson's laboratory at the University of Wisconsin.[18] They discovered that there was a greater relative activation in a particular part of Ricard's brain. In fact, Ricard had the highest recorded activation of anyone tested to that point, thus earning his "happiest man" title. How did he get there? It is suspected that it's due to, paradoxically, welcoming in all feelings. His meditation practice involves watching all feelings without prejudice, simply allowing and observing whatever arises in his awareness. In addition, his practice also involves engaging in compassion meditation, in which he extends his sense of compassion to both himself and to the entire world. He has developed an inner state of equanimity that allows him to welcome what feelings come to him, he is very engaged in the service of humanity, and his work is profoundly meaningful to him.

Although everybody is different and what makes us happy can change over time, we've got a pretty good idea of the kinds of things that can engender enduring feelings of fullness and flourishing. Friendships and love are high on the list, as well as creative and authentic expression, engagement, immersed activity, taking time for simple pleasures, doing work that you consider meaningful—basically, finding what, for us, is good or true or beautiful. Those of us who are the most satisfied with life are often those who attend to the pleasant, engaged, and meaningful life, with engagement and especially meaning carrying the most weight.[19] Although each person experiences this differently, these approaches tend to consistently trump status and stuff over the long haul.

There is one more vantage point that may be helpful in taking stock of what makes a difference in life, and that is death. Writer

Bronnie Ware worked with people dying in hospice care. She listened to what had brought them happiness, and maybe most poignantly, she also heard their regrets. What are the top five regrets of the dying?

1. I wish I'd had the courage to live a life true to myself.
2. I wish I hadn't worked so hard.
3. I wish I'd had the courage to express my feelings.
4. I wish I had stayed in touch with my friends.
5. I wish that I let myself be happier.[20]

If *your* moment was at hand, would you have any regrets? Asking this question may help us recognize and recalibrate what's really important while we still have time.

Feelings bring color and richness to life, warmth and excitement, peace and passion, marking all of human experience. At their most essential, feelings let us know we're actually alive; so welcome them all.

Feeling
Tuning in to our own feelings without being overwhelmed by them gives us a chance for the full experience of humanness.

Quiz
For each statement or word, circle the number that describes you best.
(least like me)   1   2   3   4   5   (most like me)

I am able to identify and name my feelings.   1 2 3 4 5
I find ways to express my feelings
    constructively.   1 2 3 4 5

I am in touch with my passion.	1	2	3	4	5
I feel joy.	1	2	3	4	5
My fears do not stop me.	1	2	3	4	5
I most always know what I'm feeling.	1	2	3	4	5
I have a rich feeling vocabulary.	1	2	3	4	5
I enjoy my feelings.	1	2	3	4	5
I do not hold grudges.	1	2	3	4	5
I let myself have all my feelings, including difficult ones.	1	2	3	4	5

Add up the circled numbers.   Total: _____

10–19	20–29	30–39	40–50
A trailhead	**More is possible**	**A good ally**	**A great strength**

....

PRACTICES

Sounds Good

Music captures and evokes feeling. This exercise is done in a group or with one other person as a way of touching into our own feelings and sharing them with others. It is a quick way to get to know one another at an emotional level.

Pick two songs that really resonate with you. The process of selecting these songs can be a potent practice of reflection itself.

Once you have chosen them, play them to your partner or to the group as a way of meeting one another. Your partner or each group member will have a turn to do the same. Describe the experience of your own music. How does it affect you? What does it mean to you? Share whatever else comes to mind.

The listener or group gets a chance to reflect upon each piece of music. Because music can represent very intimate themes for us, it is very important that this exercise happens in a safe, nonjudgmental space. The ground rules for this sharing are that it should be done with goodwill and mutual respect. Responses should not come from a place of judgment but rather a place of observation and curiosity. As you listen to another's music your responses could be something like

- "What stands out to me is . . ."
- "I wonder about . . ."
- "I feel _____ when I listen to this."
- "I notice _____ happening in my body."
- "This reminds me of . . ."

The person who presents the music should have another chance to respond and elaborate in whatever way they wish.

This simple exercise does several things. It gets us in touch with our own feelings. It provides a means to bring some of our inner world to the surface to share with others in a safe way, an opportunity to practice listening and compare how we hear and feel to others, and to connect with one another at an emotional level.

A Little Space

Part of balancing your feelings is having them without letting them have you; that is, strong feelings (a moment of anger or passion, for example) can overwhelm us or become stuck. Some of us are so in touch with certain feelings that it can be difficult to see past their drama. The practice here begins by allowing feelings space in your body and mind without allowing them to take over.

First, try to relax just a bit and just welcome whatever feeling is present.

- What does it feel like?
- Where is it in your body?
- What shape does it have?
- What is the texture and color?
- How does it move?
- Does it have a sound?
- What else do you notice about it?

Sometimes just having open awareness changes this feeling. Now that you've paid attention to it:

- How does it feel?
- Has it changed at all?
- What is it trying to tell you?

Sometimes understanding its message helps move it, and sometimes we may bring the power of our imagination and intention to move it.

Finally, imagine what would help soothe, resolve, move, express, and dissipate this in your body. You could imagine it submerged in clear water, surrounded in light, or held in warmth, or you could send in tiny helpers to clear it out or transform it in some way. Go ahead and imagine this happening.

When you're finished, take stock of how things have changed.

Facing

Free write about a difficult situation that has a strong emotional charge for you. Do this exercise for five days in a row, taking time to give voice to whatever emotions and thoughts are present. At the end of the five days, notice if there is a change in your relationship to this difficult situation.

Consult Your Death

There are a number of ways we might consult our own death. As with most of these exercises, first relax and find yourself falling into stillness and silence, taking some deep breaths, clearing out surface thoughts, and releasing any tension in your body.

Now imagine that you are watching a scene as if it were a movie. The scene is your funeral. Take in the gravity of the situation for a few moments, watching what is happening from a little distance away. Who and what do you notice? Sense what others are experiencing. Just watch the scene play out. Most importantly, notice what you are feeling. What is your sense of having to leave now? What comes up in your mind about your life? Are there things you wish you still had time for? If you were given a reprieve, what would you do? Take stock of this life. What stands out? What's really important? Give yourself some time to notice, feel, and reflect on this life.

After several minutes, gently return to today, being sure to remember that you are still very much here, alive, and well. What's important about what you just observed? Is there some attitude, action, or goal you want to remember? To fully return to the here and now, try making eye contact or speaking a bit with another person, taking a drink of cool water, walking around, or otherwise moving your body.

The opportunity in this exercise is to bring to the surface what is most important in your life. These feelings can provide direction for living your life as fully and vibrantly as you can.

10

CONNECTING

TAKE CARE OF YOURSELF,
TAKE CARE OF EACH OTHER,
TAKE CARE OF THIS PLACE.

—Painted on the wall in the main entrance
to the Champlain Valley High School,
Hinesburg, Vermont

Our lives move between forest and garden, between a wild, unknown, unpredictable frontier and our cultivated, familiar home base. Both of these places are important for our well-being.

The frontier challenges and stretches us to new possibilities, keeping life an open, growing system. The lure of the forest activates the curious and transcendent impulse we see in every great explorer and every child. Without it, we keep circling around our own cul-de-sac.

While the forest pulls us toward something new, home base gives us the safety, rest, support, and confidence to reach out and experiment, knowing we can return home to lick our wounds and count our treasure. Without this haven of belonging, we remain refugees in our own lives, always searching for a refuge.

With it, we're connected; we belong. These spaces—forest and garden—exist in the spaces of our minds and hearts and especially in the space of our relations with one another and with the universe.

One tradition from a tribe in Africa that helps its members know that they are connected to home and home to them.

When a woman in a certain African tribe knows she's pregnant, she goes out into the wilderness with a few friends. Together they pray and meditate until they hear the baby's unique song. As they attune to it, the women sing it out loud. Then they return to the tribe and teach it to everyone else.

When the child is born, the community gathers and sings the child's song to them. When the child enters school, the villagers gather and sing the song. When the child passes through the initiation to adulthood, the people again come together and sing. At the altar of marriage, the person hears their song. Finally, when it's time for the soul to pass from this world, the family and friends gather at the person's bed, just as they did at their birth, and the sing the person to the next life.

There is one other occasion upon which the villagers sing the to child. If, at any time during the person's life, they commit a crime or socially aberrant act, they're called to the center of the village. The people in the community form a circle around the person and sing their song to them.

A friend is someone who knows your song and sings it to you when you've forgotten it yourself.[1]

Familiar rituals like singing a special song together let us know we are welcome. From our very beginning to the very end, we need to connect, to know we are rooted in some way in the gardens of our lives, to that and those we belong to.

Hardwired to Connect

A sense of belonging and connection is fundamental to our human nature and ultimately to our flourishing and fulfillment. To get a better sense of this, let's look at a few ways in which connection is embedded in our lives, from the most down-to-earth to the most transcendental.

When you touch or stroke a newborn's cheek, the child immediately turns its head and moves its mouth toward the touch, searching for a nipple, that first garden of nourishment and comfort. This is called the rooting reflex. In the 1950s, British psychologist John Bowlby theorized that humans, like other mammals, are born with a drive to be in contact with one another, to attach.[2] A short separation of a puppy or a child from her mother may lead to loud painful protests, and a prolonged separation will lead to despair. This bond, typically between mother and child, promotes safety. When the child or the puppy is separated, hungry, or otherwise uncomfortable, it cries to bring the mother back into contact. As the child grows and explores, during times of stress, the child will hide behind Mom's legs or bury his head in her shoulders. Dad, a special stuffed animal, or blanket may be a good second choice, but the goal is the same: to make contact and thus feel safe.[3]

Even when supplied with food, water, hygiene, safety, and shelter, without this primary contact, we may not survive. In the 1940s psychologist René Spitz discovered great hygiene and healthcare without tender contact leads to withdrawn, sickly, and underweight children.[4] He also saw that at a time when measles resulted in a death rate of about half of 1 percent in the general population, the death rate in very clean but emotionally cold institutions was astronomically different. In hygienic institutions, there was overall a nearly 40 percent death rate from the disease, and in the most sterile institutions where children were less exposed to harmful biological conditions but also less exposed to human touch, the death rate was as high as 100 percent.[5] We need contact just to survive.

Not all contact is created equal. How we make contact with one another, not just that we do, matters tremendously.[6] One of the first places we notice this is in the contact between caregiver and child. The most securely attached children—those well-rooted in the garden, who were secure and had the confidence to explore the world, who were socially competent, happy, resilient, likable, and empathic as grade schoolers—were those whose primary caregivers responded to the child's needs accurately and on demand. Mom knew when he wanted to be held or to be put down and gave what was asked for when appropriate. When he was hungry, she sensed it and fed him, and when he was sleepy she moved to tuck him in. The child who is cared for and protected is more likely to grow up with both a nervous system and a psychological pattern that is secure and balanced. Parents, in turn, benefit from this reciprocal interaction; they feel not only a sense of relief but also a deep satisfaction that comes from successfully reading the cues and responding in a way that satisfies the child.[7]

Successful early attachment links to nine key capacities:

1. Regulation of the body, especially balancing the parasympathetic nervous system that helps us settle down
2. Attuned communication
3. Emotional balance (not too little or too much feeling)
4. Fear modulation
5. Response flexibility (being able to pause and ponder for a moment before responding)
6. Insight
7. Empathy

8. Morality

9. Attuning to our own flow of felt sense[8]

This is an extraordinary testament to how valuable that attuned resonance between parent and child is to our long-term potential. Maybe the most central message here is that if we want citizens with a more balanced, empathic, attuned, moral, flexible future, we'd better be taking good care of our caregivers so they can take loving care of us.

But what if our rooting is not so ideal? Can we still move toward this high end of balance and integration, fulfillment, and flourishing? The same fundamental process of attunement between persons works throughout life. Whatever our age, whether in our family or with a friend, with a therapist or a boss, when we have someone who can read our moods and needs and respond appropriately, we feel seen and cared for. We belong.

In adults, this same need can directly impact physical health. One study found that social isolation tripled the death rate following a heart attack.[9] In dozens of studies, solitary individuals have a three to five times greater likelihood to die earlier than those with caring ties to family and friends.[10]

In addition, the most basic form of contact, touch, has an extraordinary effect on the sense of belonging. From the massage of premature infants who gain substantially greater weight over non-massaged infants, to mothers who significantly improve their postpartum depression by massaging their infants, to cardiac patients petting a puppy, resulting in a decrease in blood pressure and cardiac readmission, touch calms us down, links us up, and provides life-sustaining nourishment. It appears that with favorable touch (holding hands, a gentle caress, a good hug, a puppy on our lap, and so forth) levels of oxytocin—the so-called love hormone—increase.[11] With an increase in oxytocin comes a decrease in sympathetic nervous system activity, those systems that are ready for action. The result: increased calm, a greater sense of trust, comfort, and connection. Simply connecting with what we love—immersing ourselves in favorite music, sounds of birds chirping, kind words from someone, smells of our favorite meal or flower, or imagining our loved ones—increases our sense of calm and connection.

Remarkably, these nine capacities are also the capacities that have been tied to the effects of sustained meditation practice.[12] Attunement seems to be important not just between us but also within us. When we attune to ourselves and to the world around us, we balance our brains and our hearts in profoundly useful ways, making ourselves more available for connections with others.

Our connections can come in all shapes and sizes, out of the blue, and even from inside a bowl. In a residential psychiatric facility near my home, middle-grade boys in a classroom (who attended school at the facility) were each given a colorful Betta fish, also known as a Siamese fighting fish. The boys were entirely responsible for the care of the fish, and through earned credits for good behavior, they could purchase items like a larger bowl and accessories for the fish (a tiny treasure chest, colorful stones, and so forth). The relationships that emerged were transformative for nearly all the boys. Eleven-year-old Justin explained the role he had with his fish, Sparky. "I have to feed him and take care of him. He depends on me." Some of the children will speak in therapy about how the fish won't yell or abuse them. All the children who were given fish were extraordinarily attentive and gentle with their little charges. They also developed respect and empathy toward other students, as they felt how much their own fish meant to them and imagined the same for their peers. This simple process of connection and care has been a powerful guide for these boys. They parent a fish with the kind of gentle concern that in many cases they did not receive from their own parents. Justin also understood the two-way nature of the relationship. "When I feel hyper, I just put my finger on the tank, and Sparky looks at me," he said. "It calms me down."

A Hero's Journey

In many spiritual traditions and the mythic legends, there is a common theme of venturing out to the wilds of the world to be tested or tamed—Jesus's forty days in the desert, Oedipus wandering the world after his inadvertent transgressions—but these stories don't end with the outward journey. There is the homecoming, the return. Home is the place where they have to take you back. The hero (each one of us on our own life's journey) goes through stages of separation from the garden of the familiar and from their own immaturities, the initiation into a larger world full of challenges and dangers, and then the return home with a greater sense of who you are and how you might now belong to the world. In a sense, the journey's goal is to become master of two worlds. The hero comes to understand their belonging to the human and the divine by reconciling the inner and outer, the physical and spiritual. The insight, the revelation, is that the two kingdoms are actually one. The task upon returning home is then to share the treasure of this insight to help others on their journeys.

As we wander on our own hero's journey, we look for the ideas, people, work, and places that resonate with us. Sometimes, we find it in the familiarity in our own family or hometown. Sometimes a different sense of belonging is uncovered far from the familiar. We may not understand this attraction, but it pulls us like a magnet—the longing to visit some unknown destination, a skill or know-how that comes naturally to us, or that specific kind of attraction, recognition, and resonance we experience when meeting someone we sense some deep connection with. We don't fully understand how these connections work. Maybe the Greek gods have placed these magnetic breadcrumbs on the path to help us find our way home. In Eastern traditions, this phenomenon of recognition is explored through the concepts of karma and rein-carnation. Whatever the explanation, the opportunity and the art is to look for and feel into that deep coherence in order to find the elements we belong to. That's what the journey is for.

But there is still another level of belonging named across time and tradition. Mystical experiences, from unitive moments to near-death encounters, are often described with a profound and unexpected sense of homecoming, belonging, and interconnec-tion of another order. This realization of unity, or oneness, is the mystic's insight into the most fundamental interconnection of all. One person described the following experience to me that is common among unitive experiences across time and culture:

> I was fifteen, sitting in silence in my "special spot" outside a short walk from my family's house. I was just sort of tuning in to nature, the little birds and insects here and there. Then suddenly I had this experience of everything being connected. Both in the sense of just part of the same, but then, what was most amazing to me was there was also a sense of everything being equal—the majestic mountain, the blade of grass, and me.

Whether triggered by nature or through some other means, a person having such an experience "does not come to believe merely; but he sees and knows that the cosmos, which to the self-conscious mind seems made up of dead matter, is in fact far otherwise—is in very truth a living presence."[13] This revelation is not just that we are *on* the earth but that we are *of* it. This is the great paradox of humanity, that we are both individual and unified, the many and the one. Unitive experiences are often described as providing a kind of touchstone and initiation, reminding us that we belong to this larger mystery, helping us to broaden a narrow view of our existence.

Eben Alexander is an accomplished neurosurgeon, steeped in the reality of science and the brain. One day his own brain led him down an unexpected path. He developed a brain infection and fell headlong into a deep coma. His priest, who happened to also be a friend, was called to perform last rites, as Alexander was not expected to recover. But he did, and upon his return, he described an encounter with another world. Like others who have had near-death experiences, he came to believe that there is more to us and to this world than meets the eye. His biggest takeaway was that we live in a place where we are all loved and where we are all enough. His overwhelming experience from this bigger view was the profoundest sense of connection and communion, that he was complete and completely loved, as are we all.[14] My friend Peggy, who had a near death experience as a child and was hospitalized for nearly four years, during which time she moved easily between this world and that, put it this way: "Nothing about you is being judged. No one upstairs is keeping a scorecard. You're completely known . . . this is a schoolyard, and we're in a semester. We're all connected, we're eternal . . . and we are loved."[15]

We belong.

Community

In her autobiography, *The Long Loneliness*, Dorothy Day, social activist, radical journalist, and founder of the Catholic Workers Movement, describes her solution for her lifelong spiritual hunger for communion: "We have all known the long loneliness and we have learned that the only solution is love and that love comes with community."[16]

Communities represent a natural ecological structure of humanity. We have institutions and organizations, nations and states, but it is the quality of communities and of our communion with one another that gives us a home. A society dominated merely by institutional life is not satisfying or sustaining in and of itself; a culture of communities evaluated by the quality of human relationships is required for human fulfillment. Institutions offer the trappings of community yet occlude the essentiality of community, sometimes leaving us confused and longing for a kind of relationship and care that institutional structure alone does not provide.

I remember walking into a school in Vermont where a motto painted high on the wall caught your eye as soon as you walked in the lobby. It was not the noble *Veritas* ("Truth") of Harvard, or the *Lux et Veritas* ("Light and Truth") of Yale, or the *Studiis et Rebus Honestis* ("Through studies and upright affairs") of nearby University of Vermont, or my all-time favorite, Warren Wilson College's "We're not for everyone, but maybe you're not everyone." Instead, at this rural high school the message was "Take care of yourself, Take care of each other, Take care of this place." During my visit, I was convinced that this was more than a nice motto. This community of care was working by all accounts I could see, no doubt imperfectly but in the way that human communities can work. It was not the fact that this was a school; it was the infusion of care that grew it toward community. Service and care are important not just to fill the needs of the society or because it is the moral or good thing to do but because freely given care actually opens our consciousness and connects us to one another.

The essence of community is an integration of the concerns of the individual—agency, democracy, individuality, diversity, rights, dignity—and the needs of the group—republic, membership, cooperation, sharing, common good. Overemphasis on individuality, the self, and individual rights can tend toward a narcissistic preoccupation, social Darwinism, and a sense of isolation. At its worse, it leads to selfishness and rampant competition, where relations with the world are distorted into opportunities to serve the self, to meet "my" indulgences. On the other hand, overemphasis on the collective, with its agendas and institutions creates not a community but a crypt or a cult that is often restrictive and intolerant of diversity. This creates a hive mentality in which individuality and difference are seen as a threat rather than the essential catalyst of evolution and growth. The challenge of creating community is in balancing the personal and the communal.

These days we are presented with the particular challenges that engender fragmentation both within us and between us: the great centripetal force spun by technology, information overload, mobility and relative wealth, diversity and multiplicity, individualism, deconstruction, scientism, and flexibility of identity, among many other things. Like the infant lacking a home base of care whose biological and psychological system remains in a constant state of anxiety, in an age of fragmentation we may find ourselves displaced or dispossessed, going through the motions but not sure where we're headed or where we belong. This can be like living in a state of chronic low-grade shock of all sorts, including

- Culture shock (Where is my home?)
- Value shock (What do I believe in?)
- Environmental shock (Is this safe to eat?)

- Meaning shock (What is my life about?)
- Security shock (Am I safe here?)
- Identity shock (Who am I?)
- Information shock (How can I keep up with this information?)
- Time shock (Where did September go? How can I keep up?)
- Schlock shock (How much stuff do I need to feel satisfied?)

When an individual does not feel the basic sense of belonging that a community engenders, alienation and anxiety rule. In a classroom, living room, or boardroom, this may leave us wary, causing us to expend our energies on self-protection—on closing down rather than opening up, trying to dominate or escape rather than partner with.

If we are to survive, it is necessary to work and live together as a community of diverse individuals. We begin to recognize that the housing development becomes a neighborhood only if we know our neighbors and offer care for them. The workplace becomes a place we either look forward to or dread, not only because of the work but especially because of the quality of our relationships. The classroom becomes a community when understanding the material, ourselves, and one another becomes our mutual responsibility.

Today community is no longer just the place where we reside but has come to mean the web of relationships we are embedded in. From online communities to work environments, communities are no longer bound by geography or nearly anything else. Maintaining a priority on fostering community—from urban planning to celebration, from facing conflict in a nonviolent way to finding common goals, from taking care of one another to breaking bread together—provides the deep current for a home base.

When we genuinely see and hear one another, finding what we share in common and simultaneously respecting and staying curious about our differences, we manage the delicate balance of individual and community, bonding without losing ourselves. This practice is very simple, very powerful, and found at the heart of successful peacekeeping efforts between nations as well as between marriage partners. This kind of understanding leads to a culture of civility, one in which we can find common values and work toward common goals in a safe way. This move toward understanding and honesty begins simply with a risk to reach out in order to come together.

Connecting isn't just about addressing *our* need to belong or overcoming our loneliness. It is about how we serve our role in the home, family, town, and world, fulfilling our partnerships in the living community. Author and systems scientist Riane Eisler explained,

> If we stop and think about it, there are only two basic ways of structuring the relations. . . . All societies are patterned on either a dominator model—in which human hierarchies are ultimately backed up by force or the threat of force—or a partnership model, with variations in between.[17]

Our recorded history is one that emphasizes the violent subjugation of one tribe, group, color, gender, or religion over another. All too often, difference means threat. However, it is clear that there is another reasonable alternative: "that there can be societies in which difference is not necessarily equated with inferiority or superiority."[18] Eisler's partnership model emphasizes "linking rather than ranking" and provides a powerful template for community.[19]

The central theme of Martin Luther King Jr.'s teaching challenged us to go beyond limiting viewpoints to work toward the "Beloved Community" where "our loyalties must transcend our race, our tribe, our class, and our nation,"[20] where love and justice prevail. The word "love" here is not sentimental affection but the binding power that holds the universe together. In this community, we would know that "we are tied together in the single garment of destiny, caught in an inescapable network of mutuality."[21] As psychiatrist and community builder M. Scott Peck offered, "In and through community lies the salvation of the world."[22] Our work is to find those ways through which we can connect within and without and, in doing so, create our own beloved community.

Connecting

A sense of connecting and belonging to oneself, one another, a group, humanity, the earth, or to the divine mystery that is a fundamental human need.

Quiz

For each statement or word, circle the number that describes you best.

(least like me)   1   2   3   4   5   (most like me)

I work toward resolving conflicts.	1	2	3	4	5
I often learn from conflicts.	1	2	3	4	5
I belong.	1	2	3	4	5
I feel I am part of a community.	1	2	3	4	5
I have rich and satisfying friendships.	1	2	3	4	5
I feel loved.	1	2	3	4	5
In whatever form, I feel I am part of a family in my personal life.	1	2	3	4	5
I have meaningful partnerships.	1	2	3	4	5
I see myself as part of something larger than myself.	1	2	3	4	5

I feel seen and understood.   1   2   3   4   5

Add up the circled numbers.   Total: _____

10–19	20–29	30–39	40–50
A trailhead	**More is possible**	**A good ally**	**A great strength**

....

PRACTICES

Gift Someone

Service is a way of knowing our connection with a reality larger than ourselves. Often, our hearts open in the midst of freely given service. Is there some opportunity for service that you might try? "Gift" someone. Give this person an unexpected gift of some sort such as food, kindness, a flower, or your caring attention and careful listening. What was the process of making the choice of the gift and giving it?

Ceremony

There is something about rituals and ceremony—the symbols, the witness of community, the energy of intention and commitment—that strikes a chord beneath rational consciousness. Whether for marriage, graduation, death, birth, or even little moments such as breaking bread together or bedtime, a little ritual helps make and mark the event. There are formal rites in various traditions and made up ones with infinite variations. A rite can be elaborate, like a grand wedding that brings family and community together. It can also be as simple as writing down something you have been holding on to that you are genuinely ready to let go of and throwing it into a fire while perhaps speaking your release or good-bye aloud. In constructing or modifying a ceremony, you might want to consider the following questions:

- What is the intention or purpose of the rite (to honor a graduate, remember a loved one, celebrate someone or something, let go of something)?
- What is the prime attitude or feeling this space is anchoring (love, appreciation, respect, gratitude)? What would help engender that feeling (music, silence)?
- What or whose energy do you want to invoke? You might call upon the energy of a religious figure or the power of love, the highest and the best, or a loved one.
- What is an action that will symbolize your intention? What might help mark this as a special moment (singing, clothing, location, objects, food, prayers, time of day, movements, the ring of a bell)?
- What words, yours or others, such as a poem or story, would help mark this moment?

Forgiveness

Unresolved conflicts with others can shrink the range of our safe community, especially because they contract our heart. Sometimes we simply need to stay away from a person whom we have difficulty with. Sometimes the anger can serve as moral fire, but nearly always, holding on to the hurt poisons us. As St. Augustine wrote in *Confessions*, "Imagine that our enemies can do us more harm than we do to ourselves by hating them."[23]

When have you been wounded by someone or some circumstance? What happened? How did you react? Are you still responding to this in some way? Does this still live in you, and, if so, how? Has this closed your heart in some way?

Is there a bigger picture here—that is, something to learn? Is there something to do, write, or speak about? Is there some way to move or release part of this? How might you let go and what do you want to hang on to? You could write a letter, for example, speak the truth, create a ceremony, imagine letting this go in some way, or ask the divine for this to be taken and healed. Pseudo-forgiveness (forgiving someone before you have dealt with the anger and hurt), does not work and simply pushes the pain underground. But once we begin to loosen up the energy, we are freer to connect with the world and ourselves.

Homecoming

In a relaxed, contemplative state, consider the following statement deeply and with curiosity and just see what arises: "You are welcome here." As responses emerge, go even more deeply and see what comes. If you are in a group or with a partner, it can be powerful for another person (and perhaps others) to say this expression out loud several times. Once you've spent a little time looking inward, you may want to share what came up with someone or journal about it.

Presence

Heart

Wisdom

Creation

PART III

11

THE TRUE

The Truth must dazzle gradually
Or every man be blind.

—Emily Dickinson

Who comes to mind if you take a moment to imagine someone wise? Who (or what) rises to the surface? What's it like to be in this person's presence? What is it that makes them wise?

When I've asked these questions, I've heard about plenty of wise elders who have managed to stay steady somehow, people whose decency was palpable and at times courageous. Some describe persons familiar or famous who have had great heart or great insight, those who navigate with an inner compass, who seem to do the right thing when others may not. Sometimes a child is mentioned who seems unusually deep and profoundly open. Sometimes it is not a person at all but instead the natural world.

The meaning of wisdom is difficult to pin down. In considering wisdom, we're not speaking of merely amassing information or even practical know-how, although both knowledge and

know-how are frequently described as an important component
of wisdom. Instead, wisdom may be thought of less as something
we possess and more as a way of knowing and being. One does not
have wisdom; one *acts* wisely.

Thirteenth-century Dominican philosopher and theologian
Thomas Aquinas said that wisdom involves *gnome*, the ability to
see into the heart of things or see from a greater height.[1] While
intellect lives in complexity, wisdom cuts through the cloud of
complexity. It stretches beyond shrewdness or calculation and
gets to the heart of the matter. It can involve seeing the forest for
the trees or taking into account the long haul. For example, the
great law of the Iroquois was to consider the impact of all delib-
erations on the seven generations to follow.

In addition to this big or long view, Ralph Waldo Emerson
described wisdom as a blend of the perception of what is true
with the moral sentiment of what is right.[2] In a similar vein,
both Plato and Aristotle implied that being wise involved striving toward moral perfection or virtue (*arete*) by which balance is
found and adopted in all the significant affairs of life. The courageous and very risky acts of people like Gandhi, Jesus Christ, and
Martin Luther King Jr., three figures sometimes named as wise,
imply that wise action can move beyond self-interest. And while
the consequences can be loving and harmonious, they can also be
disruptive: Christ was said to have turned over the tables of the
moneychangers who were doing business in a holy temple; King
organized a sit-in at a segregated lunch counter in Montgomery,
Alabama; Gandhi's radical nonviolence took on the authority of
the British Empire. On the surface, we might not have recognized
these actions as conventionally "smart," but they were profoundly
wise in some way. In this sense, wisdom does not simply serve
individual growth but also the growth of the world. The actions
of Christ, King, and Gandhi helped change their societies. For

these souls, wisdom had something to do with finding a way to carry the heart—love, justice, and compassion—into being.

My friend John Reid was a professor of geology in Western Massachusetts. He could frequently be found with students on his Boston Whaler powerboat in the Connecticut River reading the sediment layers and on the riverbank studying erosion. I'm pretty sure that his life flowed best in these moments of being close to the earth and his students. Though he had an impressive academic pedigree (Exeter, Williams, Harvard, MIT) he maintained a childlike streak that was endlessly curious, and he loved helping others engage their own curiosity. I remember asking him one time about his spiritual life, and he described an uncertainty about any theology or theory, but like a good scientist, he knew what the empirical data showed him. What he had experienced firsthand now and again was a sense of connection with nature that seemed to have more gravity to it or current in it than most other moments in his life. Along with it, there was a sense of communion, wonder, and fullness that was hard to put into words but seemed so clear nonetheless. Noted transcendentalists Emerson, Thoreau, and Whitman were also of this ilk, I suspect.

On the stern of his Boston Whaler, where it is customary to put a boat's name, was this curious word, *Thalweg*, that always gave me pause as I tried to imagine what it meant or where it came from. It wasn't until after John's death from cancer that I looked this word up. In hydrology, the term *thalweg* comes from the Old High German *tal*, meaning "valley," and *weg*, meaning "way," sometimes called the "valley line." It's basically a line of the lowest points along the entire length of a streambed or valley, the deepest channel and often fastest current of a watercourse.

In these moments on the Connecticut River, John looked for the deep channel where the current quickened and carried him a bit faster into an experience that he reverently described as having both fullness and joy. Opening to wisdom involves tapping the deep current life flows through. There is both a quickening and a clarifying that occurs as the denser material settles out. Wisdom involves the art of raising or deepening our level of being in order to see the forest for the trees, to see the long haul, and to integrate the heart, and in doing so, to recognize more than we had understood before.

The Taoist's goal is to live in alignment or balance with the Tao—the way, the *weg*, that mysterious life force that flows through all. For Aristotle, the end game of life is *eudaimonia*, that bright mysterious signal that lets us know we're on to something. As my friend John did, in some moments we may recognize that deeper way through a sense of fullness. Following it is acting wisely.

We know people who are brilliant intellectually but far from wise. Smart and knowledgeable people sometimes act unwisely, falling prey to fallacies of invincibility or narcissism. Some individuals may be able to navigate with "success" in the world. Such "pragmatics of life" are certainly valuable and have even been described as a component of wisdom, but they do not necessarily integrate the heart, see beyond self-interest, or take a bigger view.[3] Consequently, lives guided only by such pragmatics can be left wanting in some very central ways.

We also know that the amount of information available today with a flick of a finger is stunning and easily overwhelming. The mysteries of the universe are on the Web. And yet with all this information at hand, it does not seem that we are taking better care of one another or have greater peace of mind or that our actions are wiser. It is not just knowledge or know-how that is required for a meaningful life and not simply information or bigger bandwidth that will fulfill us. Wisdom opens us to the deeper current our lives flow through, and this is required for our satisfaction and, increasingly, for our very survival.

In an age where information and calculation are the high-water marks in the quest for what is true, religionist Abraham Heschel spoke of a radically different understanding of how we come to wisdom.

> The loss of awe is the great block to insight. A return to reverence is the first prerequisite for a revival of wisdom. . . . Wisdom comes from awe rather than from shrewdness. It is evoked not in moments of calculation but in moments of being in rapport with the mystery of reality.[4]

Awe, wonder, and reverence are drawn forth not by a quest for control or measurement but by appreciative and open-ended engagement with the questions. This is why such qualities as the ability to listen, empathize, and be comfortable with ambiguity are associated with wisdom.[5] This is how the understanding heart and the open, aware mind set the stage for wisdom. Heschel wrote,

> Awe enables us to perceive in the world intimations of the divine, to sense in small things the beginning of infinite significance, to sense the ultimate in the common and the simple; to feel the rush of the passing of the stillness of the eternal. . . . The beginning of awe is wonder, and the beginning of wisdom is awe.[6]

This was what my friend John must have been searching for.

Truth

Wisdom entails a quest for truth, which involves knowledge over ignorance and insight over illusion, whether about the nature of the universe, the meaning of our lives, or the motivations of the person in front of us, including the one in the mirror. It is driven by human curiosity and the search for meaning. It is our nature to make meaning of the world. A young child's constant questioning, "Why? Why? Why?" reminds us of this innate need to know and how much this curiosity drives so much of life.

Truth comes to us in different ways. Sometimes truth is remembered. Plato used the word *anamnesis* (the soul's remembrance of truth) in which there is a felt sense or recognition that something is right or true. Truth is revealed as we suddenly seem to be in receipt of insight or a clearer view. The mystic revelation and the creative breakthrough are so often described in this way, whether this is thought to descend as some kind of grace, through the whisper of the Muses or from an expansion or opening of mind. Truth is also discovered, and we venture out and explore the borderlands between the known and the unknown—studying in the laboratory, sailing among the Galápagos, or on our next date. And truth is constructed, a story we build to try to capture reality.

When we say something is true, we mean that it is not bent or distorted. When we speak the truth, it is aligned with what we know to be an accurate representation of reality. But reality is not always so easy to pin down once and for all. Truth is both relatively absolute and absolutely relative. The reality is that some of my truths may be different from yours. Think of blind men standing in different places around an elephant. The truth for each is based on what he feels and deduces from where he stands. From a greater vantage point we understand a more encompassing truth, and this is the work of wisdom, to find a more encompassing, penetrating, and open-ended view, realizing that what we can see is always partial.

Even in that realm of hard facts, the history of science helps us understand that what was once established, even self-evident truth, sometimes turns out to be dead wrong (the world is flat, the sun orbits around the Earth, and light must be either wave or particle, for example). Our capacity to see limits our truth. We reach the limits of our sight especially when we become so invested in our truth. There is a saying that physics progresses by funerals. The latest ideas are not fully adopted as true until that previous generation and their individual truths are out of the way, making space for an upgraded version of reality, Truth 2.0.

Truth as a representation of reality is a story. Newton's story overturned the church's proclamations. Einstein's story overturned some of Newton's. Modern quantum physics has updated some of Einstein's. The stories we live by are worldviews, maps of reality that help guide our perceptions and actions. But as author Umberto Eco's Franciscan sleuth William of Baskerville said, "The order that our mind imagines is like a net, or like a ladder, built to attain something. But afterward you must throw the ladder away, because you discover that, even if it was useful, it was meaningless."[7]

Upgraded worldviews *are* important for wisdom; they are the truest maps we have, and necessary, but they are insufficient too. As author Morris Berman said, "Getting trapped in a worldview . . . ultimately prevents us from finding the world."[8] What wisdom requires is not only a worldview but also a world presence—openness to the world that is immediate, alive, and does not fixate in any particular worldview but may borrow from any or all as needed. Ultimately we live out a dance between worldview and world presence. They constantly shape one another in an ongoing dialectic. Truth is revealed at the edge of map and mystery. The requirement is that we must cultivate a friendship with the unknown in order to find our true way.

A mother once described to me a moment when she and her daughter were sitting on their couch in front of the television.

"I was laughing at something on TV, and my eight-year-old was scared by it, and she said, 'You know, Mommy, I don't know yet what's real and what's not real.'" How *do* we know what is real? What are the requirements to determine truth?

Our wisdom quest is like this little girl's. Reality, like a parable, is dimensional. Truth is revealed based on our capacity for seeing and understanding. While we are often told what is true, wisdom operates as an open system constantly on the lookout to update our story of reality and to live true (aligned) to this understanding. Wisdom holds truth as an ongoing process, a constant, unfolding, progressive revelation held up against and lived out in the reality of this moment or this situation. What is true in this sense is not something that sits on a shelf but is lived out, revealed, and explored throughout the day and in life. It requires our world presence to unravel it.

Part of what wisdom does that is different from just knowing a lot of stuff or thinking cleverly is that it takes in this larger, more integrated view, seeing from a greater height or seeing into the heart of something, as Aquinas said. Inherent in this seeing is recognizing that truth is an unending dialectic. Whether in the scientific or moral quest for what is true, wisdom involves overcoming our own limited capacity to see, integrating multiple truths and staying awake at the edge of the unknown.

Science provides a radical method for requiring evidence to determine if a thing is true or not. It was the shining key to overcoming superstition of the Dark Ages and, to the extent that it and we remain open to the evidence, it is an egalitarian tool of empowerment. No longer do you need to consult priest, professor, or prophet; this kind of truth is available to anyone who follows the code—that is, the scientific method. But this kind of truth has its limits. While we may be able to measure the blood flow through a heart with good numerical precision, we have difficulty meaningfully measuring the flow rate of our compassion. The scientific method has been so valuable and effective in modernist, materialist culture that it spilled into other domains where it is inadequate and inappropriate. This leads to a kind of tyranny of one kind of truth: scientism. The materialistic, modernist, reductionist worldview that has been reinforced by this confusion ends up treating the world merely as a collection of objects. You are surely more than that, and so am I. Wisdom recognizes a larger net of truth, as we will explore in chapters to come.

Ultimately, the *true* is bound to the *beautiful* and the *good*. By some accounts when we recognize or capture a deep reality, it is truly beautiful. When Picasso captured the essence of a bull with a few sparse lines, stripped of all but something essential, the result was both true and beautiful. When Rosa Parks decided she could no longer collude in her own diminishment and remained seated in the whites-only section at the front of the bus, it was an act that rang true and opened the *good*. Each cardinal direction taken deeply enough can open to all others.

Light

Light is used throughout human history and across cultures to describe what is both deep within us and the source of consciousness. "I see the light," the light at the end of the tunnel that provides hope and a beacon, the light in her eyes, the fire of inspiration, the lamp of knowledge, a candle in the wilderness. All are phrases that reflect some deep recognition of light as allowing us to see better.

We use words like enlightenment, illumination, and radiance to describe some special quality of knowing. Religious texts claim that, as written in the Qur'an of Islam, "God is the light of heaven and earth."[9] In the book of John in the Bible, Jesus was reported to have said, "I am the light of the world." In Tibetan Buddhism, the "clear light mind" is referred to a capacity of a kind of pure, unobscured consciousness. According to the Jewish *Zohar*, both the individual and the universe as a whole are composed of ten dimensions, the ten Sefirot, (emanations), of light. Think of waves of light emanating out from "a never-to-be-exhausted fountain of light."[10]

- Light feeds us; it provides energy for plants.
- Light reflects paradox, as it is both wave and particle.
- Light sets our biological clocks, and at the speed of light, time stops.
- Light allows our cells to communicate and our eyes to see.
- Light has no volume; it is energy without mass.
- The amount of light is what we measure; we cannot measure darkness.

In order to reveal itself, light needs an object like a body or a wall. In this way, light as wisdom is revealed through our action and interaction with the world. We do not possess wisdom (light); instead, we act wisely (shining light on the situation). Light as wisdom comes into being at the center of paradox, where time stops, where we find nourishment, where our cells touch and our eyes meet.

Maybe the process of wisdom involves, as Jacques Lusseyran said, "looking from an inner place to one further within." In this way of knowing, we come to see "wisdom [as] the process by which we come to know that the limited thing we thought was our whole being is not."[11]

In the midst of this information age, we realize that knowledge is not enough. This age is desperate for wisdom.

Plato claimed that the capacity for wisdom was first among virtues and the only one that is innate.[12] Whether it is innate or not, from the evidence presented by both our world and ourselves, it is clear that wisdom needs some help to rise to the surface. In the chapters that follow, let's explore those qualities wisdom rides and relies on.

12

POSSIBILITY

> I rise, I rise, I rise.
>
> —Maya Angelou

I've always had a fascination with the scenes in movies like the James Bond, Indiana Jones, and Lara Croft films where, after an encounter with a diabolical bad guy or a step too far into a forbidden place, the protagonist finds themselves trapped with absolutely no way out and only seconds remaining before all is lost. Our hero is doomed, surrounded by a mote of hungry crocodiles or in a plane without parachutes, fuel, or any hope whatsoever as it is about to crash into a mountainside. I loved these scenes, but it took me a while to realize why they grabbed me so completely. Sure, there is the drama with its rise and release of tension, but there is something more. They are metaphors related to doing the impossible. The hopeless suddenly manage against all odds and all reason to transcend their fates and, in so doing, remind us of this possibility within us. Our hero sees something fresh, takes a risk, and finds a way out. This resonates with the energy of transcendence, possibility, and hope.

But it can be hard to stay open to possibility. Neuroscientist Walter J. Freeman concluded that the neural activity due to sensory stimulation (sound, taste, sight, and so forth) essentially disappears in the cortex.[1] That means we are not really seeing what we think we are. Some stimulation, like the sight of a car heading our way or the sound of a partner's oft-repeated complaint, flows into the brain, and it evokes in its place an internal pattern already in place, which the mind uses to represent the external situation. We think we see the real world, but we actually see what is already in our own minds. In the face of a new situation, we tend to replay the maps in our heads rather than seeing the landscape in front of us. But wisdom involves staying both aware of this tendency and open to fresh input and seeing in new ways.

My wise friend Carolyn had her family coming for Christmas dinner. Several of the grandchildren had to be off to their mother's family in the early afternoon (the result of a divorce), and it had been carefully calculated that they would all have to be sitting down to eat promptly at one o'clock if they were to make their obligations and maintain harmony between all parties. So that they might best enjoy one another on Christmas morning, Carolyn decided to prepare all the food the day before. She then wrapped everything in foil and left it overnight on the glassed-in porch, which served as a large refrigerator on that cold night. One of her sons brought their large retriever with them along with the rest of the family to spend the night. Let's see, retriever, overnight, food on the porch—well, you know where this is going. Although Carolyn had been sure to lock the door to the porch, one of the grandchildren had taken a phone call there for some privacy. She apparently didn't close the door tightly. By midmorning on Christmas day, the discovery was made: turkey bones, bits of foil, and a sheepish, lethargic golden retriever. The Christmas meal was ruined. Since her son's dog and daughter were the unwitting culprits, her son quickly offered to get another turkey. Carolyn was sure that it would be impossible to cook in time and told him not to bother. He offered again, and that offer hung in the air. If she refused, the mood of the day looked pretty grim. Instead of taking the reasonable course and abandoning the turkey idea, she paused and then said, "Go for it." He rushed to the store, got the last unfrozen turkey at Food Lion, and called from the car to say, "Preheat the oven!" The turkey was done, quite impossibly and against the laws of culinary physics, at one o'clock. Except for the retriever, who was not feeling so great at this point, the day was saved, and everyone was really delighted.

Whether in saving the world from evildoers or saving the Christmas dinner, whether in responding to someone who has trespassed against us or stuck at the edge of our own impossible situation with no way out, there is often a moment that hangs in the air when we can either default to our reasonable views and pre-programmed reactions already etched in our minds or hold open another possibility. Those hanging moments are like little portals just waiting for us to step into them. They take us beyond expectations and odds to some new possibility. They can also be contagious.

Ladies and gentlemen, here is the result of event nine, the one-mile: 1st, No. 41, R. G. Bannister, Amateur Athletic Association and formerly of Exeter and Merton Colleges, Oxford, with a time which is a new meeting and track record, and which—subject to ratification—will be a new English Native, British National, All-Comers, European, British Empire, and World Record. The time was three . . . [2]

"Three" was all the crowd needed to hear as it burst into a roar. On May 6, 1954, at the Iffley Road track in Oxford, England's Roger Bannister broke the world record by running the first sub-four-minute mile. For years, the four-minute mile was considered not merely unreachable but also, according to physiologists of the time, dangerous to the health of any athlete who attempted to reach it. When he crossed the finish line with a time of 3 minutes, 59.4 seconds, Bannister broke through not only a temporal barrier but also what seemed to be a collective psychological barrier. John Landy, one of the great milers of that era, had never gotten closer than 1.5 seconds to the four-minute barrier before. Within forty-six days of Bannister's breakthrough, Landy set a new record with a 3:57.9 minute run in Finland. Bannister and Landy raced later in the year in the "Mile of the Century." Bannister won in 3:58.8 to Landy's 3:59.6, the first time two men in one race had broken through the four-minute barrier. By the end of 1957, sixteen runners had logged sub-four-minute miles.[3]

Once we see that something is possible it may be just the ticket to open up our own consciousness and capacity. Examples of the extraordinary and the novel (Bannister and Bond, turkeys and underdogs) can free us, shattering our internal image of what is not possible. Wisdom is constantly on the lookout for a new way of looking, for another possibility.

Hope

Physician Jerome Goopman explores the role of hope and possibility in the practice of healing.[4] He suggests that appropriate hope is a powerful tool in medicine. If a patient is told they have six months to live, the time line too often becomes a self-fulfilling prophecy. (Most physicians try not to offer that kind of death sentence.) If on the other hand the patient understands the reality of the illness but also has a glimmer of possibility for healing, there can be quite remarkable results, as Goopman catalogues from his patients. The experience of hope or possibility may motivate us to try something against the odds that just might work. Hope may affect our mental state, catalyzing healing from the inside out in ways we do not fully understand, and hope may change the quality of the time we have, however long. Goopman makes an important distinction between blind optimism, in which we may try to hold an attitude that "everything will be fine," and hope that may have a "realistic" or true sense of what is happening but still entertain a possibility that there may be a way out and that we can choose to move toward that opening.

Even at the level of our mammalian cousins, there is some hardwired survival mechanism that seems fueled by the extraordinary energy of possibility. In one study, rats were individually placed in glass jars filled with water. Researchers measured the amount of time the rats were able to keep swimming. Rats are proficient if reluctant swimmers, and many in this case kept themselves afloat in their little torture chambers for eighty hours. However, in other instances rats died within minutes, described as a phenomenon of unexplained sudden death. In trying to eliminate all sorts of variables, researcher Curt Richter and his associates discovered that rats who were removed from the water, placed on dry land for a minute, maybe given a little pep talk before being placed back in the tank, would consistently swim for hours and even days. While I don't suspect that rats experience hope in the same way humans do, an experience of possibility clearly activates some latent capacity for endurance. Some sense or experience that this was not a hopeless situation kept the rat swimming for remarkably long periods of times, while many of their cousins who had no experience of being rescued died within minutes.[5]

(In the next world, some bathing-suit clad experimental psychologists will no doubt face a natatorium where the bleachers are filled with white laboratory rodents waiting patiently to return the favor.)

Believing Before Seeing

Seeing before believing is the credo of modern science. We are encouraged to believe something only after we see it for ourselves. For the most part, this works just fine, providing the kind of verification that helps us avoid foolishness and superstition. However, it is sometimes necessary to believe *before* we can see. More precisely, this means suspending disbelief in order to open ourselves to some new possibility, perhaps like Bannister or Bond's achievements. This does not mean abandoning our critical mind or being a naïve convert to some belief or doctrine; rather, it means turning off critical judgment for a moment and turning down our sense of certainty in order to see possibility. This is my favorite definition of faith—the suspension of disbelief. And what faith does is open our consciousness and allow us to see new possibility.

As he entered high school, Hugh was a troubled and troubling underachiever. He was on the fast track to a disappointing life. But his school had an unusual experiment at the time that involved periodically busing Hugh and a group of his peers to the nearby Princeton University campus, where students listened to presentations by distinguished scientists of the day, Einstein among them. The idea was that these wise, or at least smart, men might have a positive impact on the lives of these difficult teens, sparking some inspiration or motivation.

One day, after a particularly long, dry talk by one of the physicists, a young girl sitting in the back of the tiered lecture hall raised her hand and wryly asked these men of science what they thought of ghosts. Her question was entirely off topic, but after some chuckles in the room, the physicists took it on. The first fellow stood up and with an air of absolute certainty entirely dismissed any possibility of their existence. When he was done, the second scientist stood up to take his turn at her question. With great authority, he rejected any chance whatsoever of ghosts, citing a lack of any hard scientific evidence. When they had finished, the third member of the panel took his turn. It was Robert Oppenheimer, who had directed the Manhattan Project that developed the atomic bomb and then, once he saw what he had done, became the staunchest opponent of its use. He stood up, paused for a moment, and then said, "That's a fascinating question. I accept the possibility of all things." Given what he had seen already in his life we can suppose this was a statement borne out of firsthand experience. He went on to explain that "it is necessary to find one's own required evidence before accepting or rejecting a possibility."

For Hugh, hearing this response as he sat in this Princeton lecture hall was an absolute moment of revelation that forever changed his life. Instead of closing down and accepting the world as prepackaged, which was the impression he had received from school, Oppenheimer's perspective opened it back up to mystery, to the possibility of all things, and to one's responsibility to discover its validity for oneself. This gave Hugh permission for two things. The first was the openness to infinite possibility that comes from what poet W. B. Yeats called "radical innocence"— that moment of suspending disbelief and opening ourselves.[6] And simultaneously, there was the necessity to find out for oneself, to be true to one's own standards rather than simply swallowing someone else's truth.

Hugh's inner life began a fundamental shift as he came to define himself from the center of his own direct experience.

Hugh told me that he began to believe in possibility and mystery again and to rely on his own standards of verification rather than shutting down and merely conforming to what others said was real or true. He dialogued with truth and reclaimed responsibility to evaluate it for himself. Life became about discovery, adventure, and invention instead of simply accumulating information that was "certain" or "true" and ultimately foreclosing of new possibility. Hugh Gunnison went on to become a distinguished, innovative, and irreverent professor who helped open up possibilities for others, including me, as he was my very first graduate school professor. Essentially, this moment helped him believe in the possibility of all things—to believe so that he could see.

Deep in a Dark Forest

Meaning has a role in opening up possibility. If something is meaningful to us, we find a reservoir of relevance and power to move toward the future. If we have a reason, we can show up to where possibility has a chance of opening up. Nelson Mandela was imprisoned for nearly thirty years in South African jails. What he lived for and was willing to die for was the liberation of South Africa from apartheid. While in prison, he maintained a strict exercise regimen and refused any collusion or negotiated conditions for his release. He organized political education classes at Robben Island, which actually became a center of learning during his imprisonment. In a remarkable turn of events, Mandela was released in 1990, awarded the Nobel Peace Prize in 1993, and became the first democratically elected president of South Africa the following year. The clear vision of his goal and the congruence of his means helped achieve what by all odds looked impossible.

Physician and Nazi concentration camp survivor Victor Frankl declared that meaning is not so much found as it is created. Our opportunity, our responsibility, and our ultimate freedom is to create meaning in any situation. Frankl said, "Ultimately, man should not ask what the meaning of his life is, but rather must recognize that it is *he* who is asked. In a word, each man is questioned by life; and he can only answer to life by *answering for* his own life; to life he can only respond by being responsible."[7]

The meaning we make of something shapes perceptions and thus possibility as it did during both Mandela's and Frankl's imprisonments. The possibility is not only in our social circumstance but also in our body. For example, the phenomenon of the placebo effect demonstrates that our beliefs can affect experience and even health. When given an inert pill—a placebo—instead of the actual medication, typically one-quarter to one-third of those participants have the same change as if they were given the actual medication. The mind-body unity has been so well established that if researchers are testing a new medication, and there is improvement in one-third of its users, it is considered ineffective—that is, no more effective than a sugar pill. It appears that if we have an idea that something will effect a change in us, in many of us in many ways, it actually does.

A related phenomenon has to do with how we make meaning of an illness or injury. For example, if we come to view illness as just punishment for some transgression, we may not get better or work to do so. We may accept the "punishment" and consider ourselves undeserving of healing or redemption. Esther, a patient of physician Jerome Groopman's, had breast cancer that resulted in a radical mastectomy. A devout orthodox Jew in a very disappointing marriage, she confessed to her doctor that she had committed adultery. She saw the cancer as God's just punishment and simply refused treatment because of this belief. She died at age thirty-four.[8] Our meaning is shaped by our assumptions about our history, about the nature of illness that the medical community or our physician holds ("How long have I got, Doc?"), the sense of responsibility for our own healing, our sense of helplessness or personal agency, which is in turn shaped by social status, history, and on and on. In other words, as philosopher David Michael Levin argued, the body is more than physical substance; it is essentially a "discursive formation" shaped by various stories of meaning.[9] Our sense of possibility or hope is often tied to the stories we come to believe in. Thus medicine or any kind of healing or learning or living in general misses a key ingredient if it does not consider meaning at the center of healing and flourishing.

As it did for Mandela, meaning gets us out of bed in the morning and focuses us on a target. It gives us the internal fuel source to carry on and thus puts us on course to possibility. Without it, we may stay under the covers and miss the chance to meet halfway. Meaning shapes perception and thus can foreclose or open possibility. Sometimes, though, meaning just slips away in the middle of our night.

On the night before Good Friday in 1300, Dante Alighieri was in trouble.

> Halfway through the journey we are living
> I found myself deep in a dark forest,
> For I had lost all trace of the straight path.[10]

As with Dante's *Divine Comedy*, it is not so uncommon to find ourselves lost in our own dark wood, trapped in a way that seems like there is no way out. Meaning and hope seem to have disappeared; light has grown dim and cold. My friend Tara shared with me about such a time in her own life.

It had been a tough winter filled with cold, gray days and I had been battling serious depression. I had just gotten out of the mental hospital a few weeks before, and getting up each morning seemed to be a momentous accomplishment. Part of my depression was admittedly situational as I was working as the sole professional minister in a dysfunctional church, so getting up on Sunday was even more difficult.

Anyway, one Sunday morning, I woke up and made my way to the kitchen to make coffee, and as I glanced outside, I noticed just how gray and cold it looked. After making my coffee I went back to gazing out the window, searching for the horses in the meadow that always seemed to lift my spirit. I did not see the horses, but I noticed a tree, and my eyes just sort of became glued to this tree. It was a tree that had no life, stripped completely bare of leaves, and for all intents and purposes, it was dead, and yet something about the tree was so beautiful set in front of the gray sky. I could see the shapes of each limb and noticed how artistic it looked in my window. I noticed squirrels running over the limbs, jumping from one to the other, the way the absence of leaves allowed me to see more clearly the interesting shapes it formed, and I began to see myself in this tree. Even in the dead of winter, stripped bare, it still was beautiful and made the landscape complete. That was how I saw myself at the time, depressed and stripped bare of any defenses, and as I looked at that tree I had this sudden realization that even this time of my life was beautiful and that in the grand scheme of the world, this was just as important as the times when I have blossomed.

That moment really shifted my whole perception of depression, and I was able to embrace more fully the winter of my own emotional life. I was even more surprised that it took a dead tree to shift me into a more hopeful and helpful space. To this day, I still look at winter trees, the way the sky accents their limbs, the way they reach to me, and I remember that whatever shape I am in is the shape I am supposed to be in. I remember the way a tree spoke to me and gave me hope to finish my season.

In the dark woods, possibility comes from the act of befriending the unknown, risking looking deeply enough and facing it long enough to see something we hadn't seen before. Friedrich Nietzsche wrote, "When you gaze long into an abyss the abyss also gazes into you."[11]

Some chemistry of friendship is catalyzed in the interaction. Transcendence is possible not because of running away or trying to solve the mystery but because of making a turn in that hanging moment to stay with it in order to see something we had been missing. Wisdom seeks to change nothing but the way we look at things.

Wisdom rises on a current of possibility. Through the continued practice of suspending disbelief, befriending the unknown, and risking having our maps changed and through creating meaning and finding hope, we come to see in new ways. As we do, as Maya Angelou said, we come to sense that we have within us the possibility of nearly everything: "I rise, I rise, I rise."

Possibility
The idea that something is possible helps us transcend our current state and current situation and create a future.

Quiz

For each statement or word, circle the number that describes you best.

(least like me)   1   2   3   4   5   (most like me)

I see old problems in new ways.	1	2	3	4	5
I dream big.	1	2	3	4	5
I take constructive risks.	1	2	3	4	5
I don't often feel stuck.	1	2	3	4	5
I like a challenge.	1	2	3	4	5
Anything is possible.	1	2	3	4	5
The world is full of mystery.	1	2	3	4	5
Generally, I am hopeful.	1	2	3	4	5
The world is full of endless possibilities.	1	2	3	4	5
I befriend the unknown.	1	2	3	4	5

Add up the circled numbers.   Total: _____

10–19	20–29	30–39	40–50
A trailhead	**More is possible**	**A good ally**	**A great strength**

....

PRACTICES

The Art of Pondering

The ancient Greek philosophers were bold in asking questions like, "Who am I?" and "What are we here for?" Pondering big and radical questions, what theologian Paul Tillich named "ultimate concerns," has the capacity of opening to unexpected insight, essentially using the intellect to go beyond intellectual understanding. In conversation or journaling or simply musing to oneself, we might ponder

- *Big things.* "What is life about?"
- *Both local and distant influences.* "What would make your workplace, your family, the world better?" "What do you wonder about and worry about?"

- *Ethics.* "How do you know what's the right thing to do?" "What would you do if you were the president or prime minister?"
- *Identity.* "What is the most important thing about being you? What's the most fun?" "What will your life be like in ten years?" "What would you like as your epitaph?" "Who are your heroes?"
- *New perspectives.* "What if you had only a week to live?"
- *Limits.* "If I had a million dollars (or whatever you think you are missing on the one hand or chained to on the other), what would your life feel like? Be like?"

Bucket List

Before your time is up, what would you like to do, be, or experience? What's on your bucket list?

Dream Big

We often adopt others' visions, perhaps our parents' or peers' or images from the mass media. Sometimes we are so focused on realistic goals (which is by no means a bad thing) that we forget to keep in view that dream we have within us. A vision compels and propels toward some horizon.

Move yourself into a contemplative state and imagine you are living your dream. Dream big: see it, feel it, taste it, hear it, touch it; see what arises spontaneously in your consciousness. It may surprise you. It may not be entirely clear. Take a look. Soak it in. Enjoy it. Does it have some meaning for you?

A Vision

Possibility is activated when we gain clarity on both our personal vision and the reality of our current circumstances; that is, the dynamic tension between our ideal and our reality may provide the energy to reach out for that vision, take creative risks, keep our eyes on the prize, and commit to the life we want.

A vision and a fantasy are not quite the same thing. The recognition of where we are helps ground the vision in this world, keeping us from the narcotic effect of an otherworldly fantasy. At the same time, too much emphasis on the current situation without a strong enough sense of vision may feel discouraging, like the mountain of our vision is too distant or big to climb. See if you can find the right balance of real and ideal. Ask your deepest self,

- What do I truly want?
- What really matters to me?
- What do I really want to create in my life?
- Where is my life now?
- What is the gap between where I am and where I want to go?

Represent this ideal and the reality with words or maybe an image. Deep down is there something about this vision you want to make a commitment to? Go ahead if this seems to be the right moment to do so.

Goal

A dream and a vision provide hope and direction. They are made manifest, at least in part, through our commitments and effort. Goals take the big vision and help move us from the reality of where we are nearer to where we want to go. Consider the following questions and free write a response to each:

- A goal I have for the next (hour, day, month, year) is

  _____.

- Why is this important? How important is it?
- If necessary, how can I adjust my goal?
- How will I know if I have achieved it?
- What it would feel like to have already achieved this?

- Obstacles to achieving this include _____.
- I will try to achieve this goal by _____ (specific plan, time table, concrete steps, details, action steps, and so forth).
- What part of me is "all in," ready to move forward? What part of me is doubtful, dragging its feet, or even likely to sabotage these efforts? Have a dialogue with these parts, perhaps free writing a conversation or giving them voices, especially to the doubter, in some way.

Exposing and acknowledging our inner resistance up front helps foster more complete agreement with our goals and actions.

13

GUIDANCE

When Michelangelo did the Sistine Chapel he painted both the major
and the minor prophets. They can be told apart because,
though there are cherubim at the ears of all,
only the major prophets are listening.

—J. C. Gowan

Wisdom involves recognizing the limits of what we know and seeking some help to reach beyond those limits. But where do we go for guidance?

If we're sensible, we seek advice from experts we think we can trust, from tax talk to car talk. The ancient Greeks who could afford the visit consulted the Oracle at Delphi for her cryptic pronouncements. Wise elders are typically sought out in many traditional societies for their counsel. Spiritual guides and teachers steer in religious or moral contexts, while therapists and executive life coaches dot the landscape of contemporary allies. Experts in every field from financial planning to home repair expound advice ("Do this." "Don't buy that." "Move here."), but wise allies often also spend plenty of time listening, which helps us find, activate, and clarify our own views. Wise guides tend to draw us out and, in doing so, help us see more clearly.

Wise guidance is more than bits of information or technique, however helpful. Instead, it activates a shift that moves us from a limited, denser, reactive or off-center state like fear, anxiety, or discouragement to see from a greater height or perhaps with greater heart. The exchange essentially raises, deepens, and opens our level of being. In this sense, wisdom seeks to change nothing but the way we look at something.

A Pathless Land

Beyond experts, ideas also provide guidance. From fiction to philosophy, we may find a compelling story or an inspiring line that has the effect of expanding the way we look at our situation, such as Gandhi's "Be the change you want to see in the world" or Oppenheimer's "I accept the possibility of all things." The great texts of the wisdom traditions or a great line of poetry or prose, or even a simple phrase, can serve as living words that activate and shift awareness to take in a new view or affirm a new day.

Values and virtues can serve as important guides. Our actions are often guided and measured by the values we hold dear. If we see the world as a place to win at all costs or instead as an opportunity to care for one another, we tend to act according to these values. But values, virtues, and aspirations do not come to life by themselves. Recall that wisdom is not something we have; it is instead something we do. We act wisely or not. What we learn very quickly about values or virtues is that they are *enacted*. They are breathed to life by our choices and our actions, our words, and our deeds. But how do we proceed? Which ones should we choose?

At thirteen, Jiddu was discovered on a beach in a small town in southern India. He and his brother were soon adopted by Annie Besant, then president of the Theosophical Society. Besant and others proclaimed that Jiddu was to be the "World Teacher" whose coming the Theosophists had predicted. To prepare for the teacher, a worldwide organization called the Order of the Star in the East was formed, and soon the young man was made its head. At a large annual gathering of the order, the crowd hushed as Jiddu Krishnamurti prepared to address his followers, who had waited for this moment in great anticipation of receiving inspiration for their spiritual quest. What happened next was unexpected, to say the least. In one sweep of his words, Krishnamurti renounced his role, dissolved the Order with its huge following, and returned all the money and property that had been donated for this work. He had come to see that

> Truth is a pathless land. Man cannot come to it through any organization, through any creed, through any dogma, priest or ritual, not through any philosophical knowledge or psychological technique. He has to find it through the mirror of relationship, through the understanding of the contents of his own mind.[1]

In this powerful act of spiritual integrity, Krishnamurti invites each of us to take active responsibility to find our own way.

Virtually all the wisdom traditions have a list of values or virtues that we are invited to abide by, from the Ten Commandments to the Three Jewels of Jainism. Serving as guideposts to be consulted and lived by, most of these tenets seem like pretty good ideas. The challenge isn't to find good values; it's to find how the values live in us and see how well we can live them out. "Truth is a pathless land" implies that full responsibility is not only about living in alignment with some set of values but to also assume responsibility in constructing our essential values, making them ours, ensuring conscious ownership at each step. They require us to enact them and to coconstruct them, examine them, tend to them, and grow them.

Business consultant Fred Kofman outlined a few simple questions he uses as a way of helping to clarify our values.[2] Give them a try:

1. Think of three characters, real or fictional, you consider admirable.
2. Ask yourself, What is it that I admire about each of these individuals? What makes them special to me?
3. How or where did that character express that quality in some situation?
4. Would I put myself on my list of people I admire?
5. If not, what's missing? How do these three characters live or what do they have that seems to be missing in my life?

In posing these questions to thousands of individuals, most who were in the field of business—a domain associated less with virtue and more with achievement and success—Kofman said that *not once* has anyone identified success or its trappings as the admirable quality.[3] Instead, qualities of the order of courage, compassion, and the like are what folks recognize as significant and worth aspiring to. The gap between the virtues our heroes embody and how many of those qualities we embody is a trailhead for our conscious growth.

To live from these admirable virtues is to live less with our worth tied to an outcome, which is something we do not have full control of. The stock market goes up and down, accidents happen, the world turns. To tie our satisfaction, meaning, self-worth, or happiness to a particular outcome is to set ourselves up for who knows what. But these virtues we identified come largely from the inside out. They are journeys, not outcomes. While we cannot often be assured of an outcome (winning a game, getting the date, landing that job) we can assume complete responsibility for how we go about it, maintaining our integrity of values in the process. Regardless of the outcome, at the end of the day or the end of life, we can usually live with that.

In a world that can seem out of control and certainly beyond our control, the central hope for a sense of peace and integrity lies in staying true to our values and ensuring that they are worth being true to. This means radical and ongoing responsibility to be accountable for the values we live by.

A Second Knowing

Many traditions and plenty of wise souls describe two general aspects of the human being. We will simply call them the "big self" and the "small self." The small self is understood as the ego in Western psychology or the "lesser self" in several traditions. It's not hard to recognize a small self as it develops into an orchestra of parts. The small self generates the internal dialogue that occupies so much of our daily existence: "Do I like this?" "What should I say?" "He's hot!" This "monkey mind" chatter offers nearly incessant commentary and judgment ranging from worries about the past to plans about the future. Sometimes one or another dimension of this voice seems to dominate, and we hear plenty of self-criticism, judgment of others, or maybe fear. This is the ego-generated voice that is simply a part of being human. But in the sacred traditions, the lesser self is not mistaken for our whole being.

As a source of wise guidance and insight, the Indian sage Sri Aurobindo called the big self the "Inner Guide."[4] Meister Eckhart, the thirteenth-century Dominican priest, referred to the "Inner Man."[5] Ralph Waldo Emerson spoke of the "Oversoul."[6] Italian psychiatrist Roberto Assagioli wrote about aspects of our greater dimensions as the "Higher Self" and "Transpersonal Self."[7] Time and time again, we are asked to loosen our identification with the chattering self and raise our level of being in order hear the voice of our deeper nature, and sometimes the means are very simple and very quiet.

As a teenager, George left home to try to find the person who would inspire him and serve as guide and mentor. He came away from his visits with each candidate more disappointed and discouraged. Finally, sitting in silence one day he began to hear a deep inner source, what he called the "Inner Light." George was George Fox who founded the Society of Friends in the seventeenth century, better known as the Quakers.[8] In recognition of the Inner Light, Quaker worship services proceed largely in silence so that participants may listen for that inner voice. The power of presence that we spoke of in previous chapters helps set the stage for our availability to guidance. We hear this wellspring described throughout the wisdom traditions and wise souls. Fellow Quaker William Penn, for whom Pennsylvania is named, described what arises out of the silence "as the word in the heart from which all scriptures flow."[9]

Discerning the difference between the inner voice and the ego's voice is a little tricky. Even when the ego-generated voice sounds reasonable and logical, it will typically prejudge a situation with a tone of self-interest, lack, and fear (of missing out or perhaps being hurt). By contrast, that deeper voice generally feels more generous rather than self-interested, works from abundance and possibility rather than lack and limitation, feels more peaceful than fearful (although it may offer warnings), and is open-ended rather than prejudging. With practice and awareness, we can recognize the different timbre and tone of these voices. In addition, the inner voice is often accompanied by a felt shift—a feeling of things falling into place and a sense of flow. It often emphasizes a way of being rather than simply doing, holding an attitude of openness or forgiveness rather than specifying the precise action, for example.

Guidance in the form of an inner sense, insight, or inspiration comes unbidden; you cannot will it to be. The opening can come unexpectedly, perhaps while in the shower or in that liminal space just as we are waking up or as we relax and let go. Although not willed, such guidance can be wooed and welcomed. A variety of contemplative invocations ranging from poetry to radical questioning to certain meditations create a recipe that welcomes insight, which generally includes

1. focus, as when we have a problem to solve or a question we're pondering;
2. an open, receptive soft-mind; and
3. listening.

Wise Guys

Sometimes we have to get out of our own way in order to find another approach to guidance. Sometimes it helps to find an ally ("What would [one of our admirable characters] do?"). Wise historic figures or loved ones can serve as touchstones and powerful sources to dialogue with through our imagination, and in so doing, they can call forth wisdom. When the question or concern is posed honestly and deeply, it can serve as a surprising invocation and activation.

However, guidance might not only come through an elder before us, a rich encounter with a good book, the depth of our values, or an imagined ally. It can also arrive in a fashion we could hardly have imagined.

Beginning when she was thirteen, Jeanne saw a brilliant light and said that she touched, smelled, and heard various saints.[10] Her first encounter occurred in her father's garden when, as she explained, "God sent a voice to guide me. At first, I was frightened." But in time, she came to trust and rely on this guidance. At seventeen, the voice, steady throughout her teens, instructed her to leave home and join the army. This was simply an outrageous suggestion at that time. Even more extraordinary was that in time, she was put in charge of the entire army. Under her leadership, this army led the defense and liberation of France from the invading British. Jeanne is better known as Joan of Arc, who lived in the fifteenth century. Jeanne was later persecuted and ultimately executed because she refused to deny the source of her guidance, her inner voice.

Great sages and mystics have recognized the possibility for hearing deep sources of guidance. Abraham, Moses, Mohammed, and Mary all claimed to hear, see, or feel a deep source of wisdom. So, too, did Martin Luther King Jr., Mahatmas Gandhi, George Washington Carver, and Winston Churchill. Socrates called his inner voice *daimon*, meaning "divine." The Hebrew prophets claimed to have received illuminated truth through a connection with the divine. In first-century China, individuals called the *wu* received guidance from inner voices. Christian mystics attributed their inner guidance to the Holy Ghost, deceased saints, and angels.[11]

The word *genius* (from Latin) once meant "guardian spirit," and each of us was meant to have at least one. Genius is the origin for the word *genie*, and in the Middle Ages, the genius came to be known as a guardian angel. The notion has changed over time from the ancient idea of everyone *having a genius*, a personal guide, to extraordinary poets in the Middle Ages as *having genius* itself, to the contemporary understanding that an unusually talented individual might *be* a genius. The notion of guidance and guardianship has been supplanted with the idea that our minds are self-contained and that insight becomes self-generated—a kind of noetic narcissism, we might say. But in an age desperate for wisdom, it may be time for a rehabilitation of that ancient notion of genius as involving a kind of intimate dialogue. We don't have to make any commitment to the ultimate source of such insight. We only need to decide its value based on how functional it is—that is, the quality of the information provided and the impact it has on life.

Across traditions, sometimes even animals are claimed as wise allies. In most traditional explanations of animal guides, you do not choose the animal; it chooses you. It pays you a visit. For example, the animal is seen as a power or "medicine," as some Native American tribes refer it, which serves as a link, symbol, or totem between the invisible world and the physical one.

Seven-year-old Laura's dog, Adam, had just died, and Laura was having a very difficult time getting over the loss. She had really loved Adam, and she didn't know how to deal with losing him. According to her mother, "Over many days Laura was crying a lot about him, and I just didn't seem able to comfort her very well." One day they were driving in the car, and Laura was talking a lot, as she often did. "I was tired and I asked her to please just lie back and rest for a few minutes. Thankfully she did, and after about twenty minutes she sat up and said, 'Mom, something wonderful happened! I left my body and went to talk with Adam. He told me that my being so upset about him dying was making it harder for him, and if I really wanted to help him, I should send him love and light. So I did, and it feels better.' Laura paused and then added, 'Adam said the reason he came to see me is that when somebody close to me dies, I'll know what to do.'"

A few weeks later, Laura's aunt gave birth to a baby with a terminal illness. It was a very difficult situation for everyone. Laura insisted on visiting the baby in the hospital. Her mother said was not too sure about this. "Normally, given Laura's emotionally charged personality," she said, "I would have expected her to fall apart, to be really hysterical, and I didn't think this was what the family needed." But Laura was so persistent that her mom finally relented, deciding that it couldn't really hurt at this point. "We went to the hospital, and in the middle of all this grief, Laura insisted on holding the dying baby. She was unbelievably calm and clear; she was not upset or crying, but was working hard to help this dying baby by sending him love and light. She helped all of us."[12]

There are certain states of consciousness that tend to reduce the amount of mind chatter and open us to more internal imagery and sometimes insight. In a sudden "Aha!" moment, consciousness has shifted, opening to some current that a moment ago was out of reach and, a moment from now, may slip away. Those moments at the edge of sleep, or in a deep relaxed state, or maybe in the midst and mist of a long shower are times when this kind of consciousness becomes available on its own as well as through intentional meditative means. We don't know the whole story (or even close to it) about how the mind operates, but we do notice that these kinds of breakthroughs are often associated with an increase in theta brain wave activity, a state of deep relaxation defined by brain activity between 4 and 8 hertz (cycles per second). It is also intriguing to realize that the high end of theta waves, around 7.8 hertz, is also the resonant frequency of the earth itself, the Schumann Resonance, first recognized in the eighteen century and scientifically confirmed in the 1950s. In a very real sense, we seem to be in tune in moments of insight.

Field and Stream

The contemporary stories that form our understanding of the mind are shifting. The mind is contained inside the head in most contemporary accounts, virtually indistinguishable from the physical brain. But a more expanded story from across science has been emerging that helps give a bigger account of wisdom and of ourselves. We mentioned this renewed story of interconnection in the previous discussion on compassion; it has particular implications for wisdom as well.

From computing and biology to physics and neuroscience, we are increasingly describing how the world works with words like "networks," "webs," "fields," and "streams" instead of simply individual parts, bits, and components reduced to their lowest independent nature. The forward edge of technology, for example, isn't bigger computers; it's better networking—ways of tapping into webs of information. In biology, interactive field[13] and systems theories[14] are more complete (as opposed to the atomistic "component") explanations for understanding the mechanisms of biological organisms, from the cellular to the social level. The flourishing field of brain science tells us we operate as a neural web, one that even networks with others, underlying our interconnection in the field of consciousness. This has come to be understood as a neurological reality through the emerging field of social neuroscience.[15] In physics, field theories explain the subatomic world (nonlocal influence and electromagnetism, for example) in a more satisfactory way than, say, Newton's description. Theoretical physicist Michio Kaku captured this sense of unified field when he claimed, "The Universe is a symphony of vibrating strings."[16] Physicist Erwin Schrödinger concluded, "Mind by its very nature is a *singulare tantum*. I should say: the overall number of minds is just one."[17] And as William James recognized, with just a little self-awareness we come to notice that consciousness itself does not exist as chopped-up bits but instead as a constant flowing stream of experience.[18]

If the mind and the universe are indeed webs and networks, fields and streams, then cultivating wisdom is not about merely *filling us up* with more information (the typical goal of contemporary education) but it is especially about *opening us up* to this inherent interconnection—that is, cultivating the skills to open and expand the range and reach of the mind so that we can see more and more richly, tapping streams of consciousness as a source of information and guidance.

In this sense the capacity is to raise, open, or deepen our being to expand the reach of the mind. Through clarifying values, thinking rationally, seeking allies, asking earnestly, listening for that inner light, and resting in the larger self, we stretch past the gravitational pull of the chattering mind and tap the stream of consciousness we are all a part of.

Guidance
Uncovering inner and outer sources of guidance.

Quiz

For each statement or word, circle the number that describes you best.
(least like me)   1   2   3   4   5   (most like me)

I have a source of guidance I can
   depend on.   1   2   3   4   5
I know whom I can ask for help and advice,
   and I ask them.   1   2   3   4   5
I listen and sense my inner voice.   1   2   3   4   5

I have friends I can bounce ideas off of.	1	2	3	4	5
I have sources of guidance I use on a regular basis.	1	2	3	4	5
I can access my higher self.	1	2	3	4	5
My values are clear.	1	2	3	4	5
I stay open to new information.	1	2	3	4	5
I listen to my heart of hearts.	1	2	3	4	5
I make good decisions.	1	2	3	4	5

Add up the circled numbers.   Total: _____

10–19	20–29	30–39	40–50
A trailhead	**More is possible**	**A good ally**	**A great strength**

....

PRACTICES

Higher Self

Write a dialogue with your "higher self" or the wisest being you can imagine.

Begin first with entering a contemplative state and then write the following: "There is something I would like to tell you; it's time for you to hear _____." Continue writing both the part of the higher self and how other part responds. Go back and forth in the dialogue. It might feel awkward at first, but allow yourself to go with it and give enough time to let it unfold.

Angel

Draw a picture of a guardian angel or spirit in your life. When you are done, answer the following questions: What stands out to you about this drawing? Is there anything you specifically want to remember, hold near, and carry with you?

Ask

Consider the following question: Who would be a trustworthy and wise guide for this current situation or for my life at this time? It does not matter whether they are in your living room or in your mind. Ask them what you would like to know. If they are physically available, you could ask them. If not, begin a dialogue in writing with them. You might begin by writing your question or difficulty and begin to free write a response.

Inspiration

As we have explored, inspiration cannot be willed, but sometimes it can be wooed. What inspires you? Is there a movie, song, poem, person, activity, or something else that raises you up? Find something that inspires you. It might just sneak up on you, or you may call forth a memory or music, an image or word, a sense of mission or founding principle, or an inspirational figure or motivational sight. Or maybe an action helps invite it. It can be stepping outside for a moment, reading a poem, or being kind, generous, or courageous, or whatever takes us beyond our limited self and into our deeper nature.

This does not need to be too fancy or formal, although that's fine as well. It's just a moment of shifting, welcoming, wooing, and being filled. What inspires you?

Perhaps this could be a way to start or end the day, reading from a special text, calling forth the images and feelings we want to hold and convey to the world. As a daily practice, this shapes our consciousness.

14

CLARIFYING

After the mind is . . . freed of certain blocks that are inherent in its accumulated knowledge, it is able to operate in new ways.

—David Bohm

When my wise friend Carolyn and I talk after months of absence, she always asks, "So what's become clear?" I don't often have a ready answer, but I do notice that the question sends me immediately scanning inward to see if there is something I see clearly. Wisdom involves moving toward clarity, understanding, or a bigger view, and Carolyn's question invites us to look for this. Clarity reflects understanding of what is true and often what we value.

We know people who are not intellectually brilliant or those who do not have much experience in the world but who nonetheless act wisely. They have insight into what is important and what is less so, and they act accordingly. At times, they may tap into a vein of wise simplicity in the midst of perplexity. In fact, while intelligence is often equated with complexity, wisdom sometimes emerges as elegantly simple. This is not a simplicity born of ignorance but a simplicity that stays close to what is essential. It cuts to the chase; it sees through the cloud of complexity to see clearly what is really important.

Just Stop

Mattie Stepanek seemed to have a remarkable embodied wisdom.[1] The clarity and simplicity of his being and his single-minded mission to "spread peace in the world" characterized his life. Mattie had Multiple Sclerosis and, for years, had been precariously poised between life and death. His three older siblings had already died from MS. Mattie had three crystal-clear wishes for his life: (1) to get his book of poetry published, (2) to meet his hero, Jimmy Carter, and (3) to be on Oprah Winfrey's show so he could "spread peace." All three wishes were accomplished by the time he was eleven years old. When asked about his meeting with Carter, Mattie described it in a lively and funny way and said they'd had a wonderful one-on-one conversation. He said that Carter is his hero because he is a "humble peacemaker." At the time, he said they were still in touch and are on first-name basis, and he likes to "make sure that Jimmy stays on track" with his peace work.[2]

In response to the 9/11 tragedy, Mattie wrote three poems that day. (He started writing poetry at three years old.) The first poem was when the World Trade Center Towers were falling, and he was "very, very sad and scared." The poem expresses this sadness, almost despair, about what is happening to people and their suffering, without in any way getting stuck in the "good" here and the "evil" there. Essentially, he tried to experience and express the fullness of the feelings, just as we spoke of in part 2. In the third 9/11 poem, "For Our World," he called on all people to stop and stay still before we do something that inflicts more hurt, recognizing how much we are actually alike. He wrote that we should just be before making any move in reaction to what just happened. The clarity of his advice rings wise and true. Mattie died some three weeks before his fourteenth birthday.

Stella's life was quite different from Mattie's. While blessed with the good health that Mattie lacked, she faced her own adversity. Eleven at the time, Stella lived in a very difficult situation with her mother and stepfather. Week after week, the stepfather would beat the young girl, often severely. One day, she was pushed to her limit and found herself in a moment of brilliant clarity. Later in the evening following one beating, Stella sat down on the living room couch next to her stepfather. As they both looked straight ahead in the direction of the television, she calmly said to her stepfather, "Do you know the big knife in the kitchen? I want you to know that if you ever touch me again that I will get that knife and will kill you with it in your bed at night." The stepfather never touched her again. This girl has grown into a flourishing professional helper and healer. Nothing could have prepared her for that moment. It is difficult to say exactly where that impulse emerged from and why she took control of her life at that instant. From some deep center, wisdom arose that understood with razor-sharp clarity just what the situation called for.

Recall Aquinas's notion of wisdom as seeing from a greater height or seeing into the heart of something. Both Mattie and Stella seemed to move into this kind of awareness. We know times when we see more clearly and those times that seem pretty cloudy. Mattie kept a clear focus over much of his time with us; Stella spontaneously rose to the occasion in response to radical necessity. But is there a way for us to cultivate clarity?

In Buddhism, *prajna* is clarity in the sense of "seeing the way things are," which involves a kind of constellation of discernment, insight, wisdom, and enlightenment. It is more likely to emerge if the mind is pure and calm. This in turn follows from mental development (through practices like meditation) and also, like our friends the ancient Greeks advocated, from living with virtue, from a clear sense of our values. For example, we might consider the impact of our choices on others as we factor in the reciprocity of compassion ("How would I want to be treated in this situation?"). We might, like the Iroquois, look into the future as we factor the we and the *world* in our decisions ("How will this affect the next generation or the seventh?"). We might consider the underlying impetus behind a decision as we unpack our motivations ("Is this about revenge or self-interest?"). We might take Mattie's advice and just stop and let the dust settle in our consciousness in order to see what comes clear.

The Bible tells us that a change toward clarity is indeed possible, "For now I see through a glass darkly, but later face to face; now I know in part, but later I will know even as also I am known."[3] This movement toward clarity has something to do with a more intimate ("face to face"), complete ("now I know in part"), participative, and reflective knowing ("to know . . . as I am known"). Let's see how we might do so.

Unseeing

To a large extent, the world appears as we expect to see it. We know our perception is not a snapshot taken by the senses but is instead a highly filtered construction based on what we have seen before and what we expect to see. The inner art required in the quest for truth and clarity, whether scientific, personal, or moral, is not only about *seeing* but also about *unseeing* or *unknowing*.

The practice of unseeing involves exposing our habits of thinking and our expectations of what we will see in order to be free to see more clearly what is actually there. In the following sections, we'll briefly name six approaches to unseeing, several of which we've explored in some detail already.

The Ridiculous

There is an old story about a man clinging to a branch high in a tree as floodwaters rapidly rise to swallow him. He prays to God and asks for help. Soon a makeshift raft floats by, and he thinks about jumping on but tells himself he is waiting for God to deliver him. As the water rises, a man in a boat comes to his aid, but the treed survivor assures him he is fine; he's waiting for God to save him. As the waters are nearly upon him, a helicopter comes and throws a line to him. His response: "No, thanks. I'm waiting for God. I'll be fine." The helicopter flies off. The man drowns, and ends up at the gates of the next life. Incredulous, he confronts God and asks why He did not answer his prayers, especially as he had been so devout. The reply: "Who do you think sent you the raft, the boat, and the helicopter?"

Sometimes, our expectations and fixation on seeing things in a certain way keep us from seeing clearly. It may take a jolt—sometimes a silly one—to shake us up.

In Sufi tradition, Nasrudin was a wise sage often in the guise of a trickster. In tales of his exploits, we often find that the Mulla has put himself in strange situations to shake thinking loose.

For example, one evening a passerby notices Nasrudin crawling on the ground, apparently looking for something. The fellow stops and asks, "Mulla, what are you doing crawling in the dirt?"

"I've lost my key," Nasrudin says.

The man offers to help, and together in the half light they crawl in the dirt on hands and knees, carefully searching for the lost key.

After they've spent considerable time looking without any success, the man finally asks the Mulla, "Do you know where you lost your key?"

Nasrudin responds with an emphatic "Yes!" As he points some distance away, he says, "Over there, near the house."

In disbelief, the helper asks him why in the world they have been looking for it over here. Nasrudin responds, "The light is better over here."[4]

Like a good joke, the punch line catches us by surprise, disorienting and exposing our chain of thinking and thereby freeing us to consider something in a new way. Exposing ourselves to what is radical, unfamiliar, surprising, or ridiculous can shake our thinking loose and ultimately help us see more clearly.

Mindful Awareness

Beyond the ridiculous and unexpected, the second approach common in contemplative traditions is noticing what arises without overreacting to it. We've spoken of this in some detail in part 1. As we bring ourselves into a mindful state, perhaps in still silence or through reflective contemplation such as writing in a journal, we may notice, for example, anger arise toward something or someone. If we can find that delicate balance of staying with it without overreacting to it, we may notice that under the anger is perhaps hurt. The fixation on and reaction to the surface—the anger, in this case—may have kept us from seeing more clearly what lies underneath. Mattie's advice to just stop captures the spirit of pausing so as not to be at the whim of our initial reactions. Conflict, especially between couples, often gets stuck at the surface reaction. When there is presence to move beneath the immediate emotional reaction, beyond our justifications, and look at the underlying patterns of thought and feeling, there can be a deepening of honesty and clarity about what's really going on. This is really very simple; it's just that we are so often captured by our reactions that we have trouble seeing anything else. Just stop.

Questioning Assumptions

The third approach to unseeing uses our good thinking to question and unpack the assumptions we live by. In Plato's *Apology*, Socrates wrote that "the unexamined life is not worth living."[5] We're told that in order to live the good life we should examine not only what we believe but also why we believe it. In the Socratic method, we see if our thoughts, perceptions, behaviors, and biases are rooted in clear seeing and come from some form of truth or instead are simply rooted in habits of mind. Socrates told us that our personal beliefs are conditioned by our culture. And much of our personal beliefs and values are simply habits of mind, habits that are so often repeated that we take them to be true.

Today we've come to understand that politics and power, ego and economics, religion and relatives inevitably shape accepted truth. We now know to ask questions: "Who funded the research?" "Why do I want that?" "Who says that is true, and what's in it for them?" We may be reasonably suspicious if, for example, research reporting that cigarette smoke is harmless is funded by a tobacco company. These challenges to knowledge, power, motivation, and authority can work to help us see under the surface. As a practice of unseeing, this kind of deconstructive questioning accepts nothing at face value. Its starting point is a kind of rejection of the surface proposition or at least a questioning of what lies behind it.

In many spiritual traditions, similar kinds of radical questioning are also used to gain fresh insight. Thomas Merton called this unraveling a "dark knowing," by which he meant it was mainly an "unknowing"—taking down rather than adding to.[6] The Buddhist Madhyamika method intentionally deconstructs core concepts, even of Buddhism itself.[7] The approach called negative theology in Christianity systematically suspends core beliefs, even the basic tenants of Christianity, as a way of arriving at the most profound knowing. In a similar fashion, postmodern deconstruction and critical theory help us explore the origins of beliefs and the structures of power and knowledge they may be shaped from. Clear seeing requires us to question where an idea has come from.

Empathizing

The fourth method of unseeing involves taking another's point of view, a move that can expose our particular egocentric bias. I've noticed that when we have guests coming to stay at our house, imagining how things might appear through their eyes, I suddenly see the layers of clutter or giant dust bunnies that have been hiding in corners and under furniture. While this happens spontaneously in these moments, the intentional practice of imagining the world through another's eyes (the houseguest, the neighbor, the terrorist, the child) is a practice of unseeing. It helps provide alternative ways of viewing a situation, thus exposing any particular implicit biases or vantage points. This can be very simple and very revealing. Of course, we can see through another's eyes by asking them about their views. The chapter on empathy in part 2 emphasizes this general approach.

Paradox

A fifth approach to unseeing is through paradox. A paradox is a self-contradictory or absurd statement or proposition that in reality expresses a possible truth. There can be a shift of knowing and clarity through holding paradox. Jungian analyst Robert Johnson speaks of this in spiritual terms: "When the unstoppable bullet meets the impenetrable wall, we find the religious experience. It is precisely here that one will grow. Conflict to paradox to revelation: this is the divine progression."[8]

In other words, holding paradoxical or contradictory perspectives long enough may frustrate and then transform normal thinking. The absurdity of a Zen koan, "What is the sound of one hand clapping?," is fashioned to invite us into another kind of awareness. In the case of Zen, a moment of *satori* (clear insight) is the goal. In more down-to-earth terms, we might ponder the conflicting issues of fairness involved in a contemporary issue like affirmative action. Could we take both the position of the disadvantaged youth as well as the privileged child who was denied admission to college despite their higher performance? The point is not to win an argument as in a debate; it is to see beyond the various sides in order to take in the whole of the issue and synthesize a larger perspective. Holding contradictions serves as activation. As author Morris Berman wrote, "The mind is moved to unfold itself in the space between contradictions."[9]

In the nineteenth century, German philosopher Georg W. F. Hegel devised an approach—dialectics—that became formulated into a simple process that involves thesis, antithesis, and synthesis. The *thesis* is an intellectual proposition. The *antithesis* is simply the negation of the thesis, a reaction to the proposition. The *synthesis* solves the conflict between the thesis and antithesis by reconciling their common truths, and forming a new proposition. Importantly, the point of the process is to recognize the limits or partial nature of understanding in any side. Hegel said that the purpose of dialectics is "to demonstrate the finitude of the partial categories of understanding."[10] Wisdom has the capacity to hold truth lightly, and in recognizing that any singular view is inevitably partial, we may move toward greater clarity.

Interdependence

Finally, unseeing might begin by recognizing that the thing in front of us is not quite what it appears to be to us. A professor of physics tells us that the table is a matrix of vibrating molecules, a woodworker tells us the table is mahogany, the geographer or ecologist reminds us of the threatened Amazonian forest from which the wood was likely sourced, our mother tells us to use a coaster lest the condensation from our iced tea glass mar this family heirloom. Unseeing allows us to suspend completely buying the surface appearance to consider a larger web of understanding. That "great deal" on that discount shirt looks like not so great a bargain if we learn that it was manufactured using child labor. Things exist not only as their surface appearance but also as part of a complex, dynamic web through time and space. The choices we make in our family may carry a legacy from generations past as we consider cycles of violence or habits of handling our emotions. Our global economy and ecology are interdependent. A blip in Beijing affects markets on Wall Street. Hydrocarbon emissions in Iowa affect plankton in the South China seas. Everything is part of a limitless web of interconnections and is in a state of dynamic flux. Every appearance arises from complex causes and conditions and in turn combines with others to produce countless effects. Keeping interdependence in view helps us unsee what is only the surface so that we may take in a larger view of what lives beneath and beyond.

Whether through the surprise of the ridiculous, the spaciousness of mindful awareness, seeing through another's eyes, deconstructive questioning, the conundrum of paradox, recognizing the interdependent origination of things, or some other means, the goal is to unsee—exposing our habits of mind—so that we may see more clearly.

Centering

In one of my classes, I asked my students how many of them were feeling frazzled, since they looked a bit harried that day. Nearly all of them said they felt this way regularly. They described the sources of their frazzle as pressure to keep up with school, work, and relationships, as well as other particular things, like a court date or family member's illness. Those bigger, longer-term concerns ("What will I do with my life?") also seemed to hang over the vast majority, like some high-gravity force pressing down on their lives. Feeling anxious, scattered, and distracted characterized this unsatisfying, off-kilter state. It is no news that this is common among so many of us. And the consequence of frazzle is that it inhibits quality of life and, ultimately, our ability to see clearly.

The neurobiology of being frazzled involves the frontal and prefrontal cortices of the brain, those locations that are most associated with higher-order processing, to basically go off-line in a frazzled state. Minds then become driven by more defensive, primitive systems rather than those that can think in larger, more creative and agile ways that lead to clarity. We might also recognize from our own experience that sadness can have a similar effect as frazzle on performance.[11] As most of us know firsthand, in sadness, the world ends up looking gray, limited, or narrowed in some way. But if we can find a way to stay centered, we may avoid being frazzled and keep the most nimble parts of our mind engaged. This movement inward provides the basis for moving outward with integrity, clarity, and symmetry.

We know that taking care of ourselves—exercising and getting a good night's sleep, a reminder of what is most important, a nap, good meal, hot shower, or even good joke, can take the edge off frazzle and re-center us a bit. This can be extremely important day in and day out. Beyond this kind of frazzle management, we can keep a clear pivot or hub in view that helps us stay centered. This is an act not of force but instead one of coordination such as that of a potter or a ballerina.[12] What are the coordinates that help you or me center? We may recognize the heart as one common pivot. We may also center ourselves in some coordinate like:

- *Kindness.* The Dalai Lama says his religion is kindness.[13]
- *Curiosity.* "Lead with bewilderment," as Einstein said when he approached problems with a sense of wonder and curiosity[14]
- *Hope and strength.* "I can do this."
- *Commitments.* "I will be a good parent."
- *Mindfulness.* Staying in gentle awareness of the body by keeping a healthy pace or rhythm, for example.
- *Keeping meaning in view.* "This is important to me because . . ."
- *A clear goal.* This is especially useful for a group so that we may coordinate our energies and keep our eyes on the same prize.

There are endless ways to center. Because it's especially easy to lose balance these days, it may take intentional coordination to keep us from wobbling too much.

Since centering is about how we are holding ourselves, just a little shift is sometimes enough to bring us to a clear pivot. I remember a time when I felt great pressure to finish a project. It was my doctoral dissertation. We had a new home, and a new child, and there was not much money to go around. Yet we had come all this way together, and I just needed to finish writing this thing and get back to full-time work. But when I would sit down in those days, I would get a little head of steam and then quickly lose it to what felt like a kind of narcotic-induced fog. Day after day, I would find myself losing focus, lost in a mental fogbank, unable to see any way ahead. Frustration, distraction, and discouragement were creeping in. One day in desperation, I paid a visit to the office of my sage advisor, Al Alschuler. Al had his doctorate from Harvard, had been the youngest full professor ever at the university, served as a university president, written a dozen books, and had remarkable, mystical experiences in his life. After hearing my tortured tale of woe, probably a story not unlike what he had heard many times from his other students, I hoped he might have some transformative pearl of wisdom. I didn't know what he could do or what advice he would have for me, but I was getting more desperate by the day and finally brought myself to ask for whatever help I could get. But I didn't expect what he offered: "When you feel cloudy, why not just tell yourself you're clear?"

What? This was the big advice from my wise advisor? This is way too simplistic for my difficult condition and my lofty task. In disbelief, I dismissed his advice and left that day frustrated with his trite response. *Was he even listening?* I wondered.

The next morning, I found myself once again back at the dreaded desk, in front of the demon computer, being pulled into that hazy fog. At that moment, I remembered Al's ridiculous advice. Anything was worth a try at this point. So I simply took a breath and told myself silently like a mantra, "I am clear." I think I also wrote it down.

Sure enough, and despite my disbelief, I felt a shift within less than a minute. Some piece of the writing crystallized in my mind, I knew where to proceed and quickly whipped off some ideas. This would happen again and again. And whenever I would find myself in the cloudiness, which initially was several times every day during my writing time, I would repeat my little mantra—my secret antidote—and move forward.

At some points, I found that it helped if I just started free writing; other times I would switch from typing to writing on paper just to change things up a bit. Things seemed to catch fire, and I finished in what seemed to be no time at all. And what was even more remarkable was that I ended up enjoying the writing. It had always been awkward drudgery for me, but I actually became excited, not just by the feeling of accomplishment but because the process ended up being as joyful, nourishing, and healing in ways I didn't even fully understand. It became a kind of meditation, discovery, and creative play. I really couldn't believe that what got me over the hump was that simple advice. But sometimes, just intentionally shifting inside a bit is enough to shift the system and open perception in a new way. Notice, by the way, that Al directed me not toward a concept like "I can do it," but instead toward that felt sense—cloudy to clear. This provided a new center point for the wobbling pot that was me.

Like the potter or the dancer, the work is to pay attention to what is required in this instance—a little more pressure here, a tilt of the hand or head there. Our techniques can be of real help, but we change, the situation changes, and thus the old formula may not work the next time. Instead, we center by staying awake to the present moment, what is called for here and now.

Clarifying
The inner art required in the quest for truth and clarity is both about seeing and unseeing.

Quiz

For each statement or word, circle the number that describes you best.
(least like me)   1   2   3   4   5   (most like me)

I know what I like and what I don't.		1	2	3	4	5
I am usually clear.		1	2	3	4	5
There does not seem to be too much in my way.		1	2	3	4	5
I can center myself.		1	2	3	4	5
I'm not often frazzled.		1	2	3	4	5
I can step back and look at an issue from arm's length.		1	2	3	4	5

I can see through another's point of view.	1	2	3	4	5
I can usually see the big picture.	1	2	3	4	5
I can often see into the heart of an issue.	1	2	3	4	5
I take good care of myself.	1	2	3	4	5

Add up the circled numbers.   Total: _____

10–19	20–29	30–39	40–50
A trailhead	**More is possible**	**A good ally**	**A great strength**

....

PRACTICES

What Has Become Clear?

Pause for a moment and ask yourself, "What has become clear?" Repeat the question as often as seems needed. You may want to free write a response. Alternatively, pose the question to a friendly listener and ask them to pose it to you, taking turns to listen quietly and respectfully to one another.

Seeing How We See

This is an exercise designed to help uncover projections and bring what is in the background to the foreground. This exercise is best done in pairs and requires images that participants can select from. I have used a deck of tarot cards with striking and mysterious imagery. Pictures cut from a magazine or even pictures of fine art could work as effectively.

With cards or images scattered faceup on a table, participants each pick two cards, one positive and one negative. Then they're asked to take a few moments to look at their own cards and then to take turns speaking as if they were the positive card. After this, they can each move to the negative card. ("I am the Three of Swords and I am very dangerous.")

Once that is accomplished, each person speaks as if the negative and positive card were having a dialogue with each other. Again, it is important to speak as if you're the cards themselves. Once the initial hesitation has been overcome, these dialogues can quickly take on a life of their own.

Next, ask all the participants to imagine that their positive card is now negative and their negative card positive. This is followed by another round of dialogues ("I am now a positive card."). This helps reveal how subjectivity is projected onto the pictures. Switching the cards serves the additional function of bringing what was in the background into view, adding flexibility of perception.

At the end, process the whole experiment by asking what this experience was like, what was difficult and what was easy. Invite partners to reflect on how similar or different their own perceptions of the other person's cards were.[15]

Centering

What are the coordinates that help you center? We might ask ourselves, When have we been centered? What has that been like? What was the result? What helped you achieve it? We might also help clarify by asking what it was like when we have been off-center. What was the result? What tends to push us off center? Grounding or being grounded is another way we might recognize this. Being rooted like a tree or solid like a great pyramid are images that capture the stability and solidity of this state of consciousness. The role of wisdom is to coordinate these reference points in some dynamic gesture of balance that frees us from overreaction and brings us back to center.

Detachment

In a contemplative state, take a moment and think of a concern, problem, or conflict you face. Flesh it out. What is the issue, and who does it involve? "Look" at this issue from your belly, your gut. Notice how it feels and how you feel. What are the qualities as you see it from here? Take a little time to feel this. Do your best to keep the focus on your gut, even if it is uncomfortable. Once you have a good sense of that, take note of what that is like. Take a few deep breaths, perhaps move your arms or the rest of your body to shake it off.

Now bring your awareness to your heart. See if you can look at this problem through your heart instead of your gut. First, take a few moments to shift to your heart, bringing your attention to the area of your chest. You may want to place your hand on your chest to help focus your attention. Bring the problem back to the center of your awareness, feel it, imagine it. Now see if you can "see" the issue through the heart. What does this feel like? What do you notice? Take a few moments to try to see it from this point of view. When you have a sense of this, notice any difference. What's this like? When you're ready, again, take a few deep breaths.

Bring your awareness now to the center of your forehead—your "third eye." You might want to very gently tap or touch that area with a fingertip. Do your best to simply focus the attention on this area. If you find yourself drifting away with thoughts or anything else, gently bring your awareness back to that area. You might notice some tingling. You could imagine looking out as if you were looking through a window, a porthole in the forehead. Now bring the issue, concern, or problem back to mind. Don't think about it or try to figure it out from inside your head; simply try keep the focus on looking at the issue through the third eye. Give yourself a little time to try to stay on it. What do you notice

when you see it from here? What is it like? How does this compare to seeing from the gut and from the heart? Is there anything
that seems significant for the goal of clarity? You might compare
your experience out loud if you do this with others.

Most people notice that seeing from each location has a
different quality to it, impacting what we see and how we feel.
Seeing through the third eye is often described as providing
greater clarity on the situation.

15

DISCERNING

Somewhere within our life is a standard as invisible as the equator,
as relentless as the seasons.

—P. H. Elliot

When we say someone is discerning—from a wine connoisseur to someone skilled at picking out fabric for a window curtain—we mean that in some way they are making discriminations of quality or value. These distinctions imply sensitivity and standards that serve as a basis for decisions. This also implies that not all things are created equal, that there are distinctions of quality that are real and significant.

Discernment provides a balance to love, and this is why so many of the great traditions speak of love and wisdom as the dynamic duo for a life well lived. While most would concur that living a life of love or compassion is desirable or virtuous, the particularities of a situation require discernment as to how our actions may play out for the greatest good. For example, while love may be an ultimate goal or principle, sometimes it is anger or firmness, saying no rather than yes, that may be the wisest choice. Without this discrimination, we may be taken advantage of, place ourselves or others in danger, or simply make a lousy choice. When a loved one struggling with addiction asks us for money, compassion and generosity may open our pockets but wisdom might say no or tell us to offer something else. Whereas the heart is indiscriminant and accepting by its very nature, wisdom brings distinctions to the particularities of a situation. This also helps explain why wisdom is not preset (something we can accumulate) but rather lived experience and insight. We don't have wisdom. Instead, we act wisely. Together, love and wisdom walk a razor's edge between radical acceptance and radical scrutiny.

Acting wisely often involves making a choice between this or that. "Should I move there?" "Should we get married?" "Which car should I buy?" "What is true?" "What is the right thing to do?" These range from which shampoo to buy to complex moral decisions. But how do we make a wise choice, especially those bigger ones? Is there some secret formula that wise souls use?

Marry, Marry, Marry

There are plenty of sources telling us *what* we should choose. Advertisers try to sell us one thing or another; experts offer to advise us, sometimes for a fee; religions put forward various doctrines designed to shape our choices. These sources sometimes provide guidance and comfort, but unless we're careful, they can also lead to immature decision making. Instead of discerning for ourselves, we may simply default to someone else's standard, relying on dogma as opposed to our dynamic experience. Remember Oppenheimer's advice to that hall of troubled teens: "It is necessary to find one's own required evidence to determine whether a thing is true or not." It is our responsibility to make our own decisions, not in naïve or narcissistic isolation but in dialogue with the best sources we can get our hands on.

Emerson's notion that wisdom is a "blend of what is true and what is right" implies that wisdom relates to both an ability to perceive clearly and to conduct oneself ethically or virtuously. If this is accurate, then the work of developing discernment unfolds on these two related fronts. First, we try to perceive reality as clearly and fully and with the best information and guidance we can. The second element involves recognizing and integrating the heart.

In Christianity, the term "discernment" is generally described as the practice of attuning to God's will, receiving and following grace: "Thy will be done." But we also seem to have free will, and thus must also determine what is asked of us. Ignatius of Loyola, who founded the Jesuits in the sixteenth century, developed a systematic method for making life choices. His approach distinguishes between two opposing kinds of interior "movements of the soul." Those two movements he referred to as "consolation," which, he said, is the result of choices that are in harmony with God's desires, and "desolation," which is the result of choices contrary to God's desires.[1] Consolations might include a sense of joy, vitality, or freedom, whereas desolations might include a sense of burden or discouragement. Essentially, we have a built-in feedback loop and the gauge is our feelings or felt sense.

Ignatius of Loyola's method of discernment involves first forming a question clearly and appropriately. After posing a good question, the next step in Ignatian discernment is to enter a contemplative state and then sense the response. To do so we might imagine having made the decision in question and feel what it brings us or enter into a relaxed state and note the felt sense that arises in response to the question posed. What are the feelings, images, sensations, or thoughts that arise? Do they line up with consolations or desolations?

My friend Ellen decided that it was time for a clean sweep. The spring cleaning was not just shaking the rugs and airing out the house but going through and hoeing out everything in her life—a kind of psychological and spiritual purging. It's the kind of cleaning that might happen when a big change is at our doorstep—a move, a divorce, or enough dissatisfaction that we know it's time to lighten our load. Ellen had diligently worked from top to bottom through everything—old magazines, clothes, mysterious plastic bits, those stuffed "everything drawers" that accumulate the items we just can't quite part with. Finally, she got all the way down to those little scraps of paper that populate the top of dressers and between the pages of books, tiny notes of things we wanted to be sure to remember—a friend's phone number, a list of tasks to complete, a brilliant idea. One at a time, she took each slip of paper, read it to herself, closed her eyes, and drew in a deep breath as she gently held the paper in her hand. She then asked herself, "Does this bring me life or drain my life?" She would either keep or throw out the paper and what it represented depending on that felt response. In her own way, I think she caught the spirit of Loyola's discernment pretty well.

We typically might think of making a decision as a rational operation (or that it should be), gathering as much data as possible or making our list of pros and cons and stepping into our choices from there. This can indeed be extremely useful for clarifying choices, no question about it.

After his five years on the HMS *Beagle* and another two years back in London, at the age of twenty-nine Charles Darwin pondered the idea of getting married. He wrote down his list of pros and cons.

Not Married: Freedom to go where one liked—choice of society and little of it. Conversation of clever men at clubs. Not forced to visit relatives and to bend in every trifle—to have the expense and anxiety of children—perhaps quarrelling—loss of time . . . How should I manage all my business if I were obliged to go every day walking with my wife. Eheu! I should never know French, or see the Continent, or go to America, or go up in a Balloon.

Under "Marry" he wrote,

Children (if it please God), constant companion (and friend in old age) who will feel interested in one.

And his conclusion:

My God, it is intolerable to think of spending one's whole life like a neuter bee, working, working, and nothing after all. . . . Only picture to yourself a nice soft wife on a sofa with good fire, and books and music perhaps . . . Marry—Marry—Marry. Q. E. D.[2]

And so he did to Miss Emma Wedgewood. But this is not often a purely rational choice; it certainly didn't seem to be for Darwin. Wisdom uses everything at its disposal—the analytic mind, intuition, information, imagination, experience, our favorite sources of guidance, synchronicity, and felt sense—in order to land on an answer. It is too simplistic to reduce to either following the "head" or following the "heart"; these aspects are intertwined in our knowing, as we have explored. In using multiple sources, we have a chance to triangulate in on our choice.

The body is one of discernment's biggest allies. When we are somehow living against ourselves, overstressed or overwrought, it calls on us to pay attention. That knot in the stomach or the high gravity of exhaustion tells us something is not right and asks for a different response—a change of job, facing a difficult relationship, a shift in attitude. The body can be both teacher of last resort and also first responder as we notice that something doesn't quite feel right.

I like to ask whether an idea goes "bing" or "thud," sensing the potential value from that vague felt sense. We might flip a coin, pretend that we have made the decision already, much like Ignatius suggested, and notice how we feel about it (disappointed, relieved, comforted, or something else). We seem to have some internal barometer. Whether this is alignment with God's will, our own essential virtues, or something else will remain a mystery in this life, but the experience can be immediate, intimate, and visceral, like it was for Darwin ("Marry, Marry, Marry!") In time, we learn to interpret those responses even more precisely, and sometimes the consolation is something we want but not something in our best interest. Practice and the grace of mistakes help develop discernment.

Some of us have learned to distrust our inner sense in favor of a more "rational" approach. Wisdom returns a robust and resonant capacity for knowing to the center of discernment. Light, truth, and quality are recognized through our own unique constellation of knowing: thought and image, sound and feeling, intuition and analysis. For example, sometimes I get the chills in some situations that I have come to understand are a signal that something important is happening. I think this is not so uncommon. Once, someone I didn't really know well asked me to travel far away to a place I didn't know at all (I had to look up on a map), but as soon as he said it, my body responded with chills. From past experience, I take this as a positive sign of some sort. I have a friend whose tears serve a similar function at times. In the same vein, one woman described her natural childhood awareness of "light" as "the fundamental measure against which all else was measured in my life. I tested everything else. I saw people and things in terms of quality and quantity of light: the presence of light or its lack was my only yardstick of right and wrong."[3]

Whether chills, tears, light, a felt sense, or something entirely unique to you, we may have signals and processes along with our rational analysis that work for us, a bright signal that tells us we're on or off the mark. Listening, testing, and refining these signals along with our rational reflection grows the capacity for discernment.

Reading the Signs

As long as there has been need for discerning which path to take in life, there have probably been those who looked for omens and signs by throwing sticks or runes, rolling dice, consulting the stars, flipping a coin, reading tea leaves, or consulting the flight of birds or the entrails of some unfortunate animal. Humans have always used what's at hand to try to divine insight about everything from the right marriage partner to the right time to go to war. While I don't know much about reading chicken bones, I do know that wise souls use whatever is offered as an opportunity to open to insight.

One of the primary functions of the mind is actually to serve as a reducing valve. For example, we are pre-wired to hear only a certain range of sound, and this is different from the range that dogs hear, for example. Our socialization then constructs further filters that shape what we see: "This is called a maple tree; that is a holly bush." In this sense, our minds limit and sort our experiences. We would probably be completely overwhelmed if it didn't; it's often hard enough to keep focus as it is. But wisdom involves opening this valve so that we can see more of reality.

As we open the aperture of the mind, we may notice information arriving not only through a brilliant insight but also through a physical symptom, a serendipitous meeting, a feeling, a fleeting

thought or image, a song that does not seem to go away, a problem or a passion, sometimes through the symbolism of a dream.
Jungian analyst Robert Johnson described one of his own dreams.

> I am standing next to a one-hundred-story building. There is no
> earthquake, but the building begins to collapse of its own weight.
> The building has been built up far higher than the underlying
> structure is capable of supporting. I can see the building begin
> to tremble, and people on the ground floor begin streaming
> out of the front door to escape. Then the second floor collapses
> downward, becoming the new ground floor. One by one, the
> floors come crashing down on top of the one below, in each case
> leaving just enough time for the people to get out safely.[4]

For Johnson, this dream represented a "clear signal that my
overblown psychic structure was in danger of collapsing."[5] He
had gotten too big for his britches, and he understood that his
dream warned him of the impending danger.

Marie, highly intelligent and well educated, had a bad car
accident in which several of her lower vertebrae were injured. She
was diagnosed with herniated discs that left her in steady agony.
She spent nearly three years in chronic pain and was forced to quit
her job, since she could not sit still for more than fifteen minutes
at a time. The only real medical hope offered was back surgery.
Despite encouragement, support, and even pressure from friends
and family to go ahead with the surgery, the prospect just didn't
sit right with her. One day, she got an idea from a particular book
about back pain.[6] The advice invited her to see what the pain
might be offering. The idea she took away was that she might not
be getting better because she was not seeing something clearly.

She said, "When I stopped resisting it and asked what the
pain was trying to teach me, my life absolutely changed." She

explained that her unresolved pain was not about herniated discs at that point but about unresolved emotions. She began to work through those feelings, and with no further medical intervention, she says that the pain left her once she listened to what it was offering. Eight years later, she remains nearly pain free. When there has been a rare twinge of pain, she remembers to look for the message, the unresolved emotions, and when she finds them the pain abates.

Wisdom uses whatever is given as a kind of divination practice. On one day, I put my shirt on backwards three times, and then a tire flying through the air shattered the windshield on my car as I was driving on the highway. *What am I not paying enough attention to? What is trying to get my attention?* I wondered. Once I paused and asked myself, I knew that I was avoiding dealing with my ailing and aging father and my feelings about him. It's not necessary or possible to prove any ultimate source or external agency of the tire or my backward shirts. In fact, this is often where we get stuck. Instead, we can avoid any metaphysical conundrum and use whatever is given as a reminder to listen and pay attention and, in so doing, focus and expand the valve of our mind. Listening of this sort is a kind of divination that requires a conversation with the message. We have to be present and dialogue with it to read the signs. The good news is that maybe everything is waiting for us to do so.

Questioning

Ideally, through an examined life, a clear and virtuous mind, the feedback loop of consolations and desolations, and learning from mistakes, our decision making matures. But we know even the saints of Ignatius's and other traditions sometimes find themselves confused, in the dark. You'd think that these saintly figures would have discernment nailed down, and if Ignatius was entirely right, then they would be full of clear choices and consolations. But this is not quite so. St. John of the Cross, from whom we gained the term "dark night of the soul," used the term *obscura* (obscured) to describe his predicament, and he has had plenty of good company.[7] Sometimes, we just can't see what the universe or our own heart has in store for us, but we are invited to step into the unknown nonetheless. In these situations, we continue to seek the clear way, clarify our values and our mind, use our best logic, look for the signs, and seek guidance, but our main work may be to tolerate the unknown, keep asking questions, to welcome the mystery, and not get too freaked out.

Philosopher Richard Rorty suggested that the Cartesian shift some four hundred years ago marked the "triumph of the quest for certainty over the quest for wisdom."[8] The goal thus became rigor, prediction, and control rather than wisdom or peace of mind. The endgame became finding the answer rather than living the question. The result is, in part, heightened anxiety when facing the questions that life provides and a demand for immediate answers—the right answer.

Instead of always grasping for certainty, wisdom takes a different approach. Wisdom seeks questions as if looking for the best fruit on the tree. It then bites into the question, living it, allowing it to fulfill its purpose as nourishment. Whereas intelligence will cut, dismantle, and reconstruct the question in order to work toward certainty, wisdom rides the question to see where it goes, where it came from, and what it turns into. Author M. C. Richards offered this image of the ride as an alternative to control of the unknown and impatience with it:

> Let us ride our lives like natural beasts, like tempests, like the
> bounce of a ball, or the slightest ambiguous hovering of ash,

the drift of scent: let us stick to those currents that can carry us, membering them with our souls.[9]

Wisdom and the practice of discernment seeks and creates questions as much as answers. "Problem finding," identifying the most salient problems, has been closely associated with wisdom.[10] Problem finding allows us to move beyond conceptual limits (the problem as given) in order to reconsider the question in a new way. Physicist David Bohm explained,

> Questioning is . . . not an end in itself, nor is its main purpose to give rise to answers. Rather, what is essential here is the whole flowing movement of life, which can be harmonious only when there is ceaseless questioning.[11]

Wisdom asks questions about questions, not so much to close in and trap the answer but to see what the question has to tell us about ourselves and our world.

- "What if we knew that?"
- "What is the lesson here?"
- "What is the big picture?"
- "What can this teach me?"
- "What other ways can we look at this?"

In this way, the question (as well as the universe) serves as a mirror. Our reaction to the question, our feelings of superiority or inferiority, and our solutions themselves reveal the limits or edges of our seeing or insight. Often statements are embedded within questions such as, "Are you really going to wear that?!" Questioning helps disclose these implicit values. This includes the questioning of the questions themselves, as David Bohm said, "For in the beginning these usually contain the very presuppositions that are behind the unclarity and contradiction that led one to question in the first place."[12]

Reflective questions ("I want that; what's that about?") help us consider our own motivations and desires. In the realm of love, Shakespeare suggested that we "go to your bosom: Knock there, and ask your heart what it doth know."[13] Ethical questions ("What's the highest and the best that I can do here?" or "What would Spider-Man do?") help clarify our standards of conduct. Sherlock Holmes uses pondering and questioning in a process of inductive reasoning, generalizing elaborate conclusions from some small particulars in his cases. Existential or spiritual questions form the whole basis for philosophy and religion ("What am I here for?" or "Who am I?") just as our questions about the natural world provide the impetus for science and discovery. ("How does that work?")

Socrates, the wisest of the wise in ancient Greece, admitted that he knew nothing.[14] He essentially taught through questioning instead of through answers. Like Socrates, wisdom acknowledges that we don't know, or at least that we know incompletely, and once this is accepted, it frees us for learning. This is the great power and utility of humility with respect to truth as it keeps us open to revision and refinement, to seeing something new. Anthropologist Gregory Bateson said that in this way it is not certainty but instead "ambiguity [that] potentiates learning."[15] Once we stop fighting the question and give up the need for domination and certainty, we are really free to see what it has to offer. Ultimately wisdom invites us, as poet Rainer Maria Rilke wrote, to "live the question."[16]

Discerning

Discerning involves developing the capacity for wise choice and recognizing distinctions of quality.

Quiz

For each statement or word, circle the number that describes you best.

(least like me)   1   2   3   4   5   (most like me)

I know what I like and what I don't.	1 2 3 4 5
I am a good judge of quality.	1 2 3 4 5
I am a good judge of people.	1 2 3 4 5
I can cut to the heart of a decision.	1 2 3 4 5
I'm not hesitant to ask questions.	1 2 3 4 5
I have a signal that helps me know what's right.	1 2 3 4 5
I can see the forest and the trees.	1 2 3 4 5
I listen to what the universe tells me.	1 2 3 4 5
I have an internal sense of what seems better or worse.	1 2 3 4 5
I evaluate things effectively.	1 2 3 4 5

Add up the circled numbers.   Total: _____

10–19	20–29	30–39	40–50
A trailhead	**More is possible**	**A good ally**	**A great strength**

....

PRACTICES

Ignatian Discernment

This method of discernment involves forming and posing a question clearly. Take some time to form and hold the right question. Next, enter a contemplative state and then sense the response. To do so, we might imagine having made a decision in question and feel what it brings us or alternatively enter into a relaxed state, pose the question, and note the felt sense that arises in response to the question posed. What are the feelings, images, sensations, and thoughts that arise? Do they line up with consolations or desolations, such as the following:

Characteristics of Consolations
- courage, strength
- delight, deep joy
- satisfaction, "rightness"
- sense of freedom
- gratitude
- energy, vitality
- desires are rooted deeply ("true self")
- choices are life-giving

Characteristics of Desolations
- discouragement
- sadness not due to crisis or depression
- anxiety
- feeling of being trapped, imprisoned
- sense of burden
- enervation
- desires rooted shallowly ("false self")
- choices are life-draining[17]

Lifeboat

This practice is for a group. In your group ask for three (or more) volunteers.

The last spaceship is leaving to safety. Anyone left behind will perish. The problem is there is only one seat left. Ask each of the volunteers to make an argument of why they should be taken to resettle the population. Once they've each made their case, the remaining group members can discuss and then vote on whom they would select. The ensuing discussion may reveal or clarify values, logic, and assumptions that help clarify and expose our patterns in decision making.

Clearness Committee

The Quaker tradition provides a method of clarifying decisions called a clearness committee.[18] A member of the community can simply call upon other members of their choosing to sit together and ask questions about a concern or choice being faced (for example, "Should I take this job?" "Should I marry this person?" "What should I do with my life?" or maybe even something like "What should I write my paper on?"). The committee is not there to offer opinions or advice but simply to pose honest questions and listen. The point is to help one clarify and discern one's inner knowing.

Active Imagination

Bring a scene to mind. In Jungian practice, this is typically a dream that seems significant or curious and leaves us hanging a bit. Instead of a dream, you could also take up some unfinished situation in your waking life. Take a moment and see if a scene comes to mind. Try to trust the wisdom of whatever emerges.

Once you've found the scene, move yourself into a relaxed state. Take a few deep, clearing breaths, get comfortable, close your eyes, notice any tension in your body, and let it go. Notice tension in your mind and let it go. Allow yourself to fall gently and safely into relaxation. Take a few minutes to go deeper as you float gently into calm and quiet.

Once relaxed, bring the scene you selected to your awareness. You may be able to watch it like a movie. Let the scene come to life as you recall the faces, sounds, the surroundings, and especially the feelings that are there. Using your imagination, see where the scene has left off or, if you prefer, start the scene wherever you think would be most revealing. You don't have to figure anything out or plot out the story line; just allow your imagination to complete the next part in your mind. Even if this feels contrived or forced, allow yourself to suspend judgment for a moment and just let it unfold. If it seems helpful, you can steer the next scene in a direction where you would like to see things go. See what emerges and spend some minutes being curious and watching this screen inside you.

What does this have to tell you? What can you see now that you may not have seen previously? What is revealed or resolved? Does this have any meaning for your life or concern?

Reading the Signs

The art of divination involves reading the signs the universe presents. They can be the flight of birds, the configuration of tea leaves, or most anything else. Traditionally, the seeker would bring a question to the diviner, hoping for some discerning guidance.

In this playful version, take a magazine that has a variety of kinds of images. (The *New Yorker* magazine, my personal favorite oracle, has good cartoons and artwork scattered throughout, but not so much imagery on each page as to confuse.) Take enough time and quiet focus to clearly formulate the right question you want direction on. Once the question feels just right, consult the "oracle" for an answer; that is, randomly open the magazine and notice what presents itself to you. What is the image or the words that catch your eye? What is it trying to say to you? How might this be an answer to your query? How does that answer seem to you? Does it seem right or off the mark?

Ultimately, whether the gods use the *New Yorker* as a conduit for the divine or you project meaning on whatever image comes to you will be best left for the oracle to decide. But regardless of the answer, this kind of focus, asking and reflecting on the response, may help move our decision making. Of course, there are any number of devices you may use. Perhaps there is a sacred text that serves as an ally, a holy book, or a collection of poetry. Or maybe a wandering walk in nature presents something that has meaning for you. Everything is speaking to us. We can use anything as a point of reflection.

Courageous Questions

Questions can help stir the pot and reveal new perspectives. Here are a few that might work in journaling or out loud in a group or family.

- What is a question that I have not yet had courage to ask?
- What questions do we feel uncomfortable asking around here?
- What questions never seem to get asked or answered?
- What is life's purpose?
- How can I more openly express who I really am?
- Why do I want that?
- Why am I in this relationship now?
- What question should I be asking?

Presence

Heart

Wisdom

Creation

PART IV

16

VOICE

If you bring forth what is within you, what you bring forth will save you.
If you do not bring forth what is within you,
what you do not bring forth will destroy you.

—The Gospel of St. Thomas

There has been a great hunt throughout human history. Beginning at least with Aristotle and continuing through today, people have been trying to understand the nature of the universe by tracking down the ultimate "stuff," the primary substance that makes up the world. The discovery of atoms and the like have been benchmarks on the quest for this Holy Grail of existence. Though we've discovered ever-tinier bits, it turns out we may have been searching for the wrong thing.

Modern science, especially in light of quantum reality, acknowledges that "stuff" or "substance" is an incomplete explanation for the underlying nature of the universe: Our minds, for instance, are abstract patterns formed by moving atoms. But the atoms themselves are also patterns, woven by the movement of subatomic particles. And those particles—the electrons and quarks—are patterns, too, but patterns in what? Some other force is operating that makes up minds and mountains beyond that of location of an object in space. That other force looks more like a movement, a process or aliveness that makes things go. Sure, there are atoms and quarks, but they are considered secondary physical manifestations of these underlying patterns and processes. We're coming to recognize that the primordial stuff may not be stuff at all.

Instead, it looks more like a process—that is, a process of creativity, said philosopher Alfred North Whitehead.[1] Life is a process constantly re-creating itself in a kind of endless cosmic renewal.

In various traditions, creative force is represented as sound. Sound represents the power of manifestation, of bringing something into being. "In the beginning there was the Word" that called the universe into being, or so the story goes. In another familiar creation story, another sound, the Big Bang, brought matter to life. In Indian spirituality, *Nada Brahma* are primal words. In Sanskrit, *Nada* means "sound" and is also defined as sounding, droning, roaring, or howling, while *Brahma* is the primal creative word and thus the source of the world and the fundamental element of all natural and historic things and events—everything.[2] Essentially, then, *Nada Brahma* means that creation, the cosmos, the world is sound. The world is created from this sound, this idea, this consciousness, this process. Sound carries consciousness into being. Thus, the universe is, we might say, a great song.

Our humble human counterpart to this ultimate force is our own creative expression, as that great universal roaring takes on the timbre of our own voice, our unique creative expression in the world. Mystery becomes manifest in the moment of creation— the conception of a child, the birth of an idea or piece of art. Meister Eckhart, the fourteenth-century Dominican priest, philosopher, mystic, and big fan of an overflowing God that cannot hold back its abundance speaks of our stunning role in this creative process: "We are all meant to be mothers of God."[3] Eckhart says we are midwives to the divine, bringing forth the many from the one. We midwife mystery, divinity, and ourselves through our creative expression. "To be mothers of God" is not hubris, although it was no doubt heresy in Eckhart's time. It is recognition that we, as part of creation, are infused with that current of aliveness, that word, the sound, the drive, the power to create. The remarkable thing about Eckhart's insight is that we are both the matrix, the womb out of which life flows and evolves, and we its manifestation, its child. We birth ourselves and the world through the creative impulse. Our personal responsibility is to be drawn forward by that aliveness, and we channel it as we will.

When our youngest child was little, we had a three-foot-long plastic thing called Crazy Daisy. It was basically a plastic pipe with a giant yellow and brown plastic daisy head on the top with little holes at the center of it. On a warm summer day, we attached the bottom end to the garden hose, turned on the hose, and let 'er rip. The giant daisy head would spurt out water all over the place, flopping randomly this way and that as squealing little people (and sometimes big people, too) would run about like, well, little kids. That flopping, wild gushing water is like the creative energy that the likes of Whitehead and Eckhart identify. Our creative opportunity is to take that hose and use it as we will, maybe to hold steady for a drink or maybe to water the tomato plants or maybe just letting it get us wet. That's when we find ourselves in that current of aliveness, that elusive thing we've been trying to track.

Expression

As Ralph Waldo Emerson wrote in his journal, "You are there in that place to testify."[4] Channeling this life force is about finding and using our unique creative expression in the world—our *voice*. This is not reserved for the artist or inventor but the way each of us expresses our abilities and creates our lives out of what we're given. Using our own voice as we create, speaking our truth, holding ourselves to our words, being authentic—all are acts of integrity. If we speak someone else's voice or keep our own silent, we live against ourselves and ultimately suffer. Our well-being is dependent on our ability to bring our voice to the world.

As a young boy, Native American elder Black Elk had visions that would shape his life and the life of his tribe. But in and of themselves, the visions were not enough. Black Elk reported that for a person who has a vision, you do not get the full power of that vision until you perform it on the earth for people to see.[5] The power and medicine comes both to us and to the world when we bring forth our authentic voice and take action in the world.

From the very beginning, we have not only a *capacity* to express ourselves but also the *drive* or push to do so. As infants, we cry if we need something and coo if we have that need satisfied. Children are usually always ready for a chance to play, whether it's coloring, building with blocks, making up silly words and songs, or constructing a world out of a pile of sand. When my children were young, the neighbor boys would build all sorts of jumps and ramps for their skateboards out of scraps of wood and even highway debris. They would then do the thing that boys sometimes do, especially when fueled by the presence of one another: they invented all sorts of new risky, radical, and sometimes even beautiful moves on their boards. In the same creative vein, I remember one day our youngest child, with the aid of a new glue gun, started spontaneously making people, fairies, and tiny household essentials (beds, dishes, clothes, and so forth) out of sticks, flowers, and all sorts of little found objects. This natural abundance of imagination is not rationed out but overflows. This is the nature of the creative force—diverse, overflowing, endless, abundant beyond measure.

The drive to express ourselves, to create in the world, is an innate need like beauty, love, and the search for truth. It seems almost biological, like the need for food and water. In the Nazi concentration camps of World War II, deprived of nearly everything, many prisoners composed songs, wrote poetry, and even found ways to paint. A concentration camp survivor himself, Victor Frankl suggested that these were meaning-making activities but ones that were not so much consciously planned as spontaneous outpourings from that deep current, that creative impulse.[6]

The drive for creative expression is so great that we can invent new ways to express our voice. Professor Ursula Bellugi discovered a form of poetry invented by people who are deaf and use American Sign Language to communicate. Instead of signing with a single hand to make certain signs, they use two, "holding one sign in the air with the left hand while the right creates an overlapping visual. The signs are altered, creating repetitions that . . . are analogous to verbal repetitions, phrasing, and meter in verbal poetry."[7]

Even when we have no voice whatsoever, we are waiting and working for the day when we do. Christopher Nolan, born in 1965 in a hospital near Dublin, Ireland, was brain damaged at birth, leaving him "with useless limbs, uncoordinated movements, and a voice that [was] generally incoherent."[8] Nolan could communicate only with his eyes and mainly to his mother, Bernadette. He would sit propped in his wheelchair, listening to his family and their friends. At eleven years old, he was given a new drug, Lioresal, that relaxed the muscles in his neck, giving him some small measure of control for periods of time. He then painstakingly began pointing to letters on a typewriter by the use of a "unicorn" pointer attached to his head. Nolan let loose what he called a "dam-burst of dreams," the title of his first book of poetry, which one critic called "a jubilant, lawless debut."[9]

What burst out was a remarkable flow of highly original inventive poetry that, in his mother's words, from the age of three he had "spent his long days composing poetry, learning it by heart and then storing it away in individual compartments in his mind, whilst at the same time praying that someday, somehow, he would find the means to express those poems in written words."[10] The first poem he wrote, bowing his head with its unicorn pointer toward the typewriter, was "I Learned to Bow."[11] His work has been compared to that of James Joyce and John Donne, among others. His imaginative use of language, alliteration, archaic meanings, and the metaphysical continually describe the world in fresh ways.

His mother explained, "It is as though he had been playing with words all his childhood as other, able-bodied children play with toys."[12] In his autobiography, *Under the Eye of the Clock*, Nolan wrote that during the years when his voice was in bondage to an "alien, lock-jawed world,"[13] "despondency never could stop [his] mesmerized woldwaddling in ink-blue heaven's busy mobility of secrets."[14] When he finally could express his thoughts and feelings, he said he "gimleted his words onto white sheets of life,"[15] that he "felt the glow lighting glimmering candles in his . . . mind,"[16] and that "spooned secrets hurrahed in his mind"[17] as he expressed "hollyberried imaginings."[18]

White sheets of life indeed!

We may not all have Christopher Nolan's particular talent, but we do all have the need and capacity to find and use our own voice, our unique self-expression in the world.

Adventure

As we've previously noted, we all live between a forest and a garden, between the wild, untamed, and uncertain on the one hand and the known, cultivated, and predictable on the other. Both of these are necessary to us. The garden is safe; it is our home base. By contrast, the forest stimulates and challenges us to grow and learn at the edge of our understanding. This is not just so we adapt but also so that we have adventure.

Alfred North Whitehead emphasized the opportunity for *adventure*, and he suggested that it is the courageous, spontaneous response to the events of our lives that grows our lives and the life of the world. Without this response and subsequent growth, civilization would fade into a state of tameness and vapidity, toward prepackaged, reconstituted, homogenized juice boxes, rather than just being naturally juicy.

Between forest and garden is this growing edge of adventure. Every action we take exposes us in one way or another. When we speak our *voice*, we take a risk that we may not be heard or that if we are, someone may not like what we have to say. When we risk asking someone out on a date, or risk committing to a marriage, a mortgage, or a move, or just risk being who we are, we enter the extraordinary field of creative energy.

The amazing thing is that every action we take actually activates the world, setting the forces of creation in motion. Just like a pebble thrown into a pond, our actions enact movement. Between forest and garden is where we tap into the stream of creation and come alive. Recognizing this remarkable process, Goethe offered this advice: "Whatever you think you can do or believe you can do, begin it. Action has magic, grace, and power in it."[19]

Speaking our voice also has risk, as we just don't know how things will work out. We can avoid some of the anxiety and excitement of uncertainty by staying with our familiar responses and routines and doing our best to keep things, including ourselves, as they are. But creative expression calls for voice and action in the world. We grow through challenge; our best-learned lessons usually come from failure and our strongest motivations from discomfort and desire. The world will do its part, bringing challenges and invitations. Our job is to live up to our end of the bargain. It does not mean we all need to take up hang gliding or some other risk of that sort. It does mean that our particular ongoing adventure is unique to us and is enacted in the little moments of telling someone the truth or trusting our gut, looking within to see what is uncomfortable or locating our deepest desire, making a commitment and risking failure or perhaps walking away and seeing what comes of it. The frontier is always at hand.

The movement of our four cardinal points culminates in this direction. We listen for the tug of aliveness in the silence to the East (presence), feel the courage, passion, discomfort, and yearning that heats us up from the South (heart), look to the North (wisdom) for the light that helps us find direction, our steps, our commitments, and now to the West (creation) we harness the capacity to take action and bring our voice and vision into the world and create the world as we do so.

This final step brings the inner life to full contact with the outer world and, in so doing, enacts it. It cannot be done otherwise. The most recognizable line in all of literature speaks precisely to this extraordinary opportunity and responsibility: "To be or not to be. . . . Whether 'tis nobler in the mind to suffer the slings and arrows of outrageous fortune . . ."[20] or, basically, to go to sleep. That is the question.

This compass point (Creation) is about finding a way to bring forth that aliveness (ideas, visions, voice, and self) into the world. It involves developing the strength and clarity of *Voice*—meaning the capacities and courage for creative, authentic expression. It involves directing our energies and developing the power of *will*, that energy that moves, manifests, and makes things happen, and along with this, recognizing the *willingness* to allow those currents to move through us. It requires the power of *imagination*, celebrates difference and *originality*, and brings forth our *calling*, where our lives connect deeply with the world.

17

WILL AND WILLINGNESS

Let us ride our lives like natural beasts, like tempests, like the bounce of a ball, or the slightest ambiguous hovering of ash, the drift of scent: let us stick to those currents that can carry us, membering them with our souls.

—M. C. Richards

When our alarms go off, we glance at our clocks and will ourselves out of bed to start the day. At the end of the day, we flop back into bed and, with a little luck, surrender to a night's sleep. These two internal qualities—the power of our *will* and the release of our *willingness*—speak not just to the start and finish of the day but also to the call of any moment in our lives where we must ask whether this is a time for us to tighten up and persevere or just let go and allow. Our lives are a dance between will and surrender, yang and yin, masculine and feminine. Will involves the power of intention that throws (or holds back) our weight, heart, and effort in one direction or another. However, the power of will alone is insufficient to find the intersection between human creativity and the flow of the life current through us, which is where willingness comes into play. In the pages ahead, we'll take a look at the qualities of will and of willingness and find their balance within us.

Will

Qualities of perseverance, dedication, intention, and stubbornness constitute the will. Climbers dragging themselves up Mount Everest or a student staying with a difficult problem or a long study session both involve the power of the will to keep moving.

The creative process involves framing questions, focusing our energies, engaging, committing, and moving forward despite odds and uncertainty. The painter returns to the canvas day after day, the scientist to the problem or laboratory, the writer to the story. We all have a frustration threshold, whether it's reached while working through a complex mathematics problem, learning a new language, or staying with a commitment like an exercise regimen—most anything that requires sustained effort and delayed pleasure. It is the ability to take a breath and keep plugging that gets us through. The successful problem solvers stick with it, whether it takes hours, days, weeks, years, or even decades. This brings together the power of focus we considered earlier with the power of perseverance and drive. This requires us to deal with our frustrations, manage our expectations, and keep plugging.

It should come as no surprise, then, that will and work have a great deal to do with success. In *Outliers* Malcolm Gladwell made the case that the reason that Asian children in the United States generally perform much better on average in mathematics and in school in general has to do with what my Asian American friend (who is a medical student, a virtuoso violinist, pianist, and humanitarian with degrees in English and psychology) called the Asian algorithm. It is a work ethic and, Gladwell argued, it also has to do with rice paddies.[1] The argument is this: Growing rice is extraordinarily labor intensive, requiring daily attention unlike, say, growing wheat or corn, which is seasonal. For wheat, you plant it, you wait, and then you harvest it. Rice yield is directly related to effort and skill. If you work harder, you get more rice. This is not so for the wheat that European ancestors grew. While fully aware of the danger of stereotyping, Gladwell argued that it is not IQ or neurological differences that account for the high achievement gap but instead that this cultural history imprints a work ethic revealed in the hard, sustained effort that results in high achievement. Gladwell argued that it is precisely this long-term sustained effort that so often leads to success.

When we think of successful people—the Beatles or Bill Gates—we generally assume their success to be the result of great talent, ambition, and some good luck. But something else also seems to be at work. It's exactly that, in fact: work. No matter the field, from computer programming to playing music, it takes about ten thousand hours—roughly ten years of practice—to reach world-class mastery. Neuroscientist and former music producer Daniel Levitin wrote, "In study after study of composers, basketball players, fiction writers, ice skaters, concert pianists, chess players, master criminals, this number comes up again and again. . . . It seems that it takes the brain this long to assimilate all that it needs to know to achieve true mastery."[2]

Even prodigious achievers like Mozart may not be exceptions to the ten thousand–hour rule. Psychologist Michael Howe offered this: "By the standards of mature composures, Mozart's early works are not outstanding. The earliest pieces were all probably written down by his father, and perhaps all improved in the process." He reported that "many of Wolfgang's childhood compositions—the first seven of his concertos for piano and orchestra—are largely arrangements of works by other composers. Of those that only contain music original to Mozart, the earliest that is now regarded as a masterwork, Piano Concerto No. 9 (K. 271), was not composed until he was twenty-one: by that time Mozart had already been composing concertos for ten years."[3] Certainly there was no denying Mozart's talent, but it took these years of practice to bring his work to master level.

By 1960 John Lennon and Paul McCartney had been playing together for three years. Their struggling high school rock band was invited, along with a number of other bands, to play at strip clubs in Hamburg, Germany. It wasn't that the band was particularly good at the time; it just happened that one of the German club owners was visiting Liverpool, and through a bit of luck, they were among several bands that were asked to play. The formula was to bring music groups into clubs to drive in business. And they weren't being asked to play a set or two. They were typically on stage seven nights a week, playing nonstop hour after hour. Lennon described the Beatles's experience at a club called the Indra.

> We got better and more confidence. We couldn't help it with all the experience playing all night long. . . . In Liverpool, we'd only ever done one-hour sessions, and we just used to do our best numbers, the same ones, at every one. In Hamburg, we had to play for eight hours, so we really had to find a new way of playing.[4]

In a year and a half on five separate trips to Hamburg, the Beatles performed 270 nights. Before they had their first real hint of success, they had performed live an estimated twelve hundred times.[5] The lesson: If you want to really master something, practice. A lot.

The will allows us the power and self-discipline to stick with our goals, pursue our dreams, and persevere along the path. Our intention focuses and becomes like a vow ("I will finish this or do that"). There will always be things that get in our way—crises of meaning or confidence, crises of money and time, limits of ability, and all sorts of sirens of pleasure that lure us away. But it is the capacity of the will, this *intention* and *self-discipline*, that allows us to stay on path or fall off. We engage will every time we maintain our focus, work through our frustration threshold, and persevere. We discover that free will is actually a great discipline.

In addition to strength, the will also gathers even more power by being skillful. We may need some down-to-earth *plan* ("What are the steps I need to take to move toward my goal?") and certain *habits* or practices ("What are the habits or schedule or situations I need to keep me going?"). When we get a little lost in the woods or tired from the trek, the habits of work or schedule help keep us on track. We show up to work each morning even though we may not feel like it. At times, we may also need to *reaffirm* the goal, especially by remembering that felt sense or vision that moved us in this direction in the first place ("Now, why is this important to me?"). And we may need to re-evaluate along the way ("Is this still what I need and want to do, or do I need to adjust this goal a bit?").

And while we want to succeed and so often measure, or at least mark, our lives by outcomes and accomplishments, sometimes it is sheer effort, regardless of outcome, that demonstrates the integrity and honor of the creative will. American author Anne Lamott related a story about watching a Special Olympics event. She wrote of one player on the men's basketball team, "You could tell he was [the star] because even though no one had made a basket, yet his teammates almost always passed him the ball. Even the people on the other team passed him the ball."[6] She described the game as joyfully loud and crazily beautiful, even though long into the second half no one had yet scored. She wrote that as she sat in the packed auditorium, "I could see that it was about tragedy transformed over the years into joy. It was about the sheer beauty of effort."[7]

However noble and powerful, will has its limits. It doesn't usually turn out well if we try to control, direct, or force every bit of our life. Life happens. No matter who we think we are, we just don't control or manage all the forces of the universe. They carry us into expected and sometimes unwanted places despite our every effort. We just can't force everything. Doing so leaves us tight, too controlling, even violent, especially when we try to impose our will on others. Power, as opposed to mere force, involves a balance of will and willingness.

Surrender

There is an old story of a bright young man with impeccable academic pedigree who traveled from afar to work with a revered teacher. Upon his arrival, he asked the teacher how long it would take to learn tai chi.

"You're very bright," the teacher said. "Seven years."

To which the young man replied, "What if I work especially hard?"

The teacher answered, "Then it will take you fourteen years."

The student said, "But what if I work really, really hard? How long will it take me then?"

The teacher answered, "Then you will never learn."

However essential and powerful the will is in directing our efforts, there is a clear sense that it is not by effort alone that we find our way. Freshness and spontaneity, insight and creativity come not only as the result of our will but especially through our willingness and wakefulness.

The creative process swings back and forth between directed, focused effort and the willingness to allow something to arise in us and flow through us. Scientists, artists, and others regularly describe the directed focus needed to work toward some project and the effort to refine their ideas. But equally common among those who have made extraordinary accomplishments is a description of allowing—not forcing—something to arise on its own accord. For example, some writers have spoken of a common experience of allowing ideas in, rather than forcibly dragging them back as if from some hunting expedition. Lewis Carroll of *Alice in Wonderland* fame, for example, wrote,

> Sometimes, an idea comes at night, when I have had to get up and strike a light to note it down—sometimes when out on a lonely winter walk, when I have to stop and with half frozen fingers jot down a few words . . . but whenever and however it comes, it comes by itself.[8]

Likewise, William Blake described his poem *Milton* as coming from beyond his will.

> I have written this poem from immediate dictation, twelve sometimes twenty or thirty lines at a time, without premeditation, and even against my will.[9]

Goethe wrote of being overtaken or surrendering to the words, that

> The songs had me, not I them; the songs had me in their powers.[10]

Perhaps this capacity for receiving the creative process describes the difference between talent and genius. Willingness opens a space that allows ideas and feelings, images and senses to rise into view. We relax our defenses and loosen our grip on a particular way of being or seeing, allowing more to come into awareness. The spaciousness and graciousness of presence helps us open to and stay aware of whatever may present itself.

The concept of *wu wei* from Taoism is described paradoxically as the action of non-action, or choiceless willing. It involves consciously aligning ourselves with the natural and essential ebb and flow of things—with the Tao or life force. Without effort, we are awake enough to respond to whatever arises, not as an act of will but more as an act of alignment and balance, which is described as spontaneously virtuous. In fact, *wu wei*—this acting without a sense of self—is the highest virtue in Taoism.

If Alfred North Whitehead was right and the ultimate building block of life is the creative process, it is in part through willingness that we drop into the current of creation. "Letting go" or "allowing" follows naturally from trust, but while trust or willingness implies an attitude, letting go is closer to an action. It is paradoxical in the sense that we must be intentional (willful) as we move toward letting go, but we release in this moment of willingness. German philosopher Martin Heidegger used the terms *resoluteness* and *releasement* to capture these dimensions, not only in creative acts but also in our lives in general.[11]

One day, I got an assessment of my own balance of will and willingness in an unexpected way. In a workshop many years ago, it was suggested that someone feed me. I immediately balked at the suggestion. I was an adult, after all, and adults are not generally fed like infants. But as the idea lingered in the air for a few minutes, my growing resistance confirmed that there was something here for me. Now, there are some who would have no problem at all with this, like our little family dog, Bella, who at any moment will roll on her back to have her stomach rubbed. But some of us don't let go of control so well, and as a young in-control man, the idea of being fed was not so easy to stomach. I had learned to be in control, not to give it up. Control meant power and safety; surrender was weakness and vulnerability. And I didn't want to be weak and certainly didn't want my weakness to show. I found myself continuing to resist the idea, but despite my protests, we gave it a try. Even as my feeder proceeded to give me my dinner, I found myself trying to help out and stay in some measure of control by spontaneously reaching for the fork on several occasions, moving my body and head toward the approaching food, and directing the process. My muscles were taut, not yet willing to give in. But with a little coaxing and with a growing trust in the goodwill of my helper, I started to relax and allow this to unfold. It was a surprisingly powerful experience for someone like me, who was really trying to control my life. I got a very immediate taste of both my willful resistance and, eventually, the gentleness and even delight in conscious, willing surrender. There was a metaphor here about control and willingness that begged for a recalibration in my life.

Willingness is an act of faith and can be a statement of hope. It can occur out of deep trust and sometimes great desperation, when we are brought to our knees to ask for help. It also can be cultivated consciously and intentionally. Willingness closes the space between us and the other; that is, it lessens our self-separateness as we say yes to join in that flow of the universe. In doing so, we may even find that it reduces our fundamental loneliness, our disconnection.

For young children, this willingness is often a natural way of being. We may catch hints of this as a little child spins and spins out of control just to get dizzy, or explodes into uncontrolled giggles and silliness, or trusts being held in a loving embrace. However, our overly willful, in-control cultural norms often exclude the possibility of constructive surrender, teaching us that willingness must be replaced by will instead of complemented by it. This shrinks the possibility for letting go, mystery, and adventure. Willingness or surrender says yes to belonging; it joins life as we give ourselves over to a certain flow and lean toward communion and unity. The wise use of the will can move us to the edge of aligning with these currents, but joining with them occurs through willingness to enter the mystery.

Einstein claimed that it is appreciation for mystery, not for nailed-down certainty, that is at the heart of creative drive.

> The fairest thing we can experience is the mysterious. It is the fundamental emotion that stands at the cradle of true art and true science. He who knows it not and can no longer wonder, no longer feel amazement, is as good as dead, a snuffed-out candle.[12]

Willingness, of course, requires discernment, as discussed in part 3. It just doesn't turn out well if we go around surrendering to everything and everyone. We become a leaf in the wind, carried by the currents of parents and peer groups, society and sex, marketing and meaningless pursuits, and those whose agendas involve using us for their own desires, like a manipulative friend or a leader. Such blanket willingness can be a way of avoiding making a choice, avoiding taking responsibility that stems from a sense of learned helplessness. It leads to submissiveness, oppression, and victimization. This is not exactly the place where we want to end up.

One way to think about willingness is to recognize various dimensions of the self. As we have spoken of previously, we can often recognize both our small self and our larger nature. The small self remains self-interested, sometimes greedy or driven by immediate pleasure and power. Various parts of our personality live here, and we have to manage these impulses in some way. If we simply surrendered to them at every occasion, we would be a little difficult to live with.

However, it's clear that we are more than instincts and neurotic tendencies. Not all our parts are created equal or worth surrendering to. By whatever name, the deeper nature is driven by something more than the personal ego or pleasure-seeking biological drives. It represents our more expansive, moral, loving, and wise virtues. The idea is that we would do well to align our personal, conscious will with this larger current that seems to be flowing through us.

Humility

Humility is a kind of life orientation to one's self and the world that engenders and is engendered by willingness. Humility is characterized by open-mindedness and self-awareness of what we know and what we don't—that is, a realistic appraisal of our strengths and weaknesses. The humble person is open to asking for help or advice, recognizing that they simply don't know it all and never will. They retain an awareness of context and tend to see the world with complexity and diversity, recognizing there is much more happening than meets any one set of eyes. This orients us to the world so differently than an orientation of arrogance, which tends to want others to bend to our will. Thanks to humility, we might be willing to try a new idea, remain curious about other ways of being and seeing, or suspend or surrender our stance to try out a new one. We more naturally respect others and other points of view. Humility is an active—not passive—force seeking fresh perspectives to constantly renew its view. Rather than fixed or rigid, it is flexible, open, and curious. Rather than low self-esteem, humility requires great self-awareness and respect for ourselves as well as others. We begin to see why humility is considered a virtue and, in a culture dominated by domination, why it can be pushed aside as a sign of ignorance ("They just don't seem very certain in what they know.") or weakness ("They're always asking for help."), rather than be seen as a key to wisdom and creativity.

As a virtue, humility is an aspiration, an organic outcome or a trait of spiritual and psychological maturity. It serves as a valuable benchmark or goal. But to say "I'm going to be more humble today" is a tricky order. It can set up insidious swings of success and failure that may fuel the ego toward a spiritual narcissism rather than greater humility. The path to virtue is often strewn with puritanical expectations and sorry failures. So how do we go about this?

Rather than striving directly for humility, willingness gives us a more concrete action or practice that may get us nearer this paradoxical quality. To say "I'm going to try to be more willing today" invites us to notice where we resist, where we try to impose our will on others, where we close off or shut down, and where we might let go just a bit by saying yes rather than saying no, cooperating rather than dominating, listening more and speaking less. This turns the high and noble virtue of humility into a capacity of being and knowing we can experiment with.

Holding On and Letting Go

Sometimes we fear that by surrendering we'll lose something, even destroy it. And we're right. Embedded in creation is destruction. In creation, the old way, form, limit, way of being, concept is often destroyed, sloughed off, or released to allow room for something new. Something is lost and something is gained when we let go, and we are not always willing to give up that familiar security, whether it is a cherished idea, a perception of oneself, or an outgrown relationship. But creation requires this.

In this sense, willingness and surrender may even be thought of as a mini death. When we consult our death, we have the chance to deeply experience impermanence and then stop wasting time defending and propping up the identity and "the stuff" (status, possessions, and so forth) that inevitably passes away. With surrender, our priorities are rearranged or reaffirmed. Author Gregg Levoy said it this way: "We all owe God a death, Shakespeare once said, so we owe it to ourselves to practice for the occasion whenever possible." We can practice small surrenders almost daily by forgiving someone, letting go of a bad mood, letting go to kindness, dropping fear in order to tell the truth.[13]

Surrendering our expectations of how something should be creates the space for us to appreciate it just as it is. Ask the following questions when considering surrender:

- "What am I holding on to that is clotting the flow of my life?"
- "What am I afraid to let go of but know I should?"
- "What do I hold myself back from saying yes to but am most deeply drawn to?"
- "Is it time to forgive and let my resentment die in order to save my life?"
- "Can I forgive God? My parents? Myself?"

Practicing for death—and life—involves the art of surrender. This practice is a natural rhythm. The rhythm of human psychological and spiritual development involves regularly shedding our snakeskin of beliefs, attachments, and identity to make room for expansion into a larger perspective and identity. Many mystics and sages encourage us not to merely defend our beliefs and ourselves but to regularly and naturally clean house, sloughing off the dross of identity and reworking our understanding of ourselves. Eighteenth-century scientist and mystic Emanuel Swedenborg described the cleansing of his own mind and the reprioritization that came through a profound moment of surrender: "This meant that my head was being put in order, and is actually being cleansed of all that might obstruct these thoughts."[14] The result is a reorganization of being and a clearing of the baggage obscuring the heart and mind, leading to self-knowledge and even, at least with Swedenborg, mystical union.

The transformative or creative process requires consciously aligning with this rhythm of holding on and letting go, of death and birth, which is very different from chronic fortification of the self that we often learn. Rhythms of nature provide a reminder. Trees slough off their leaves; the tide sweeps the beach each day; and each breath expels carbon dioxide. Can we bring this same ebb and flow, the consolidation and the cleansing to ourselves, allowing us to accomplish our spring cleaning throughout the year?

Willingness is essential not only for creativity; it is a thread that runs through all our four directions. In part 1, Presence, we spoke of openness to experience, witnessing without judgment and the value of beginner's mind, which are all kin to willingness. In part 2, Heart, we spoke of the capacity of allowing one's feelings and felt sense to come into view and to let down boundaries of self-separateness in order to really meet another. In part 3, Wisdom, there is a willingness to seek and be open to guidance, to listen to the still, small voice and tolerate paradox and unknowing.

By cultivating a friendship at the edge of the known and the mysterious, through the movement of both will and surrender, discipline and wildness, firmness and vulnerability, we engage the creative life.

Will and Willingness
Balancing the power of will and the constructive
surrender of willingness.

Quiz

For each statement or word, circle the number that describes you best.

(least like me)   1   2   3   4   5   (most like me)

I follow through and get things done.	1 2 3 4 5
I persevere through challenging issues.	1 2 3 4 5
I can let go and relax.	1 2 3 4 5
I am open and adaptable to change.	1 2 3 4 5
I am not afraid to ask for help.	1 2 3 4 5
I can be self-reliant.	1 2 3 4 5
I can work hard.	1 2 3 4 5
I find my natural rhythm most of the time.	1 2 3 4 5
I allow things to unfold.	1 2 3 4 5
I don't always have to win.	1 2 3 4 5

Add up the circled numbers.   Total: _____

10–19	20–29	30–39	40–50
A trailhead	**More is possible**	**A good ally**	**A great strength**

....

PRACTICES

Toning

Essentially, this practice is about sounding your voice in the world. There are only two parts to this. First, the practice involves taking a deep diaphragmatic breath. Singers, trombone players, and sponge divers understand that you get the most breath in your lungs by distending your diaphragm on the inhale. Place your hand on your belly and see if you can distend your belly without raising your shoulders as you take in a deep breath. I find that this breathing really has two parts: first the belly expands and then the chest fills.

Once you've managed some diaphragmatic breaths, simply (and without worry of achieving any musical virtuosity) make a sound and hold it. Perhaps an "ah," "o," or "e." Notice the tone and timbre in your voice. Notice where the tone reverberates in your body. Take another breath and perhaps vary the pitch and volume. Experiment. Hold the tone for a minute or two, breathing as needed. A toning workout might involve holding each vowel sound for two minutes. If you're doing it in a group, you may notice the degree to which voices blend and harmonize. Notice where the sound seems to be coming from. At the end of each tone, be in silence for several moments and note your experience. You might notice overtones (sound frequencies that are generated by the interference pattern between various pitches).

This may be used as contemplative practice itself or as a kind of warm-up or a discharge when being still is difficult. It can be used as a centering exercise before some other activity, like a confrontation or a performance of some sort. It serves as both a literal practice and a metaphor for bringing our voice to the world. It involves both willed action and allowing.

Change

Select some aspect of your own life you are willing to change in some way. It may be a behavior (eating, exercise, meditation), a pattern of thinking, or anything else. What would you like to change? It should be simple to describe, identify, and measure the change. In a free-writing journal, start by identifying the desired change or goal and provide any needed context, including a history of previous attempts at change or your rationale. What steps will be used to effect a new change? Over what time period will the experiment take place? (You might try thirty days, for example.) In addition to what's impelling you forward, what are the obstacles, and how will you know if this change has occurred? Keep a log of your feelings and progress throughout. Notice what parts of you resist. Report the results and reflect on the process and your choice of areas. What was learned? What do you do next?

Aimless Wandering

Find a place of natural beauty that you can wander in. The aim (although wandering implies no aim) is to allow yourself to be touched and drawn by nature and by your intuition. This can serve as nourishment and heighten sensitivity to self and surroundings and the connection between them. This requires a delicate allowance, a willingness to follow the lead of our senses, the birdsong, intuition.

Give yourself some time in this natural setting, perhaps half an hour or more. Begin perhaps by sitting or lying down, closing your eyes, taking some deep breaths, and moving into a place of quiet stillness and connection with the ground, plants, sounds, smells, and textures—all that you find yourself resting in. Settle in, letting go of the mental or emotional baggage that came with you.

As you open your eyes, let your gaze gently scan your surroundings, taking note and appreciation of this place. Where are your senses drawn? A breeze, a scent, a birdsong? Allow yourself to be drawn into the intimacy of this moment and this place.

When your allotted time for the practice is up or when your intuition tells you it's time to end, be still for a few moments. Generate a feeling of gratitude for the time and the beauty, and notice how you feel, emotionally and physically. If you're moved to do so, you might write some ideas down, perhaps a poem or a few lines of thoughts that come to mind.

Feed Me

Have someone feed you. This is not about the groom and bride stuffing wedding cake into each other's mouth. It is about trust and willingness on the part of the person being fed as well as trustworthiness and sensitivity on the part of the feeder. Although it is tempting to be silly, try this with a contemplative, gentle, and reverent attitude in order to see what gets stirred up. This is a fairly low-risk practice. If your partner blows it, you might get some pudding up your nose or need an extra napkin. Afterward, process what this was like, what came up, and how you held yourself in this opportunity to be willing.

Holding On and Letting Go

At New Year's or a birthday, or maybe just at the end of the day, we can ask ourselves to name or write down privately what we want to hold on to (a memory, a bit of insight, even a possession) and what we want to let go of (a frustrating event, anger, hurt, or some possession that we really do not need any longer). Perhaps we put this note of what we want to let go of in an envelope, seal it, decorate it, and, with the appropriate weight and fanfare of ceremony, shred or burn it. We might be reminded of nature cleaning itself out each year with the change of seasons—how trees have to let go of their leaves in order to grow new ones and how what is left behind becomes compost for creation. It is amazing how we hold on to resentments, fears, and other ideas that clot consciousness. Instead, we can get into that natural rhythm of constructive surrender that frees us for new delights.

18

ORIGINALITY

This above all, to thine own self be true.

—William Shakespeare

The motor behind evolution, whether biological, techno-logical, cultural, or spiritual, is diversity. It is difference, uniqueness, and mutation that fills the pool life crawls forward from. Darwin really helped get this idea off and running in the modern world, but the same theme is found in virtually all the ancient creation stories where the divine wants some company and creates a universe, bursting into endless forms—the one in the many. It is diversity in what we do, in how we think and perceive, and the difference between where we are and where we want to go, between one idea and another, that creates the dynamic tension germinating growth. But there are considerable forces that work against diversity, difference, and originality, and they show up very early.

The Dark Force

On her fifth day of kindergarten, the day after her fifth birthday, one of my daughters was given a short homework assignment that required her to circle the two out of three objects on the page that were alike. There were six sets of shapes and six separate questions. She handled all without ambiguity except one group that included a small green rectangle, a green triangle, and a red square. "Which two belong together?" She circled the red square and the green rectangle. When I asked her about this, she acknowledged that they had different colors, but she saw more value in the fact that two of them each had four sides, while the other had three. The next day at school, this was marked incorrect and returned to her. Obsession with the right answer misses the opportunity to see the question and the world from multiple vantage points. In this case it was understanding that some shapes can perform certain functions. My five-year-old explained that rectangles and squares form "bottoms" of things like buildings, while triangles may form "tops." She could imagine possibilities beyond the information given. This homework assignment is a tiny example, involving a tiny kindergartner in her first days of school, but it will happen again and again and will teach her that there is one correct way of looking at something.[1]

If the creative flow is the ultimate process, as Alfred North Whitehead and others think, and if diversity is central to that flow, then perhaps the most insidious threat to human evolution is not nuclear war or global warming but instead the efforts and institutions that work to homogenize this exuberant abundance. One of the risks of overemphasis on things that tend to provide the same perspectives in similar ways is simply that they tend toward homogenization in the form of standardized testing, uniform curriculum and instruction in schools, the widespread diagnosis of mental disorders and use of psychiatric medications for attention deficits and mood issues, the proliferation of the mega-marts, chain stores, restaurants, and other monster corporations, singular literalist interpretations of texts, and concentrated mainstream media.

There are some benefits as well, and standardized airport landing protocols, computer interfaces, and such, as rules of the road, allow us to function efficiently and safely. But in the realm of living things, diversity engenders innovative solutions, creative evolution, and growth. Entrepreneurial capitalism, for example, has been successful on the local and global stages not because it is the most moral, fairest, healthiest, easiest, or even most efficient, but because more than any other approach, it engenders creative diversity and thus invites innovation. It taps the same impulse to create and risk reward or failure. Homogenization, at its best, tends toward a degree of efficiency and control. This has real value in many applications, but it's not the highest value for everything all the time. It is an incomplete goal that has sometimes been mistaken as the end goal. When homogeneity overwhelms diversity, whether in a classroom or a culture, the available intellectual and spiritual gene pool starts to dry up. When it comes to human consciousness and human creativity, unique ways of seeing and being catalyze growth and evolution.

In the quest for living a life that matters, theologian Paul Tillich said that there exists unusually powerful forces that can thwart us and even destroy us. He had a name for this kind of power, one that captures just how dangerous it can be: *demonic*. He didn't use the term in the mythological sense of the devil or little demons running about but instead as recognition that our essential or creative nature can be overwhelmed by other forces. The demonic is a force that is stronger than the individual's goodwill, a force capable of overpowering our creative nature.[2]

Addiction is an example of an individual's incapacity to resist possession by a drug. The influence of the Third Reich to turn scientists and schoolteachers into components in a genocidal machine is, for Tillich, an example of how a force can overcome individual goodwill. Today there is a mixed blessing in the ability to standardize, homogenize, and globalize. Both great good and great harm are possible when forces are so powerful and universal. The greatest threat is its potential to distort or estrange us from our authentic creative nature without our even realizing it. When forces are so pervasive, we can hardly step outside their gravitational pull long enough to recognize their influence on us.

The Integrity of Betrayal

Whether it is making a career choice or a clothing choice, there is generally pressure to conform to some expectation or norm. Some of these decisions don't really matter too much and some matter a great deal. Advertisers want us to feel discomfort unless we wear or drive or drink their product. Like never before, there is a remarkable deluge of messages vying for our attention, and few have much to do with what is good, true, or beautiful in the deepest sense. The contemporary world can be a place where

- surround sound, sexuality, and violence over stimulates;
- brand loyalty substitutes for human bonds;
- the lowest human elements, not the greatest, are too often reinforced;
- fear, greed, self-interest, and "stuff" compete with love and wisdom;
- purchasing power is mistaken for liberation;
- the road to wisdom is presumed to be paved with a faster internet connection; and

- the search for peace of mind is replaced with perpetual desire and dissatisfaction shaped by slick advertising.

It is no easy task to hear our own voice and find our own way through. Remember what M.C. Richards said: "It requires a certain amount of energy, certain capacities for taking the world into our consciousness, certain real powers of body and soul to be a match for reality."[3]

So what *is* required?

There are ways of being that are of the higher self and ways of being that are other than. In order to be original—to live near one's origin—we will inevitably face times when we are confronted with betraying another's expectations of us. Are we willing to betray our parents, peers, lovers, employers, teachers, clients, religion, culture, or vague "shoulds" that live in our heads? We often feel that we must live up to the expectations of other people. If we don't, "they" will think less of us, and deep down, we may fear that we won't be loved. Cultural norms, religious expectations, our roles, our ethnicity, and so forth—all these shape us. This is not bad; it just is. But the challenge for an original life is to find our own center of gravity in the midst of these voices. To do so involves defying the pressure of others in order to be true to ourselves. At its heart, integrity ultimately becomes a practice of creative self-sculpture. Rumi had some advice about which force is available to lead us to an authentic life; he advised us to "be silently drawn by the strange pull of what you really love."[4]

Authenticity

Martin Buber recounted an old Hasidic tale that reminds us where life's task is centered.

As an old man nearing his own death, Rabbi Zusya said, "In the coming world, they will not ask me, 'Why were you not Moses?' They will ask me, 'Why were you not Zusya?'"[5] Our work is about midwifing ourselves from the inside out, uncovering, developing, and expressing our own unique voice, not someone else's. Despite the pressure to be this way or that, the work is to find our authentic life. Finding our own voice is not only about *doing* something (getting a different hairstyle, finding a novel solution to a problem, writing the next big hit) but is especially connected with being, with being authentic. You have a way about you; what is it?

The opposite of authentic and original is fake or counterfeit. If we've experienced the real thing, we can usually recognize the difference between real and fake. A genuine smile or hug has impact, while an insincere one seems to bounce off us. Artificial food often lacks the sensual depth of the real stuff. There is a warning on hummingbird feeders that tells us not to mix artificial sweetener with water to make the nectar. The hummingbird will think it's getting the real deal (it apparently tastes good enough) and keep coming back for more. But despite a full belly, it will starve to death, as the meal is nutritionally vapid. That's the danger of counterfeits; they stimulate us on the surface but they may not provide real sustenance. They don't nourish us all the way down to our bones; they just leave us wanting more.

When a life is lived on someone else's terms, the existentialists tell us that anxiety, boredom, and despair are often the telltales of meaninglessness. Today we can recognize plenty of anxiety and despair around us, not to mention the hunger for constant distractions to quench boredom or deter restlessness. Jean Paul Sartre's novels contain characters who take action based on external pressures—the pressure to appear to be a certain kind of person, the pressure to live or behave in a certain way, the pressure to ignore one's own moral and aesthetic discomfort in order to have a more comfortable life. They go along to get along. Their lives seem counterfeit and hollow, even to themselves. Sartre also gives us characters who do not understand their own reasons for acting or who ignore crucial facts about their own lives in order to avoid uncomfortable truths. Basically, they live someone else's life, and they suffer because of this.

Authenticity is about living life on the outside in alignment or congruence with one's interior. The alternative comes from either selling out in order to fit in or remaining out of touch with this inner self. Anne Lamott, in her 2003 University of California, Berkeley, commencement address, had this to say about staying in touch with our insides:

> I got a lot of things that society had promised would make me whole and fulfilled—all the things that the culture tells you from preschool on will quiet the throbbing anxiety inside you—stature, the respect of colleagues, maybe even a kind of low-grade fame. The culture says these things will save you, as long as you also manage to keep your weight down. But the culture lies. Slowly, after dozens of rejection slips and failures and false starts and postponed dreams—what Langston Hughes called dreams deferred—I stepped onto the hallowed ground of being a published novelist, and then fifteen years later, I even started to make real money.
>
> I'd been wanting to be a successful author my whole life. But when I finally did it, I was like a greyhound catching the mechanical rabbit she'd been chasing all her life—metal, wrapped up in cloth. It wasn't alive; it had no spirit. It was fake. Fake doesn't feed anything. Only spirit feeds spirit, in the same way only your own blood type can sustain you. It had nothing

that could slake the lifelong thirst I had for a little immediacy, and connection.

So . . . I want to tell you that what you're looking for is already inside you. You've heard this before, but the holy thing inside you really is that which causes you to seek it. You can't buy it, lease it, rent it, date it, or apply for it.[6]

Ultimately, Lamott argued, the source of fulfillment is inside us. Our satisfaction is not just about what we accomplish in the world but instead is somehow tied to how close and true we stay to our deepest self. For her, this had something to do with immediacy and connection.

My friend Diane was married, had a young daughter, and was working toward a graduate degree. She seemed to be doing all the right things, but there was a weight in her life that had grown heavier with time, and without her realizing, it had relentlessly dragged her to the deep end. Her life took a turn one afternoon when the school bus arrived to drop off her little girl. There was no crash, no drama, but instead an instant of riveting clarity as her daughter approached the front door of the house. Diane was so laden with the emotional weight of her life that she could hardly get off the couch to greet her little girl. In that instant, it was excruciatingly clear that she had not been emotionally available for this child she loved so much. Her energy was being diverted (sucked away, really) into something she could not grasp. In desperation, she traded couches and entered therapy.

A few sessions in, Diane was invited to take some deep breaths, close her eyes, and relax. She was told, "Put your intellect in suspended animation and just let your imagination take over. Imagine yourself in a comfortable place in nature and take in the feel, smell, sounds, and sights around you. Notice a path moving off into the woods and allow yourself to follow the path." With more than a little skepticism, Diane followed the instructions and, once relaxed, was surprised that she could so easily imagine herself strolling along this path in the woods.

The instructions continued: "In time, the path leads to a bridge. See if you can find that bridge." Diane complied. "Once you've found it, take a good look around. Notice if you can see someone on the other side of the bridge." Diane followed the invitation, and in a few moments she was able to see a little girl approaching her from across that bridge. She was startled by how vivid and real the girl was, and suddenly she realized this girl was herself as a child. Diane's emotional memory of what it felt like to have been that little girl flooded in. She could feel her vibrant aliveness. "Welcome her, and ask if she has anything to tell you," she was instructed. Diane was jolted by what she heard next. The little girl looked her in the eye and said simply, "Just let me be me."

Diane said, "In that instant, I realized that I hadn't been me since I didn't know when. Growing up in my own household was like, 'This is how we are, and we want you to be this way, so anything outside of these lines is not permitted.' It was like you couldn't really be accepted; nothing was unconditional. The message from my family was, 'If you don't think and do like we do, then there is something wrong with you, and you will be rejected.'" She said that she had stuffed that little kid away and developed a false self for the world; "I took on a very logical, unemotional, skeptical view of the world. Everything else disappeared, got pushed under."

Diane said that what got pushed under was her natural way of seeing the world as full of wonder, awe, intimacy, and ecstasy. She had felt so alive in some moments, ones of unity and ecstasy in which she somehow understood that "everything was absolutely perfect." Yet early on she recognized that this way of knowing the world was too much for those around her. Over time, this sense of communion with the world and with herself got buried further and further underground.

Meeting that little girl on the bridge of her imagination turned Diane's life around. She learned firsthand that the more we shut down, the more we live against ourselves, the more we suffer. As this background was permitted to surface, so did her intuition and ecstasy—those ways of being and knowing that were so natural to her as a child. In remarkably short order, her depression lifted. "I started having some experiences of ecstasy like I'd had as a child and now have them frequently. In fact, at first I thought I was manic-depressive because I became so much more emotionally alive again."

Once Diane rediscovered her own original nature, she turned not only her parenting around but also steered her professional life in a different direction, something nearer her origin. She has become an elementary guidance counselor, helping children live in the world while staying close to their originality and authenticity.

In *Hamlet*, Polonius offers the ultimate advice for an authentic life: "This above all, to thine own self be true."[7] Authenticity begins as a courtship with our interior and ends as communion with our life.

Speaking a True Word

Once we're able to hear that original voice—whether it speaks to us through some suffering or deep desire, by way of outrage or swollen heart, with a whisper or from the crash of hitting a wall in life—our work is to express it. These invitations from our deepest nature are a call that requires a response.

As it did for Diane, it takes both awareness and courage to break free of the gravitational pull of others' expectations and live an undivided life. Some historians date the beginning of the modern civil rights movement in the United States to a single day: December 1, 1955. That was the day when a seamstress in Montgomery, Alabama, refused to give up her seat to a white man who had just stepped on the bus. In that singular moment, she betrayed the expectations of her role, skin color, and society in order to no longer collude in her own diminishment. She was arrested and fined for violating a city ordinance, but her act of defiance helped catalyze a bus boycott and a movement that ended legal segregation in America.[8]

Sometimes when we use our solo voice, we're really part of a larger chorus. Rosa Parks's act of resistance did not come out of the blue. It germinated in the clarity of listening to the authentic voice of justice, but it was also strategic, skillful, and part of a larger chorus. Before that moment on the bus, Parks had been active for twelve years in the local NAACP chapter, serving as its secretary. The summer before her arrest, she had attended a ten-day training session at Tennessee's labor and civil rights organizing school, the Highlander Center, where she'd met an older generation of civil rights activists.

Using our voice doesn't always get us what we want or may bring only modest results. We can't control other's responses, but with some luck and some skill, we may speak a true word, and this can bring genuine liberation.

I worked as a therapist in a mental health clinic for several years. I saw all sorts of folks—young and old, chronic mental health clients and first-timers—all with a very wide range of concerns. Many were survivors of trauma, some suffered at the hands of difficult families, others struggled with fresh grief, unemployment, substance abuse, violence, and relationship difficulty, while some had existential concerns or were working toward greater satisfaction in life. I was surprised, however, to discover one characteristic that nearly everyone seemed to have in common, and it had to do with voice. Regardless of their education, articulation, or background, I came to see that the vast majority of clients were unskilled at a particular way of using their voices effectively and authentically. On this surface, this hardly seemed anything that we would term spiritual, but in time, I was struck by the profound transformation this had on the quality and creativity of their inner and outer lives, and thus it has a psychospiritual ring to it.

Some of us use aggressive communication that blames, demands, and dictates. We may use intimidation, anger, or control to get our needs met, which can set us against each other. On the other hand, a passive style (saying yes when we really mean no, not asking for what we need, going along so as not to rock the boat) tends to internalize discomfort rather than risk upsetting others. In other words the violence is largely turned inward. When passive, we might feel taken advantage of, misunderstood, resentful, powerless, and even hopeless. Aggression tries to dominate or push away whereas passivity succumbs and withdraws.

Some of us find ourselves swinging between these extremes, swallowing what has been dished out or complying with something we didn't want to do and then spontaneously busting out aggressively, reflecting the long-pent-up frustration and anger but that inevitably seems out of proportion for the incident ("Why did Mom scream at us when we asked her to pass the salt?"). Like rising water behind a dam, when the pressure gets to be too much, it overflows, bursts through, and usually does damage. We might end up feeling foolish and revert back to the passive stance until the next time we can't hold it back.

And then there is a passive-aggressive style, where rather than direct communication, a kind of guerilla war of resistance is under operation. Perhaps it's speaking with just enough sarcasm to get away with an indirect message, being manipulative, or gossiping behind the scenes. We might reluctantly agree to do something but purposefully not do it well or completely, dragging our feet or feigning forgetfulness. The result is often difficulty in living life with a real sense of freedom.

When dealing with tyrants, petty or otherwise, or with our own desires, we need to be skillful and courageous (like Rosa Parks), and we have to be in touch with that inner life (like Diane). When it comes to using our voice clearly, there is a middle way between aggressive and passive: assertiveness. Being assertive means that in some way that works for us, we are true to ourselves, expressing ourselves effectively and standing up for our point of view while simultaneously respecting the rights of others.

I remember when my children were very little and we lived in a friendly neighborhood where adults walked and jogged and children rode bikes, scooters, and whatever else they could get on. There were no sidewalks or shoulders on these roads, nor was it a through street, so drivers were never just passing through. There was a speed limit of twenty-five miles per hour, although naturally not always adhered to. One thing about having kids, which I learned in the first few minutes after the birth of my first child, was that the protective instinct in parents is intensely primal. It's so strong that I would defend my child at any cost. My primal protector would emerge when someone would speed in our neighborhood. Whether I was with my children or not, I found myself on more than one occasion running after cars, yelling at them to slow down. The protective instinct was so strong, and my indignation so justifiable, that I just went with it.

I remember the first time I caught up to a car. As soon as I got up to the driver's window, out of breath, I started yelling at him for being such an inconsiderate jerk and to slow down. What was the effect of my intervention? He drove away, speeding. My righteousness faded quickly, and I felt like an idiot. My exchange with him was so unskilled and unsatisfying. Not a proud moment. I wondered what would happen when we saw each other again. Any hope of a neighborly relationship disappeared with my attack, however much I might try to justify my action and remain legitimately concerned about the speeding.

Although I was not yet done chasing cars, I did realize that I had to find a better way to communicate my concern and, in my mind, protect my children and all the children of the universe from these evil speeders. I came up with a different strategy, one that realizes we are in this together. On my walks, I found myself rehearsing my new "speech."

So there I was, out walking by myself and, sure enough, a speeder barreled up the hill toward me, in a spot with the least visibility in the whole neighborhood. Without a thought, I stepped out into the road with my hand up in a clear signal to stop, like some righteous vigilante traffic cop. The driver slammed on his brakes and came to a hard stop. The teenager driving looked sincerely concerned as I walked around to his window. I took a deep breath, tried to stay in my heart so as not to do violence to him with my words, and this time explained that there are lots of kids in the neighborhood, including my own, and that I feared that a speeding car might not be able to see them or stop in time. I said firmly and with as much gravity as I could muster that I knew he would never want to hurt a child and that I would like him to watch his speed.

His response: "Oh, absolutely. I'm so sorry. I wasn't thinking."

I thanked him, we shook hands, and he pulled away very, very gradually.

We see each other again from time to time (I think he's visiting a girlfriend in the neighborhood) and, unlike the first guy, we wave to each other regularly. There is even a little smile and nod between us as if we're now on the same team. Our relationship was actually enhanced by the exchange. Neither of us feels like a jerk, and all the world's children are now safe.

Assertive, humane communication will save the children, the whales, the rainforest, and everything else we hold dear. Well, maybe not, but the effect is that it liberates our own voice and does so in a way that respects instead of diminishes the other person. Efforts toward nonviolent communication, restorative justice, and reconciliation recognize the power of change through authentic dialogue. Actually, maybe this will save the world, just a conversation at a time.

Originality is about living from the inside out—that is, staying in tune with our unique and original nature in the face of a world campaigning for our attention, staying in our hearts so as to remember the humanity in the other, and speaking a true word in our own way.

Originality
Living authentically from the inside out.

Quiz

For each statement or word, circle the number that describes you best.

(least like me)   1   2   3   4   5   (most like me)

I live true to myself	1	2	3	4	5
I am one of a kind.	1	2	3	4	5
I am creative.	1	2	3	4	5
I can say no with little difficulty.	1	2	3	4	5
I am assertive without being aggressive.	1	2	3	4	5

I consider myself to be authentic.	1	2	3	4	5
My actions are congruent with my insides.	1	2	3	4	5
I am honest with others.	1	2	3	4	5
I did it my way.	1	2	3	4	5
I am honest with myself.	1	2	3	4	5

Add up the circled numbers.   Total: _____

10–19	20–29	30–39	40–50
A trailhead	**More is possible**	**A good ally**	**A great strength**

....

PRACTICES

Cosmos Drawing

Draw an image representing your full development and growth in the form of a spiral. You may capture highlights (and lowlights) from your life, significant influences, threads, and so forth that have brought you to this moment. Use whatever form or materials you like to try to capture this.

If you are in a group, you may be willing to share a brief presentation of this with others.

Who Am I?

This experiment simply invites us to ask and answer the question, "Who am I?" This is done as a contemplative exercise, so take some breaths to become centered and relaxed before you begin. Then repeatedly ask the question, "Who am I?" and see what arises. If in a group, you can easily do this in pairs, taking turns saying, "I am_____." The listener is to be silently attentive, only breaking silence to pose the question, "Who are you?" if it seems helpful to do so. You might take turns for five minutes each. As we name these aspects of self, we have a chance to disidentify with them and move deeper. This self-inquiry, in the spirit of the Indian mystic Ramana Maharshi, is designed for us to expose and examine the supposed sources of the self until those conditioned aspects recede and the deeper aspects of who we are rise to awareness.[9]

Assertiveness

There are four general ways we might respond to a difficult confrontation: passive, aggressive, passive-aggressive, and assertive.

1. When we're passive, we might say yes when we mean no in order not to ruffle someone's feathers. Or we might not ask for what we want or say what we mean.

2. Aggressive communication typically blames the other person, attacks them in some way, and sounds something like this: "You are such a jerk for doing such and such to me." It often results in a hostile escalation or shuts off communication through a defense reaction.

3. As mentioned earlier, a passive-aggressive style is a kind of guerrilla war of resistance—speaking with just enough sarcasm to get away with it but without conveying a direct message, being manipulative, gossiping behind the scenes, not showing up on time for a meeting, and so forth. We might reluctantly agree to do something but not do it well or completely or we might drag our feet or feign forgetfulness and not do it at all.

4. The fourth alternative is assertive communication. This basically means that you ask for what you need or say what you mean in a direct and non-attacking way. This can be incredibly

freeing, empowering, and respectful, helping us find our voice with difficult people or situations.

Assertive communication tends to use "I" messages instead of "you" messages. The statement "I feel _____ when you do _____" is a simple template for asserting without the attack and corresponding defensiveness of a blaming "you" statement, such as "You are such a jerk; why did you do that?" "I" messages, like "I believe I was next in line," keep the focus on you, describe your needs and feelings, are nonjudgmental, succinct, and specific, and keep your relationship with the other open. "You" messages, like "You're unbelievably rude, cutting in front of me in line!" put the focus on the other, don't usually mention what you need or your feelings, blame, generalize, and diminish the other person, and strain the relationship. "I" statements can certainly sound formulaic, but they are a way to begin developing a skill. Beginning with this simple recipe can provide a foundation upon which to develop our own clear voice.

Imagine someone you want or need to be assertive with, perhaps recalling a specific incident or imagining an upcoming one. See the scene. Feel what it's like to be there, giving yourself enough time to fully imagine yourself in the picture. Construct an assertive statement or two and then role-play with a partner. The partner can spontaneously respond (not too harshly) as if they were the person you're being assertive with. Take some time to play this back and forth, continuing with new nonviolent assertion each time.

19

IMAGINING

Imagination will often carry us to worlds that never were.
But without it, we go nowhere.

—Carl Sagan

Imagination generally means the process of forming a mental image of something not actually present to the senses. It is a capacity of interior knowing. Picasso's way of bringing his unique perception and play to art and Martin Luther King Jr.'s imagining a world of justice and equality emerge out of their aesthetic and moral imaginations and take us beyond the information given and beyond the status quo. Imagination is like a laboratory of the mind where we can play out endless possibility. For our youngest friends, and perhaps our most creative, an imagined world is often the means to figure out how the world works and how to solve problems, invent new possibilities, and ponder mysteries.

Imagination is a vehicle for everything from artistic innovation to moral revelation. The activities of the mind that produced the inventions of da Vinci, the sonnets of Shakespeare, and declarations of liberty, and so on are not adequately explained through logic and learning. It is imagination, this rich interior way of knowing, that seems central to uncovering the *Good* (think: King), the *True* (think: Einstein) and the *Beautiful* (think: Picasso).

Even in the hard sciences, imagination is central for discovery and problem solving. Einstein framed its value in this way: "To raise new questions, new possibilities, to regard old problems from a new angle, requires creative imagination and marks real advance in science."[1] Einstein is sometimes held up as the model of rational thought, but his primary research procedure involved imagination. He imagined himself riding on a light beam.("What will happen once we reach the speed of light?") While this requires some logic to anticipate outcomes, it was primarily an act of imagination that led to his radical insights. Einstein's work, like so many other great scientists', was essentially conducted as thought experiments in the laboratory of his mind.[3] He considered this way of knowing so significant that he claimed "imagination is more important than knowledge."[2]

Jonas Salk, most famous for his creation of the polio vaccine, certainly had good training and skill, but it was a particular process of imagination, something he even had his own term for—"inverted perspective"—that he described as the key to unlocking insight. "I do not remember exactly at what point I began to apply this way of examining my experience, but very early in my life I would imagine myself in the position of the object in which I was interested." When he became a scientist he said, "I would picture myself as a virus, or a cancer cell, for example, and try to sense what it would be like to be either. I would also imagine myself as the immune system and I would try to reconstruct what I would do as an immune system engaged in combating a virus or cancer cell."[3] Through the insights gained he would then design laboratory experiments. "I would then know what questions to ask next . . . When I observed phenomena in the laboratory that I did not understand, I would also ask questions as if interrogating myself: 'Why would I do that if I were a virus or a cancer cell, or the immune system?' Before long, this internal dialogue became second nature to me."[4]

It is not only scientists who leverage imagination. One spring day in Harvard Yard, J. K. Rowling, author of the Harry Potter series, one of the bestselling book series of all time, offered this in her commencement speech to the university's newly minted graduates:

> Imagination is not only the uniquely human capacity to envision that which is not, and therefore the fount of all invention and innovation. In its arguably most transformative and revelatory capacity, it is the power that enables us to empathise with humans whose experiences we have never shared . . . Unlike any other creature on this planet, humans can learn and understand, without having experienced. They can think themselves into other people's minds, imagine themselves into other people's places.[5]

As it did for Einstein and Salk, King and Picasso, and Rowling, too, imagination builds a bridge between the known and the unknown. It enables us to ponder, play with, and generate new possibilities—to go beyond the information given, beyond the facts and the maps as they exist—in order to create new ways of seeing the world and create new worlds themselves. Few human qualities may be more expansive for our own life and powerful for our evolution as a species.

Two Roads Diverged

Pop quiz: How many different uses you can think of for a brick? When we come up with a handful of conventional uses—

building a house, a walkway, a fireplace—and not much more, we're using our memory but not much imagination. Our thinking converges on the familiar. When we play with the question a little differently, we might think of a brick as a weapon, as a musical instrument, as a step to help us reach the top shelf, a stop to keep the car from rolling back or a door from swinging closed, and more.

Questions like this were part of an initiative to improve the SAT test, led by Professor Robert Sternberg and funded in part by the College Board,[6] which prepares the oh-so-influential SAT, the test designed as a predictor of who is likely to succeed in college. It has a reasonable degree of correlation but is in no way definitively predictive. But Sternberg found quite a different approach to predicting college success, and this included captioning cartoons (much like the *New Yorker* caption contest) and imagining uses for bricks. Sternberg's model suggested that success in college and in life is understood and predicted better by three interactive kinds of intelligence: *analytic*, *practical*, and *creative*. The analytic measures the familiar verbal, quantitative, and figural skills. An assessment of practical intelligence might involve a story or video of a problem and then ask test takers to rate six proposed solutions from very good to very bad. Cartoon captioning, making up stories, and the like are, as you would guess, about the creative, and they turn out to be good predictors of success. But more important than *predicting* one's success is developing the capacities to *improve* the chance of success and cultivating imagination may help to do just that.

The capacity for divergent thinking is part of what makes up imagination's ability for supposition, flexibility, and inventiveness. Coming up with as many possible uses for a brick, blanket, or any other object is an attempt to activate divergent thinking. There are a few common practices that may help enhance our divergent-thinking capability. Whether in a group or working alone, brainstorming invites us to generate as many possibilities about a question or an issue without editing or judging its value or practicality. This imaginative idea generation done alone or in a group is a kind of adventure in thinking; we're just not sure where it will lead us. A bit further into the process, we might evaluate the relevance or practicality of an idea to pursue and then test out feasibility, perhaps converging on a best next step. But creativity often involves first and repeatedly the capacity to diverge from the given, the assumed, and the familiar.

Imagination is important because it enables us to break free of the pull of homogenization, our conditioned mind, and the bank of accepted knowledge in order to stretch in any moment into that diversity that is so central for technological, social, psychological, and spiritual growth and evolution. It allows us to reach beyond the known and our habits of mind to see in some fresh way.

Mind Over Matter

Imagination doesn't just help our minds diverge but can also lead us in particular directions. We know that imagining a scene in the mind can cause the body to respond as if the scene is actually happening in front of us. In passion or anxiety, relaxation or peace, everything from our heart rate to our brain waves follows the image. If you need confirmation of the phenomenon, just imagine for a moment someone you feel passionate about in one way or another and notice how the body-mind wants to follow the lead of the image with a shift in the body, feelings, and thoughts.

Essentially, the body-mind can't easily distinguish a real event from an imagined one, so visualizing what you want to have happen can actually set in motion the desired response in body, thoughts, or actions. When we talk about "mind over matter" or "creating our own reality," we're not just talking in the abstract. For example, in a wide range of studies, the visualization of improved health actually increases immune system response and thus relates to disease recovery and prevention, from colds to cancer. It has been used successfully in everything from decreasing the recurrence of cold sores to pain management to preoperative preparation. Although not so well established in research, there is also the question of whether imagining another's well-being (prayer) has some effect. Naturally, this between-person effect of imagination is a more controversial, more complex phenomenon and more difficult to measure. Although given what we know about nonlocal influence and interpersonal neuroscience, we shouldn't think this reach of imagination is unreasonable or naïve.

In addition to impacting our health, we learn from great performers, whether athletes, musicians, or others who have created remarkable success in their lives, that they often use their imagination for a special kind of practice called positive mental rehearsal to achieve their stunning success. Like many great performers, Greg Louganis, winner of four gold medals in Olympic diving, trained his muscles and movements with great discipline and commitment. But he also trained his mind. As part of his practice, he would take some deep breaths, close his eyes, get relaxed, and then imagine himself walking toward the pool, climbing up the ladder, and stepping out onto the diving platform. He would take a deep breath and then visualize himself pushing off into the air, feeling every rotation and the pull of gravity, seeing the perfect line of his body before breaking the surface, feeling the impact, tasting the water, hearing the crowd cheer after coming up for air, and feeling the deep satisfaction of a perfect dive.[7] When the actual event took place, he'd already been there in his imagination.

Positive mental rehearsal, whether directed toward a flute performance or a math test, trains the mind to serve our goals. The mind has already experienced the success imaginatively and thus may be primed to repeat it when we get in the actual situation. Imagination does not replace studying or practice, but it can take performance from mediocrity to mastery.

This power of imagination has been used to help improve another kind of performance. In several studies, stroke victims who were left with impairment of their arms were given mental practice along with standard physical therapy. After brief relaxation, patients were asked to imagine a task that required their affected arm, like reaching for, grasping, and lifting a cup to their mouth. Upon conclusion of the practice (two or three times a week for six to ten weeks, depending on the particular study), participants who practiced the visualization technique showed significantly improved function over those who only had the therapy or the therapy and a placebo activity, and fMRI results also showed changes in brain activation in parts of the brain corresponding to improved arm functioning.[8] Imagination literally changed the brain.

Real Imagination

While imagination is often described as a function of the mind, James Hillman suggested that rather than the mind being primary, it is imagination that is so.[9] Rather than an operation of the mind, the mind is a fantasy of the imagination. We do not need to resolve this in our own minds (or imaginations), but it makes the point that our presuppositions about our minds are, well, imagined.

Imagination is usually conceived of as an individual, subjective, idiosyncratic experience. Our daydreams, fantasies, and creative imaginings are thought of as generated from our own mind. But there is another understanding of imagination. The Islamic scholar Henry Corbin spoke of imagination not only as a kind of personal fiction but also as an objective and universal realm that he referred to as the *mundus imaginalis*, "the world of the image."[10] This imaginal world is not one of individual fantasy but instead a universal world considered as real as our daily physical existence. When we strive to bring some deep expression into form, we are trying to capture that other realm and represent it in this one. A great piece of art or a heroic tale like *Star Wars*, for example, may capture universal archetypal themes or images that resonate with us in some deep way. These are ancient and enduring themes repeated over and over, from Broadway to Hollywood. The universal myths and symbols across cultures are signs pointing toward this other world. In some moments, we recognize something that both expands us and brings us toward some sense of the familiar, toward what is universal.

In this sense, imagination attempts to explicate the implicate order, to borrow David Bohm's words.[11] Imagination does not create image or art out of nothing; it reaches in to perceive and then reveal; it lifts a veil. Author Evelyn Underhill, who studied the lives of Christian mystics, understood such knowing in this way:

> [The artist] by means of veils and symbols . . . must interpret his free vision, his glimpse of the burning bush, to other men. He is the mediator between his brethren and the divine, for art is the link between appearance and reality.[12]

This is the power of great art, of heroic story, of symbol and image; they present a faint image of this universal realm. In this line of thinking, one's ability to recognize and represent that other realm relates to what we call genius. Underhill described the underlying process:

This intuition of the Real lying at the root of the visible world and sustaining its life . . . *must* be present if these arts are to justify themselves as heightening forms of experience. . . . That "life enhancing" power which has been recognized as the supreme quality of good painting, has its origin in this contact of the artistic mind with the archetypal—or . . . the transcendental—world: the underlying verity of things.[13]

Emanuel Swedenborg, the influential eighteenth-century Swedish scientist, philosopher, and theologian, wrote about the ancient metaphysical law of correspondence. He understood that all things are basically stepped-down manifestations of higher realms. And when we reach and capture a glint of the universal in some way, we grow soul. In this view, the imaginal world serves as an intermediary realm that joins the transcendental and archetypal with the terrestrial. Imagination builds a bridge between these two worlds and carries us between them, thus serving as both path and vehicle between worlds.

Whether we understand imagination as our individual image-making capability or as tapping some underlying reality, its most fundamental function is to take us beyond where we are and what we can easily see, stretching us into new possibilities, new understanding, and maybe even new friends.

Imaginary Friends

Deep into one Sunday afternoon, my daughter Haley, nine at the time, had a school report to write on a significant black figure in history. She chose Mahalia Jackson, the great gospel singer who had been a powerful voice for civil rights during her lifetime. Over the previous two weeks, Haley found a book and a couple of brief articles on the singer's life. Now late Sunday afternoon, she was trying to finish typing this report. However, she was not much of a typist. This was, after all, her first real paper of this sort, so this was a slow and sometimes painful process.

As I walked into the room where she was working, it was easy to feel the tension and imagine her teeth grinding away as she pecked at the computer keyboard. She had worked pretty hard on the paper and had done a respectable job so far. Most importantly, she seemed to have learned a few things about Jackson's life and about writing a paper. But as time and patience were running out, it had reached the point that the goal was simply to finish the thing, which was due the next morning. Frustration was setting in, and she was still in need of a conclusion and desperately in need of a mood shift. I suggested that she take a short break to clear her head. Haley, more than ready for any distraction from her typing, agreed.

Fifteen or twenty minutes later, she hopped downstairs.

"How ya doing?" I asked.

"Good. I just saw Mahalia," she announced matter-of-factly.

"You did?" I said, not sure of what she was telling me.

"I was kinda surprised that I saw her, but it was easy to find her," she said.

She then started to tell me about what Mahalia said to her. I stopped her in mid-sentence and quickly grabbed a pen and paper so I could take dictation. She proceeded to tell me a wide range of seemingly intimate information about Mahalia Jackson that I could not find in the materials she had read (I checked).

After five or ten minutes of relaying this rich material, Haley said that Mahalia had wanted to tell her a "main thing" about her life:

Mahalia said that her life was filled with three things: joy, happiness, and fear. She felt joy that black people *and* white people were giving her a lot of attention. She felt happy that she was able to do just what she wanted to do, to sing her [gospel] music and sing about love and God. She also said that she was afraid—afraid because she was getting so popular and helping black people and white people to come together that some people would not like it and might try to hurt her or hurt each other.

These specific ideas were not at all explicit in the materials she had read. But they seemed to capture Mahalia Jackson's life with riveting clarity and directness.

After I finished taking dictation, Haley then added some of this information as a conclusion to her report. She suddenly had a new sense of intimacy and excitement for this woman and for her project. Because of her very personal "chat," she now felt like she really knew Mahalia firsthand. A project that had been sliding toward drudgery now became one of inspiration, especially fitting for the nature of Mahalia Jackson's life, whose voice inspired so many.

I asked Haley how she'd gotten in touch with Mahalia. She answered, "It was easy; I just got quiet [relaxed] on my bed and asked my angel for help. Then in my mind I went to www .mahaliajackson.com, and there she was, standing right in front of me. We talked, and she told me about her life."[14]

Did Haley meet with the consciousness of Mahalia Jackson? Was she tapping into the cosmic internet? Or was this her internal fantasy, a clever way for her imagination to connect the dots of her understanding?

I don't know, but I do know that her imagination provided the bridge or portal that opened to a world of fresh understanding as it has for those great imaginers among us. Perhaps all it takes is a willingness to play in our imaginations to reach another world and, in so doing, grow the soul of this one.

Imagining
Imagining builds a bridge between the known
and the unknown.

Quiz

For each statement or word, circle the number that describes you best.

(least like me)　　1　　　　2　　　　3　　　　4　　　　5　　(most like me)

I can generate plenty of ideas.	1	2	3	4	5
I am creative.	1	2	3	4	5
I think outside the box.	1	2	3	4	5
I can easily imagine new ways of seeing something.	1	2	3	4	5
I am good at daydreaming all sorts of possibilities.	1	2	3	4	5
I can make things up.	1	2	3	4	5
I know the world is more than meets the eye.	1	2	3	4	5
I like stories.	1	2	3	4	5
Right now, I could vividly imagine being elsewhere.	1	2	3	4	5
I sense under the surface of things.	1	2	3	4	5

Add up the circled numbers.　　　　　　　　Total: _____

10–19	20–29	30–39	40–50
A trailhead	**More is possible**	**A good ally**	**A great strength**

PRACTICES

A Wisdom Walk

Guided imagery taps the symbolic aspects of the contemplative mind. You might have a partner slowly read the following instructions or record them yourself, being sure to give yourself time to gently and safely find your way. Take some deep breaths, settle into your seat, close your eyes, and relax.

Imagine yourself in a comfortable scene in nature. Feel the soft breeze on your face, notice the smells, the temperature, the color of the sky, the feel of the ground beneath you, and the feeling in your body. Take a few moments to be still and sense all that you can in this pleasant and comfortable scene.

Off in one direction is a well-worn path leading into the distance toward some woods. Follow the path, continuing to notice the texture of the ground underfoot, the sounds near and far, the light, the vegetation, the wildlife, and the smells as you move farther and farther along. The path narrows as it winds its way deeper and deeper into the woods. You cross a brook, pausing to listen to its babble and feel the cool water, and then continue along the path. Soon you emerge from the woods and into a bright hilly meadow. A magnificent old tree stands on the hillside. Walk to it and be with this tree for a few moments, appreciating its majesty. The tree may also have a message for you; listen to and feel its offering. Note the words, images, and feelings that arise from this.

Continuing on around the hillside to the far side, you discover that it becomes rocky, almost cliff-like. Among the rocks is a doorway. You approach and enter, surprised to find a few steps leading to a gently lit curved room filled with other doorways. If you like, you can pick one and look inside. You don't need to go in. You can just take a few moments in silence to observe from the opened doorway.

When you're ready, consider if there is any lesson or knowledge offered. When it's time to leave, close the inner door, exit the stone chamber the way you came in, back out onto the hillside, stopping back at the tree for a moment, listening, perhaps. Then follow the path back through the woods, across the brook, and to the pleasant place where you started the journey. Know that you can return to this place and to anywhere you visited on your own whenever you would like.

Were you able to find a place to start with? Did the tree have anything for you? What did you see through the doorway in the curved room? Was there anything unexpected (scary, fun, confusing, helpful)? What did you take away?

This can be a powerful experience for some. In a group, it is important to follow up with anyone who seems unusually agitated. For a lighter version, you can skip the doorway and simply linger with the tree. Other alternative travels include journeying to a wise woman or man, climbing a mountain (perhaps representing some struggle), visiting a special or sacred site, or any number of other images that can tug on our inner knowing.

Brainstorm

Brainstorming involves simply generating a list of ideas in a creative, unstructured, off-the-cuff manner. Rather than concentrating on a single answer, the point is to get as many divergent ideas as possible in a short period of time. There are no demands of practicality; they can be silly or outrageous. Piggybacking off other ideas or using one idea to stimulate other ideas is a key part of brainstorming. During the brainstorming process, all ideas are worth recording, and no idea is disregarded or criticized. There is no editing or discussion of the merit of an idea but simply a continuing bouncing off one idea after another. There may be lags and then fast flows. Be sure to stay with it during the slow moments—that is, don't bail out too soon, as new ideas will come along. After a long list of divergent ideas is generated, you can go back and review the ideas to critique their value or merit if you want. Identify a topic, question, or problem and begin. Even the process of choosing a topic could be done through brainstorming.

Divergent Thinking

Multiplicity: How many uses can you think of for a brick? A book? A bottle? Keep going . . .

Make-believe: Make up a story for the number 34,871.

Magic: If you had three magic wishes that had the power to change things, what three things would you change?

Mind Mapping

Mind mapping involves putting ideas in the form of a visual map or picture that shows the relationships among these ideas. Instead of simply compiling a list, use the space on the page to move these ideas into different locations, varying the shape, size, or color, playing with the ways they are connected to or related to one another. This creates a visual "map" of the topic that can be used to develop the topic further. You may need to start a fresh page once you see new patterns.

Writing Freely

Write without stopping for five to ten minutes. Then read what you've written. Pick a line, word, idea, or reaction that stands out to you as wanting to be elaborated or explored. Write again for another three to six minutes. Again, read what you've written, noting what seems surprising, unexpected, curious, or important to you. Write again for another three to six minutes. If you are with others, share out loud an excerpt (anything from a sentence to a paragraph) from your last bit of writing, and share how it sounds to you as well. If you are working with a partner, you can ask what line or word or overall sense seemed to leap out.

20

CALLING

The place God calls you to is the place where your deep gladness
and the world's deep hunger meets.

—Frederick Buechner

It is our nature to find or create meaning. The ancient creation
myths from around the world try to put a face on the mysterious origins of the universe as a way of making sense of the forces
holding sway over life. Similarly, the stories we make about our
own lives (where we came from, who we are, what we do) are
our own creation stories. We tend to live according to them,
as they provide a center our own meaning and identity orbit
around. Life feels worth living when we have meaning, whether
it's when we have work to accomplish or something or someone
to care for or who cares for us.

For the mind, meaning is a necessity, like food or water. It
gives us reason to get out of bed and move forward. Elie Wiesel
was fifteen when he and others in his small village in what is
now Romania were deported to the Nazi concentration camps.
Auschwitz, Buna, Buchenwald, and Gleiwitz became his new

addresses. His mother and younger sister were killed early on, but Elie and his father survived to see horror upon horror over the next nearly two years. His father died in Buchenwald shortly before its liberation in 1945.

Even having lived through it, Wiesel had difficultly believing that what had happened was possible. Since breaking his initial vow of silence, his dozens of books, a Nobel Peace Prize, and his vast and steady teaching testifies not only to those horrors but also to the meaning that organizes his life. "[T]o remain silent and indifferent is the greatest sin of all," captures Wiesel's driving principle for his life's work of bearing witness and testifying.[1] He came to understand a vision for his life, he saw reality accurately, and he made a commitment to the life he was to lead.

The lives of so many wise souls seem to suggest that they felt not only meaning but, like Wiesel, a sense of meaningful direction for their lives—a calling. It's not uncommon for folks to reflect on life and find an enduring thread their life seemed woven around. Mother Teresa's calling from the time she was a young girl was toward the *Good*, we might say, to serve the poorest of the poor. Einstein's quest was toward some understanding of the way things work, to find what is true. His life seemed to be drawn always forward by his imagination and his quest to know. Martha Graham, whom *Time* magazine called the greatest dancer of the twentieth century, described the quality and even inevitability of a calling:

> There is a vitality, a life force, an energy, a quickening that is translated through you into action, and because there is only one of you in all of time, this expression is unique. And if you block it, it will never exist through any other medium and it will be lost. The world will not have it. It is not your business to determine how good it is nor how valuable nor how it

compares with other expressions. It is your business to keep
it yours clearly and directly, to keep the channel open. You do
not even have to believe in yourself or your work. You have to
keep yourself open and aware to the urges that motivate you.
Keep the channel open. . . . No artist is pleased. [There is] no
satisfaction whatever at any time. There is only a queer divine
dissatisfaction, a blessed unrest that keeps us marching and
makes us more alive than the others.[2]

Like Graham, our creative friends tell us that their lives
seemed to be nudged along by some current and that they felt
adrift when they were out of the channel. We search for direction in life, that compass, sign, or opening that shows us a path
or next step. Do we have a purpose, something we're here for? It
feels like it some days when work seems worthwhile, or there is
an important connection with someone, or we seem to be getting somewhere or helping someone. But some days you have to
wonder, are we just going through the motions? Is there really
something to this?

I see three general ways that we try to make sense of this question of direction or calling. The first is the acorn theory. The acorn
already has within it the programming for what it is to be, and
given the right conditions, it will grow over time into a big oak.
Applied to us, the acorn theory implies not only that our DNA
predisposes us toward a certain height and hair color but that our
"soul's code," as psychologist James Hillman calls it, has a message
for us to hear and follow about our calling.[3] We can make sense of
this as a gift from the divine or as a duty to fulfill, or perhaps as the
consequence of karma, some seeds sown in a previous life. Whatever the source, the notion is that we are already programmed
toward certain directions. Our work is to hear that call and live it
out in order, we might say, to make our life come true.

The second idea has to do with chance. The ancients thought the Fates might be playing with us, that the gods spun the wheel of fortune to see what our lot would be. This implies not so much that we have a calling to fulfill but that life is a roll of the dice. Today we think less about the Fates and more about statistical probability, random chance, or just plain luck. Through this lens, our lot is largely beyond our ability to control or direct it very much. Stuff happens. What will we do with what we're given?

The third idea is that this is our life to choose. We have free will and agency to be able to imagine and create the life we will. Whether or not we get out of bed in the morning and brush our teeth is our choice. Even how we feel about our day ahead or the diagnosis of disease we've been given may be our choice in the sense that the meaning we make of something can shape our thoughts, feelings, health, and actions.

Based on how our wise friends described their own experiences, and taking into account that the theme of integration that is present throughout this book, let's consider "calling" as a mixture of

- seed—that which is already within us;
- circumstance—the life and the situation that's given; and
- choice—what we commit to and create with what we're given.

What Are We Here to Give?

The task here seems to be not only to uncover who we are but along with it to find (and create) what we are here to do and perhaps what we have to offer. We might even say that the job is not just to be "good" but to be good for something. What are we here to give? In some traditions, our lives are said to come with visions, a purpose, a sacred contract. We have something unique that is ours to offer the world, whether it is our particular expression of kindness or a special way we see the world, like an Einstein or Picasso. The challenge, we're told, is for us to find and align ourselves with the tug of our calling. Sometimes, we hear a religious person speak of a calling that led them to minister in some way. But all life purposes (from becoming a schoolteacher to being a caring friend to dancing our dance like Martha Graham) are callings. It means that we have come here to contribute to the world in some unique way.

Purpose does not typically come as a preset career or vocation. It has more to do with certain qualities, characteristics, capacities, or ways of seeing the world. Any number of careers or situations may allow us to express purpose. Clues to calling are more about the way we are able to listen and empathize with another person, for example, or about the way we bring delight into a room, have an ability to be calm in a crisis, or see the big picture in a complex situation. It may come from the way we see the world (Picasso) or the way we use our imagination (Einstein), our body (Graham), or our words (Wiesel). It arrives as a vague tug, a sense of injustice (like it did for Gandhi and King), a tragedy, a vague recognition, a sense of stirring, meaning, or an enduring fantasy. Callings are often identified in retrospect ("When I look back on my life, even though my jobs changed dramatically, I see a theme that ran all the way through").

Sometimes the calling or talent is so natural that it is hard for us to see it by ourselves. It may take an ally to recognize our uniqueness and reflect it back to us. At eighteen years old, my friend was both curious and beginning to get a little worried about what direction she should take in her life. She has an uncanny ability to get along with others and to brighten a room with her presence. Her keen sensitivity and what we would recognize as social and emotional intelligence make her one of the most talented "people persons" I know. She also has plenty of other talents and interests. I asked her what she thought her "best thing" was. She said that she really had no idea but then thought maybe it was being artistic. I think she does have a good eye for beauty and maybe this is indeed one of the ingredients for her calling (we'll see where her life leads), but it doesn't take much to see how natural and powerful her ability with people is. Sometimes someone sees something in us, encourages us, and reflects it back to us, helping us see ourselves in a new way.

Sometimes, the shape of our purpose begins to form very early and is organized especially around some talent. More typically, it takes time for a calling to ripen. We catch little glimmers in the form of a vague tug, anger at some injustice, an obsession, a passion, a curious affinity for someone or something, or perhaps a fantasy. Eleanor Roosevelt had a very gray and angry childhood. Both her parents, who were largely unavailable to her to begin with, died before she was nine. She was withdrawn, hostile, and isolated, yet she kept a fantasy alive that provided the clue to her purpose. She wrote, "I carried on a day-to-day story, which was the realist thing in my life."[4] Eleanor's story involved her imagining that she was the mistress of her father's large household and a companion in his travels. James Hillman described her imaginatively rich inner life:

> [Her imagination's] caring and managerial content was purposeful preparation for the dutiful life she would later live. The fantasies were invented by her calling and were indeed more realistic in their orientation than her daily reality. . . .
>
> Imagination acted as a teacher, giving instruction for the large ministering tasks of caring for the welfare of a complex family, of a crippled husband, of the state of New York as the Governor's wife, the United States as its first lady, and even

of the United Nations. Her attending to "Father" was a pre-liminary praxis into which she could put her call, her huge devotion to the welfare of others.[5]

The suggestion is that her calling was represented and kept alive until the days that she might move into her roles as an adult. Have your own fantasies at times served as a clue for identity, creativity, and calling?

As we posited earlier in this chapter, calling emerges in some mysterious alchemical mixture of seed, circumstance, and choice. The purpose seems not only given but it is constructed, and it seems we must assume responsibility for creating our expression of it. Purpose is a process, an ongoing progressive revelation crafted and clarified by our choices each day. Life seems to work so exquisitely that it provides the outer situations and inner curiosities that offer us just what we need. The lives of figures like Eleanor Roosevelt seem to suggest that when we say yes to our calling, the world says yes back. Synchronicities abound, the world seems somehow in sympathy with us. Life does not necessarily become all sunshine and ease, and we do not always get what we want, but we do seem to get what we need in a way that is deeply right.

When she was eight years old, Soraida Salwala and her father came upon an injured elephant in her native Thailand. With grave concern, she asked her father where they could take the elephant for help. He answered that there was no such place. The elephant died suffering, and the tiny girl suffered right along with the giant. Thirty years later, she amassed a team ranging from veterinarians to truck drivers to financiers to form the first hospital in Thailand devoted to elephants. She still suffers along with her very large friends, but now she can help with that suffering.[6] Seed, circumstance, and the great power of her choice created an outlet for her calling. Pursuing what we love or keeping alive a rich fantasy or dream may be preparation for the day when the calling comes to life in the world.

Our callings and visions are not static but alive, like a plant. A little bud here, a branch there, some entirely new spouts propagating nearby. They can grow and meander into fresh shapes throughout a lifetime. Maybe the heartwood of the impulse feels the same. "I had to find a way to make the world more beautiful," Miss Rumphius tells us in a children's book by the same name.[7] She ends up sprinkling her neighborhood with lupine seeds and telling beautiful stories to her granddaughter and her friends. Perhaps there is a sense of being a teacher in some way or a healer who finds an elephant to nurse, or maybe we naturally bring tender compassion and hope to those who need it, without even being fully aware of this as our gift.

We might say calling involves becoming most fully the person we are to be. Our life sounds through us, through our voice, our creative expression in the adventure of our life. Sounding through has to do with the difference between

- Being good and good for something;
- Being comfortable and being authentic; and
- Speaking someone else's voice and finding our own.

This doesn't seem to have much to do with fame or fortune as a goal, but more to do with touching into this authentic calling, drawing our life from the deep place, and making choices that align us with those currents in our own unique way. To tap our calling is to be a full person, essentially to be one "through whose life greater life resounds."[8]

But this can be tricky business. Sometimes the call just seems too big for us, stirs up too much, or we're just overwhelmed by the energy of this "greater life" and the responsibility that it implies. In the Old Testament, Jonah received a pretty demanding call from God. His call involved telling the inhabitants of the city of Nineveh, apparently not a very nice place, that their city was to be destroyed as punishment for their wicked ways. But the contact with God was overwhelming for Jonah, and instead of answering the call, he avoided it, traveling to Jaffe and then sailing off to the city of Tarshish to "avoid the presence of the Lord." God wasn't about to let him off the hook so easily and created a huge storm that threatened the ship and eventually led to Jonah being thrown overboard in order to spare his shipmates, only to be miraculously saved by being swallowed by a huge fish. He spent the next three days and three nights in prayer and petition, and decided that following the call might be the better option than staying in the fish. And so he was spit out and took the next steps to respond to his call.

Psychologist Abraham Maslow explored peak experiences— moments of highest happiness and profundity in one's life. Maslow knew that these powerful moments could serve as a life-changing call for some but not everyone, and he wondered why. "On the whole, these good aftereffects are easy enough to understand. What is more difficult to explain is the absence of discernible aftereffect in some people."[9] Eventually Maslow provided an explanation about why peak experiences may not lead to transformation. He called this the Jonah Complex and described it as the "fear of one's own greatness."[10] Sometimes we might wonder whether we're big enough for the life that's calling us.

Deep to Deep

Calling is not decided with the use of the Hogwarts Sorting Hat, directing us to the next destination ("Gryffindor!"). In some traditional societies, we're to go to the wilderness to search for the vision that will help direct us. Then we're to bring it back so that others can help us make sense of it and perhaps give us a new name, responsibilities, and privileges. Indigenous rites of passage are especially about next steps. Traditional rites in which visions are sought are about asking, "What's calling you forward?" We go to find that place beyond our yards to try to read the clues, listen for the still, small voice, and await the vision or the sign. This is an attempt to push distractions to the side in order to feel the gravity of the things that seem to live deepest within us. Thoreau explained it this way: "I went to the woods because I wished to live deliberately, to front only the essential facts of life, and see if I could not learn what it had to teach, and not, when I came to die, discover that I had not lived."[11]

The wilderness has depth: deep woods, deep sea, deep challenge, deep love, deep loss. Wilderness is alive, real, resonant, authentic. The remarkable thing, the thing we too often miss, is that the wilderness is close by, right here, right now, beneath the surface. The wilderness is inside as much as outside.

Wilderness isn't prepackaged or gated. It isn't a reconstituted juice box; it's just juicy. It is in everything, from that difficult person, to that look within, to speaking a true word. The wilderness is unconfined and unpredictable. It is risky, and it makes us vulnerable. It is precisely in that vulnerability, those constructive risks, those painful foibles, and confrontations with that difficult person or maybe ourselves that is as much wilderness as anything. We just have to meet it, deep to deep.

Sometimes the deep is felt as pain, like the little girl from Thailand who befriended elephants and now heals their suffering as an adult. Other times it is a bright signal that lets us know when we're in alignment with some calling. In other moments, it's the discomfort when we're off the mark.

Joseph Campbell used the phrase "follow your bliss" to describe a compass for living our life.[12] This was not meant as an excuse for superficial self-indulgence ("That feels good, so I'll do it."). It means following those currents within that bring deep fulfillment and deep satisfaction, even when it may be difficult or involve pain or sacrifice. When we find and align with these deep currents, our lives are empowered in a profound way. When we find what we really love to do, we find our way. Our lives become organized from the inside out, and we tap some authentic power. Pleasure and the relief of pain drive us to get nourishment, have sex, and seek security. Joy, justice, creativity, and deep fulfillment are telltales that drive us toward our greater life—the *Good*, the *True*, the *Beautiful*, and the creative. When we think of individuals living out a calling in some way, it often seems to be good not only for them but especially for the world. With practice, we see the consequences and learn the different feelings one gets from making choices from bliss, from that feeling of rightness and alignment, rather than from the feeling derived from more superficial indulgence or ego-driven aspiration.

Sometimes it's gladness that shows us the way, and sometimes it's pain, but sometimes we just seem stuck in confusion, a dark night of the soul where we seem to lose our way. Most of us have some sense of this at one time or another. We find ourselves without a sense of meaning or connection in what we're doing. We seem lost and alone, discouraged, confused, and afraid. It's so universal that it just seems to be part of the game. But as mentioned earlier, St. John used a particular word to describe the phenomenon. He didn't say it was sinful or soggy, bad or broken, although these times can be discouraging, frustrating, and anxiety inducing. He used the term *obscura*, meaning "obscured, cloudy, foggy."[13] It is just hard to see our way clearly sometimes. His solution to these dark nights was basically not to get too bent out of shape but instead to try to stay awake in our fogginess, to try and remember what's important and wait and work gently for the time when clarity returns and the fog lifts. We try new possibilities, ask for help, talk to people we trust, and especially try to listen and clarify our own perception so we may begin to see that next step a little clearer, a glimpse of direction at the edge of our wilderness and vulnerability. Writer Wendell Berry framed this whole dilemma for us:

> It may be that when we no longer know what to do we have come to our real work and that when we no longer know which way to go we have begun our real journey. The mind that is not baffled is not employed. The impeded stream is the one that sings.[14]

What Am I to Learn?

As soon as we land here, we're primed to recognize some important things. Within moments of birth, babies turn their eyes toward their mothers' faces and voices but not so much toward strangers', presumably indicating recognition. We learn what that sharp "No!" means, and we learn whom we can trust. In time, we learn to use our words, tie our shoes, and what friendship is about, and we find a place to pee that isn't in our pants. Before long, we're bundled off to school for most of the day and, if we live in a society that is wealthy enough, we spend years upon years being educated so that we can, if we are lucky, get more education. We learn on the job, we learn how to love, and with a little luck, we learn how to bounce when we've fallen. We learn to take care of others, and as our time runs out, we learn how to let others take care of us. We learn what really matters. It seems that our whole life orbits around learning.

Calling has two legs. The first, we might say, is what we're here to give. The second is what we're here to learn—chemistry and Chaucer to be sure, but also maybe other orders of lessons as well: courage, delight, the right use of power, or maybe patience and kindness. We may learn big lessons, such as

- Greed's lesson is often generosity and trust in abundance.
- Restlessness and irritation invite a deep breath toward patience.
- The antidote to judgment is often tolerance for others and for oneself.
- Hostility opens an opportunity for forgiveness.

And along the road, there are all sorts of "little" lessons, such as learning to tell the truth, the impact of kindness, or how to say no. When life is seen not so much as a competition with others that leads toward success or failure, or as divine punishment or reward from the gods, and instead as an opportunity for learning (earth school), it becomes easier to accept and even welcome what life brings us. This small shift in perspective can have a huge effect on our resilience. Being cut from the basketball team, having a friend move away, or being hurt in some way is not failure or punishment but an opportunity to learn. We are healed, transformed, and made stronger by what we learn from a situation, especially a difficult one. The victim becomes a survivor when they learn from the ordeal. We heal not to be safe once and for all, but so that we may be wounded again in some new way and learn from it some new lesson.

When she was four years old, my friend Lynn had a dream that she was in a very big and special chair. The message was that she was so special, even though her life at the time was very difficult. Nine people who seemed more like angels to her came to her through a mist of glittering light. Each brought this girl a gift. The first offered art and music, which have become so nourishing to her. The next brought love, the next kindness. In time, the last gift was presented: it was pain. Lynn was confused and couldn't understand why pain would be a gift. "Why are you going to hurt me when you tell me I'm special?" she asked. They explained that through pain you learn lessons; pain is actually a gift of learning. "You'll see," they said. And so she has. Through those ups and downs in life, we have a chance to learn what matters most.

Ultimately, calling involves a dialogue; a call requires a response. Calling is revealed not simply through a rite of passage, a grand vision, or some revelation but especially as a daily encounter with the world. The call asks us to pay attention, feel our hearts, follow our dreams, be ourselves, speak the truth, engage the adventure. The stillness of presence, the sensitivity to what we feel and what we love, listening for guidance, and the courage to take action—all enable our calling. When we meet the world deeply from that place deep within, we learn to see and to be, as Black Elk said, in a sacred manner.[15] And when we do, we make our life come true.

Calling
What are we here to give and what are we here to learn?

Quiz

For each statement or word, circle the number that describes you best.
(least like me)   1   2   3   4   5   (most like me)

I have a clear sense of my calling.   1   2   3   4   5
I am aware of my talents.   1   2   3   4   5

I have a good sense of what I am here to learn.	1	2	3	4	5
My life has meaning.	1	2	3	4	5
I know what I would put myself on the line for.	1	2	3	4	5
My life has purpose.	1	2	3	4	5
Life is about learning.	1	2	3	4	5
I stay focused on what's important in life.	1	2	3	4	5
I give energy each day to what is sacred to me.	1	2	3	4	5
I follow my dreams.	1	2	3	4	5

Add up the circled numbers.   Total: _____

10–19	20–29	30–39	40–50
A trailhead	**More is possible**	**A good ally**	**A great strength**

....

PRACTICES

Journaling a Future

Consider the following series of journaling questions. Give yourself uninterrupted time and a contemplative mind-set to consider each in a free-written answer.

1. Look at yourself from the outside as if you were looking at another person. What are the three or four most important challenges or tasks in your life at the moment?
2. What are you good at? What are all the things you love to do? What are all the experiences that make you who you are?
3. What three or four important aspirations, areas of interest, or undeveloped talents would you like to place more focus on?
4. What about your current situation frustrates you most?

5. What are your most vital sources of energy? What do you love and love to do?

6. What gets in your way or holds you back? Describe two or three situations where you noticed an inner voice of judgment, fear, or doubt emerge.

7. Watch yourself from above. What you are doing? Do your actions serve your aspirations?

8. Look upon your situation as if you were another wise soul looking back from the future on your life. What advice would you offer to yourself today?

9. What would you like to create, manifest, and bring to life? What is your vision and your intention for the next few years for your personal, social, and work lives?

10. What would you have to let go of to bring your intentions into reality? What needs to drop away; that is, what behaviors, thoughts, and people need to be shed?

11. What in your current life are the seeds for the growth you want to create?

12. Who can help bring your vision to life? Who might be your allies as you move forward?

13. What steps could you take to bring this intention into reality? What practical steps could you take this week?

14. Will you take these steps? If not, try question 6 and 8 again. See if something new emerges.[16]

Mandala

For some, a circle can symbolically represent one's self, a shape seeking wholeness in some way. For this exercise you'll need paper and colored pencils or the like.

First, simply draw a circle to serve as a mandala, a sacred circle. While in a contemplative mind-set, allow whatever imagery comes to mind to flow onto the page, using the shapes and colors you are drawn to. There is no right or wrong to this—just an opportunity to see what emerges. Give yourself some time to stay with this, perhaps 15 minutes or so. Just allow the images to come on their own, letting your hand lead the way. There are all sorts of symbolic ways you could take this up (for example, thinking about the outer circle as your outside life and the center as your inner). Or you could split the circle into four quadrants representing different aspects of your life, perhaps even the four virtues. In the image you might notice two sides of you that are seeking integration or any number of other ideas. The point is to allow the images to spring forth from within you.

See what this has to offer. If you have an opportunity, you may want to share this with others in a safe environment and see what they notice about it. What stands out? Where does this point? What surprises you? What is missing?

Sacred Work

Can you devote part of the day to activity that is sacred to you? What would that look and feel like? How can you make your work that you must do sacred? Explain how this might occur.

A Difference

Once you've relaxed and settled your mind and body, ask yourself, "What kind of person do I want to be? What personal qualities do I want to possess?" Sit silently with these questions. Then imagine that these qualities are becoming more and more yours. Now ask yourself, "What can I offer the world? How can I make a difference?" Once again, stay with these questions. Then imagine that this is realized. As a final step, make the wish that all beings are fulfilled and find their own callings.

LAST WORDS

How do we find our way and help others find theirs? How do we live in those deepest currents that bring life meaning? These were the questions we began with. For me, recognizing these universal virtues—these medicines and powers—helps me assume responsibility for my life in a way that I could not do without them. They help give us the power to risk opening our hearts and not be destroyed in the process, to be steady in the midst of pain and uncertainty, to see from a greater height and with greater hope, and to stay awake so as to recognize what is called for in this moment. The bottom line is that the ongoing process of growing, balancing, and integrating these enduring virtues (each of us in our unique way) helps us live this life more deeply and with more vitality so that in the end we don't discover that we had not really lived.

As mentioned at the beginning of our journey, these four essential virtues—Presence, Heart, Wisdom, and Creation—form a matrix for growing our humanity and finding our way. These inner arts and inner technologies do not give us wisdom but instead give us the capacity to act wisely. They do not give us beauty; instead, they enable the shift in attention and appreciation that opens consciousness to perceive beauty. They do not make us good, but they help us find the ground for compassionate action. They do not give us creativity, but they help us imagine and use our own. These essential powers manifest through the center of our lives as we embody them in the world.

This field guide to the inner life does not prescribe one path or one truth over others. We're reminded by Krishnamurti about the notion that "truth is a pathless land."[1] As Thomas Merton said, "I have no program for this seeing."[2] Nor does this guide push one formula, belief, or technique, although we may employ all sorts of practices and ideas. The bottom line is that life is the spiritual curriculum, right here, right now. Merton hinted at it this way: "Heaven's gate is everywhere."[3]

What *is* required is that we live our own life deeply. And in doing so, life itself lives through us. To realize the depth of our humanity and through it our divinity, to get the most for our money does take certain energy, certain inner capacities, powers of mind and heart, body, and soul. In turn, these help call forth the fullness of our being—our genius and joy, love and creativity—at a time when the world needs all it can get.

Our great models, such as Jesus, Buddha, and so many more, show us that this deeper life is not only possible for some but within reach for all. Jesus told us that the "kingdom is within." Buddha tells us likewise that our *true nature* is within us already—wise, perfect, compassionate—and that we must do our own work to awaken it. The greater life is both within us and within our reach. We start wherever we are, with whatever we have, and from there move inward to the depths of our being to find ourselves on the doorstep of all humanity. Once we recognize and grow these fundamental powers and medicines, we can live in an extraordinary way. This process isn't all sunshine, but it does come with integrity and energy, tenderness and insight, hope and healing. Each of our paths is our own, but all journeys require certain powers of body and soul in order for us to make the most of the trip. These universal virtues help us show up for our deepest life.

ACKNOWLEDGMENTS

Although there are many friends and colleagues who have in one way or another influenced this work and for whom I am very grateful, I want to reserve special thanks here for just a few. First, I want to acknowledge the support and freedom given from the Department of Psychology at the University of West Georgia, a place where the inner life and outer responsibility remain central. I am thankful for my colleagues and especially graduate students who have been at the heart of many dialogues this work has grown from.

My own children, Haley and Maia, have been and remain profound teachers. In many ways, this work really has been about listening to and imagining what they (alongside the rest of us) might need in order to find their way.

Special thanks to Emily Han for her sense of vision and depth. Thanks to Sylvia Spratt for her keen eye, to Henry Covey for his expert editorial touch, and to Ken Lewis and Laura Fenley for their sharp minds and big hearts. My sincere appreciation to David Rome for his important feedback on an early version of this book.

It is sometimes hard to remember exactly how some things get their start. But I think it's fair to say that this work really began with Mary Mance Hart many years ago. She had a sense of vision and wisdom for what is most important in a life and the deep commitment to be of service in the world. Although I get to put my name on it, in so many ways this has been a collaborative project of heart and mind, and she is to get much of the credit for it.

INDEX: QUIZZES
AND PRACTICES

Wisdom

Creation

NOTES

Preface

1. Martin Buber, *The Legend of the Baal-Shem*, trans. Maurice Friedman (Princeton, NJ: Princeton University Press, 1995), 36.

Introduction

1. Leading Causes of Death, FastStats for the US 2010, Centers for Disease Control and Prevention, www.cdc.gov/nchs/fastats/lcod.htm. The influence of stress on these causes of death (heart disease, cancer, chronic lower respiratory disease, and stroke) has been widely recognized. For an excellent overview of mind-body interaction, see Henry Dreher, *Mind-Body Unity: A New Vision for Mind-Body Science and Medicine* (Baltimore: Johns Hopkins University Press, 2003).

2. US and World Population Clock, United States Census Bureau: Measuring America—People, Places, and Our Economy, accessed August 2013, www.census.gov/popclock.

3. "Globally Almost 870 Million Chronically Undernourished—New Hunger Report," Food and Agriculture Organization of the United Nations, accessed September 6, 2013, http://www.fao.org/news/story/en/item/161819/icode/.

4. Ronald Kessler, Patricia Berglund, Olga Demler, Robert Jin, Kathleen R. Merikangas, and Ellen E. Walters, "Lifetime Prevalence and Age-of-Onset Distributions of DSM-IV Disorders in the National Comorbidity Survey Replication," *Archives of General Psychiatry* 62, no. 6 (2005): 593.

5. Antoine de Saint-Exupéry, *The Little Prince,* trans. R. Howard (New York: Harcourt, 2000), 63, original work published 1943.

6. John Muir, *John of the Mountains: The Unpublished Journals of John Muir,* ed. Linnie Marsh. Wolfe (Madison: University of Wisconsin Press, 1979), 92, original work published 1938.

7. "Matrix," in *Online Etymology Dictionary,* http://www.etymonline.com.

8. Matthew Fox, *Wrestling with the Prophets: Essays on Creation, Spirituality, and Everyday Life* (San Francisco: HarperSanFrancisco, 1995), 93.

9. Johann Wolfgang von Goethe, excerpt from *Atmosphäre,* cited in Paul Bishop *Analytical Psychology and German Classical Aesthetics: Goethe, Schiller, and Jung,* vol. 1 (New York: Routledge, 2008), 48.

1: The Beautiful

1. Norman Maclean, *A River Runs Through It* (Chicago: University Press, 1989), 1.
2. Ibid., 45.
3. Ibid., 160.
4. Roberto Assagioli, *Psychosynthesis: A Manual of Principles and Techniques* (New York: Hobbs, Dorman, 1965), 283.
5. Alfred North Whitehead, *Adventures of Ideas* (New York: Penguin, 1967), 324.
6. Robert M. Augros and George N. Stanciu, *The New Story of Science: Mind and the Universe* (Lake Bluff, IL: Regnery Gateway, 1984), 39.
7. Henri Poincaré, *Science and Method,* trans. Francis Maitland (Mineola, NY: Dover, 2003), 22, original work published 1914.
8. Clive Staples Lewis, *The Weight of Glory* (London: Society for Promoting Christian Knowledge, 1942), 8, preached originally as a sermon in the Church of St. Mary the Virgin, Oxford, UK, June 8, 1942.
9. William Blake, "The Marriage of Heaven and Hell," in *Complete Writings,* ed. Blake Geoffrey Keynes (London: Oxford University Press, 1966), 154.
10. Warren Zevon, "Interview with David Letterman," *The Late Show with David Letterman,* episode aired October 30, 2002 (CBS, 2002).
11. Gene Weingarten, "Pearls Before Breakfast: Can One of the Nation's Great Musicians Cut Through the Fog of a D.C. Rush Hour? Let's Find Out," *Washington Post,* April 8, 2007, http://www.washingtonpost.com/wp-dyn/content/article/2007/04/04/AR2007040401721.html.
12. Rollo May, *The Courage to Create* (New York: Norton, 1975), 46.
13. Ibid., 91.

14. Nicholas Carr, *The Shallows: What the Internet Is Doing to Our Brains* (New York: Norton, 2010).

15. T. S. Eliot, *Four Quartets* (New York: Harcourt, Brace, and World, 1971), 18.

16. John David Sinclair, *The Rest Principle: A Neurophysiological Theory of Behavior* (Hillsdale, NJ: Erlbaum Associates, 1981).

2: Sensing

1. *Wings of Desire*, directed by Wim Wenders (Cologne: Westdeutscher Rundfunk, 1987).

2. Peter Kingsley, "Common Sense: An Interview by Lorraine Kisly & Christopher Bamford," *Parabola* 31, no. 1 (2006): 24–30.

3. Candace B. Pert, "The Wisdom of the Receptors: Neuropeptides, the Emotions, and Bodymind," *Advances* 3, no. 3 (1986): 8–16.

4. Antoine Bechara, Hanna Damasio, Daniel Tranel, and Antonio R. Damasio, "Deciding Advantageously Before Knowing the Advantageous Strategy," *Science* 275, no. 5304 (1997): 1293–1295.

5. Malcolm Gladwell, *Blink: The Power of Thinking Without Thinking* (New York: Little, Brown, 2005).

6. Antonio R. Damasio, *Descartes' Error: Emotion, Reason, and the Human Brain* (New York: HarperCollins, 1994).

7. Mark Johnson, *The Body in the Mind: The Bodily Basis of Meaning, Imagination, and Reason* (Chicago: University of Chicago Press, 1990), 102.

8. Eugene T. Gendlin, *Focusing* (New York: Bantam Books, 1988).

9. Daniel J. Siegel, *Mindsight: The New Science of Personal Transformation* (New York: Bantam, 2010).

10. Pierre Teilhard de Chardin, *Toward the Future*, trans. R. Hague (New York: Harcourt Brace Jovanovich, 1975), 86–87, original work published 1973.

11. Jacques Lusseyran, *And There Was Light: Autobiography of Jacques Lusseyran, Blind Hero of the French Resistance*, trans. Elizabeth R. Cameron (Boston: Little, Brown, 1963), 16–18.

12. Ibid., 18–20.

13. Ibid., 20–21.

14. Richard E. Cytowic, *Synesthesia: A Union of the Senses* (Cambridge, MA: MIT Press, 2002).

15. Maurice Merleau-Ponty, *Phenomenology of Perception*, trans. Colin Smith (New York: Humanities Press, 1962), 205.

16. As cited in Evelyn Underhill, *Mysticism: A Study in the Nature and Development of Man's Spiritual Consciousness* (New York: E. P. Dutton, 1961), 7, original work published 1911.

17. As cited in William James, *The Principles of Psychology* (New York: Henry Holt, 1893), 255.

18. Marc O. Ernst and Heinrich H. Bülthoff, "Merging the Senses into a Robust Percept," *Trends in Cognitive Sciences* 8, no. 4 (2004): 162–169.

19. Maurice Merleau-Ponty, "Eye and Mind," trans. Carleton Dallery, *The Primacy of Perception: And Other Essays on Phenomenological Psychology, the Philosophy of Art, History and Politics*, ed. James M. Edie (Evanston, IL: Northwestern University Press, 1964), 164.

20. Marghanita Laski, *Ecstasy: A Study of Some Secular and Religious Experiences* (New York: Greenwood Press, 1968).

21. Thomas Berry, *The Great Work: Our Way Into the Future* (New York: Bell Tower, 1999), 12.

22. Richard Louv, *Last Child in the Woods: Saving Our Children from Nature-Deficit Disorder* (Chapel Hill, NC: Algonquin Books, 2004).

23. Gendlin, *Focusing*, 43–45.

3: Focusing

1. Steven Levy, "(Some) Attention Must Be Paid!" *Newsweek*, March 27, 2006.

2. Thomas Merton, *A Thomas Merton Reader* (Garden City, NY: Image Books, 1974), original work published 1938.

3. Julia Cameron, *The Artist's Way: A Spiritual Path to Higher Creativity* (Los Angeles: Jeremy P. Tarcher/Perigee, 1992), 53.

4. Ibid.

5. William James, *The Principles of Psychology* (New York: Henry Holt, 1890), 424.

6. Michael Murphy and Steven Donovan, *The Physical and Psychological Effects of Meditation with a Comprehensive Bibliography, 1931–1996*, 2nd ed. (Petaluma, CA: Institute of Noetic Sciences 1997).

7. Jon Kabat-Zinn, *Full Catastrophe Living: Using the Wisdom of Your Body and Mind to Face Stress, Pain, and Illness* (New York: Delacorte, 1990).

8. R. J. Davidson, et al., "Alternations in Brain and Immune Function Produced by Mindfulness Meditation." *Psychosomatic Medicine* 65, no. 4 (2003) 564–570.

9. Sara W. Lazar, Catherine E. Kerr, Rachel H. Wasserman, Jeremy R. Gray, Douglas N. Greve, Michael T. Treadway, Metta McGarvey et al., "Meditation Experience Is Associated with Increased Cortical Thickness," *Neuroreport* 16, no. 17 (2005): 1893.

10. Mihaly Csikszentmihalyi, *Flow: The Psychology of Optimal Experience* (New York: Harper, 2008).

11. Peter L. Nelson, "Personality Factors in the Frequency of Reported Spontaneous Praeternatural Experience," *Journal of Transpersonal Psychology* 21, no. 2 (1989): 193–209.

12. Thich Nhat Hanh, *The Miracle of Mindfulness*, trans. Mobi Ho, rev. ed. (Boston: Beacon, 1999).

13. Adapted from Thomas Keating, *Open Mind, Open Heart: Contemplative Dimension of the Gospel* (New York: Continuum, 2006).

4: Witnessing

1. Meister Eckhart, *Meister Eckhart: Selected Treatises and Sermons,* trans. James Midgley Clark and John Vass Skinner (London: Faber & Faber, 1958).

2. Francisco J. Varela, Evan T. Thompson, and Eleanor Rosch, *The Embodied Mind: Cognitive Science and Human Experience* (Cambridge, MA: MIT Press, 1993), 30.

3. Ibid., 122.

4. Jacob Raber, "Detrimental Effects of Chronic Hypothalamic-Pituitary-Adrenal Axis Activation: From Obesity to Memory Deficit," *Molecular Neurobiology* 18, no. 1 (1998): 1–22.

5. Juan F. López, Delia M. Vazquez, Derek T. Chalmers, and Stanley J. Watson, "Regulation of 5-HT Receptors and the Hypothalamic-Pituitary-Adrenal Axis: Implications for the Neurobiology of Suicide," *Annals of the New York Academy of Sciences* 29, no. 836 (1997): 106–134.

6. Christopher RK. Maclean, Kenneth G. Walton, Stig R. Wenneberg, Debra K. Levitsky, Joseph V. Mandarino, Rafiq Waziri, et al., "Effects of the Transcendental Meditation Program on Adaptive Mechanisms: Changes in Hormone Levels and Responses to Stress After 4 Months of Practice," *Psychoneuroendocrinology* 22, no.4 (1997): 277–295.

7. Marianne Williamson, *A Return to Love: Reflections on the Principles in a Course on Miracles* (New York: HarperCollins, 1992), 165. Though attributed to Mandela's inaugural speech, the original source is actually Williamson.

8. Henry David Thoreau, *Walden, or, Life in the Woods* (Boston: Houghton Mifflin Company, 1910), 101, original work published 1893.

5: Opening

1. As cited in Eve Curie, *Madame Curie: A Biography,* trans. Vincent Sheean (Garden City, NY: Doubleday, Doran, 1937), 341.

2. As cited in Evelyn Fox Keller, *A Feeling for the Organism: The Life and Work of Barbara McClintock* (San Francisco: W.H. Freeman, 1983), 198.

3. Matthew 18:3 (Gideons International Version).

4. Abraham Heschel, *God in Search of Man: A Philosophy of Judaism* (New York: Octagon, 1972), 74–75, original work published 1955.

5. William Blake, "The Marriage of Heaven and Hell," in *Complete Writings,* ed. Blake Geoffrey Keynes (London: Oxford University Press, 1966), 154.

6. Roger Walsh, *Essential Spirituality: The 7 Central Practices to Awaken Heart and Mind* (New York: J.Wiley, 1999), 231.

7. Carl Gustav Jung, *Modern Man in Search of a Soul* (Oxon, UK: Routledge, 2001), 240, original work published 1933.

8. Tobin Hart, "Opening the Contemplative Mind in the Classroom," *Journal of Transformative Education* 2, no. 1 (2004): 28, doi: 10.1177/1541344603259311.

6: The Good

1. Antoine de Saint-Exupéry, *The Little Prince,* trans R. Howard (New York: Harcourt, 2000), 63, original work published 1943.

2. Rabindranath Tagore, *Rabindranath Tagore, Pioneer in Education: Essays and Exchanges between Rabindranath Tagore and L. K. Elmhirst* (London: Murray, 1961), 57.

3. St. Aurelius Augustine from the 7th Sermon on the 1st Letter of St. John.

4. Huang Po, *The Zen Teaching of Huang Po: On the Transmission of Mind,* trans. John Blofeld (New York: Grove Press, 1958), 19.

5. Hyemeyohsts Storm, *Seven Arrows* (New York: Ballantine Books, 1972), 6.

6. Evelyn Fox Keller, *A Feeling for the Organism: The Life and Work of Barbara McClintock* (San Francisco: W. H. Freeman, 1983), 198.

7. Hillel, Babylonian Talmud, *Shabbat* 31a.

8. Mahabharata 5:1517.

9. Confucius, *Analects* 15:23.

10. Epictetus, as cited in Lucien F. Cosijns, *Dialogue Among the Faith Communities* (Lanham, MD: Hamilton Book, 2008), 130.

11. Black Elk, *The Sacred Pipe: Black Elk's Account of the Seven Rites of the Oglala Sioux*, ed. Joseph Epes Brown (Norman: University of Oklahoma Press, 1953), 74–75.

12. Jalal al-Din Rumi, *Rumi: The Book of Love: Poems of Ecstasy and Longing,* trans. Coleman Barks (New York: HarperCollins, 2003), 123.

13. Tobin Hart, *The Secret Spiritual World of Children* (Novato, CA: New World, 2003), 70.

14. C. Powers, "Get Together," performed by the Youngbloods, 1963, compact disc (London: Edsel Records UK. 1967).

15. St. Augustin, *St. Augustin Anti-Pelagian Writings: Nicene and Post-Nicene Fathers of the Christian Church,* ed. Philip Schaff (Whitefish, MT: Kessinger 2004).

16. Morgan Scott Peck, *The Road Less Traveled: A New Psychology of Love, Traditional Values and Spiritual Growth*, 25th anniversary ed. (New York: Simon & Schuster, 2003), 81.

17. bell hooks, *All About Love: New Visions* (New York: Harper Perennial, 2001), 13.
18. Peck, *Road Less Traveled*, 83.
19. Ira Progoff, *The Symbolic and The Real: A New Psychological Approach to the Fuller Experience of Personal Existence* (New York: Julian, 1963), 165–166.
20. Pierre Teilhard de Chardin, *Toward the Future*, trans. R. Hague (New York: Harcourt Brace Jovanovich, 1975), 86–87, original work published 1973.
21. Pierre Teilhard de Chardin, *The Phenomenon of Man*, trans. Bernard Wall (New York: Harper, 1959), 250–75.

7: Compassion

1. Hanna Taylor, "Who We Are: Hannah Taylor, Founder," The Ladybug Foundation, http://www.ladybugfoundation.ca/who-we-are/hannah-taylor-founder/.
2. David Loye, "Darwin, Maslow, and the Fully Human Theory of Evolution," in *The Great Adventure: Toward a Fully Human Theory of Evolution*, ed. David Loye (Albany: State University of New York Press, 2004), 10.
3. Karen Armstrong, *The Case for God* (New York: Knopf, 2009).
4. David Bohm, *Wholeness and the Implicate Order* (Boston: Routledge & Kegan Paul, 1980).
5. Ibid., 172.
6. Gregory Bateson, *Mind and Nature: A Necessary Unity* (New York: Bantam Books, 1980), 8.
7. Ervin László, *Science and the Akashic Field: An Integral Theory of Everything* (Rochester, VT: Inner Traditions, 2004).
8. Pierre Teilhard de Chardin, *The Future of Man*, trans. Norman Denny (London: Collins, 1964).
9. Rupert Sheldrake, *Morphic Resonance: The Nature of Formative Causation*, 4th ed. (Rochester, VT: Park Street, 2009).
10. Rupert Sheldrake, *Dogs That Know When Their Owners Are Coming Home: And Other Unexplained Powers of Animals* (New York: Crown, 1999).
11. Peter Senge, Otto C. Scharmer, Joseph Jaworski, and Betty Sue Flowers, *Presence: An Exploration of Profound Change in People, Organizations, and Society* (New York: Doubleday, 2005), 188.
12. Nicholas Black Elk and John Gneisenau Neihardt, *Black Elk Speaks: Being the Life Story of a Holy Man of the Oglala Sioux*, as told through John G. Neihardt, 21st century ed. (Lincoln: University of Nebraska Press, 2000), 33, original work published 1932.
13. Richard Carlson and Benjamin Shield, eds., *For the Love of God: New Writings by Spiritual and Psychological Leaders* (San Rafael, CA: New World Library, 1990), 151.

14. A. J. Deikman, "Service as a Way of Knowing," in *Transpersonal Knowing: Exploring the Horizon of Consciousness,* eds. Tobin Hart, Peter L. Nelson, and Kaisa Puhakka, (Albany: State University of New York Press, 2000), 303–318.

15. Tobin Hart, *The Secret Spiritual World of Children* (Novato, CA: New World, 2003), 73.

8: Empathizing

1. Martin Hoffman, "Empathy and Justice Motivation," *Motivation and Emotion,* 4, no. 2 (1990): 151–172.

2. Beth Azar, "Defining the Trait That Makes Us Human," *APA Monitor* 28, no. 11 (1997): 1–15.

3. Martin Buber, *I and Thou,* trans. R. G. Smith, 2nd ed. (New York: Scribner, 1958), 11, original work published 1923.

4. Albert-László Barabási, *Linked: The New Science of Networks* (Cambridge, MA: Perseus Books, 2002).

5. Steven Strogatz, *Sync: How Order Emerges From Chaos in the Universe, Nature, and Daily Life* (New York: Hyperion, 2003).

6. Ferdinand Binkofski and Giovanni Buccino, "Therapeutic Reflection," *Scientific American Mind* 2007, http://www.scientificamerican.com/article.cfm?id=thera peutic-reflection.

7. Mary Gordon, *Roots of Empathy: Changing the World Child by Child* (Toronto: Thomas Allen, 2005).

8. Ibid., 6.

9. Daniel J. Siegel, *Mindsight: The New Science of Personal Transformation* (New York: Bantam, 2010), 67.

10. Paul Ekman, *Emotions Revealed: Recognizing Faces and Feelings to Improve Communication and Emotional Life* (New York: Henry Holt, 2004).

11. Carl Rogers, *A Way of Being* (Boston: Houghton Mifflin, 1980), 129.

12. Ibid.

13. Buber, *I and Thou,* 11.

14. Martin Heidegger, *Basic Writings: From* Being and Time *(1927) to* The Task of Thinking *(1964),* ed. David Farrell Krell (New York: Harper & Row, 1977), 178.

15. Thich Nhat Hanh, *The Heart of Understanding: Commentaries on the Prajna-paramita Heart Sutra,* ed. Peter Levitt (Berkeley: Parallax Press, 1988), 3.

16. Parker J. Palmer, *To Know As We Are Known: Education As a Spiritual Journey* (San Francisco: HarperSanFrancisco, 1993), 23.

17. William James, *A Pluralistic Universe* (Cambridge, MA: Harvard University Press, 1977), 19, original work published 1909.

18. Thomas Berry, *The Great Work: Our Way Into the Future* (New York: Random House, 1999), 82.

19. Evelyn Fox Keller, *A Feeling for the Organism: The Life and Work of Barbara McClintock* (San Francisco: W. H. Freeman, 1983).

9: Feeling

1. Meister Eckhart, *Meister Eckhart*, vol. 2, ed. Charles F. Pfeiffer, trans. C. D. B. Evans (London: J. M. Watkins, 1952).
2. Romans 5:3–4 (English Standard Version).
3. Mary Caroline Richards, *Centering in Pottery, Poetry, and the Person*, 2nd ed. (Middletown, CT: Wesleyan University Press, 1989), 36, original work published 1962.
4. Jalal Al-Din Rumi, *The Essential Rumi*, trans. Coleman Barks (New York: Harper One, 1995), 109.
5. Thich Nhat Hanh, *Breathe! You Are Alive: The Sutra on the Full Awareness of Breathing* (Berkeley: Parallax, 2008), 52.
6. As cited in Mary Strong, *Letters of the Scattered Brotherhood* (New York: Harper, 1948), 34.
7. Stefanie P. Spera, Eric D. Buhrfeind, and James W. Pennebaker, "Expressive Writing and Coping with Job Loss," *Academy of Management Journal* 37, no. 3 (1994): 722–733.
8. Eugene Gendlin, "Crossing and Dipping: Some Terms for Approaching the Interface Between National Understanding and Logical Formation" (unpublished manuscript, University of Chicago, 1991), 38, in Mark Johnson, *The Meaning of the Body: Aesthetics of Human Understanding,* (Chicago: University of Chicago Press, 2007), 82.
9. David Creswell, et al., "Neural Correlates of Dispositional Mindfulness during Affect Labeling," *Psychosomatic Medicine* 69, no. 6 (2007): 560–65.
10. Daniel J. Siegel, *Mindsight: The New Science of Personal Transformation* (New York: Bantam, 2010).
11. Daniel Goleman, *Emotional Intelligence* (New York: Bantam, 1995), 35–36.
12. Christine Lagorio, "Resources: Marketing to Kids," CBS News (February 11, 2009), http://cbsnews.com/stories/2007/05/14/fyi/main2798401.shtml.
13. Stephen Levine, *Who Dies? An Investigation of Conscious Living and Conscious Dying* (New York: Anchor, 1982), 192.
14. Jiddu Krishnamurti, *Krishnamurti on Education* (New York: Harper & Row, 1974), 61.
15. Darrin M. McMahon, *Happiness: A History* (New York: Atlantic Monthly, 2006).
16. Martin E.P. Seligman, *Authentic Happiness: Using the New Positive Psychology to Realize Your Potential for Lasting Fulfillment* (New York: Free Press, 2002).
17. Mihaly Csikszentmihalyi, *Flow: The Psychology of Optimal Experience* (New York: Harper & Row, 1990).

18. Richard J. Davidson, "Well-Being and Affective Style: Neural Substrates and Bio-Behavioral Correlates," *Philosophical Transactions of the Royal Society* 359, no. 1449 (2004); 1395–1411.

19. Christopher Peterson, Nansook Park, and Martin E.P. Seligman, "Orientations to Happiness and Life Satisfaction: The Full Life versus the Empty Life," *Journal of Happiness Studies* 6, no. 1 (2005): 25–41.

20. Bronnie Ware, *The Top Five Regrets of the Dying: A Life Transformed by the Dearly Departing* (Carlsbad, CA: Hay House, 2012).

10: Connecting

1. Alan Cohen, *Wisdom o the Heart* (Carlsbad, CA: Hay House, 2002), 4.

2. John Bowlby, *Attachment and Loss*, vol. 1 (New York: Basic Books, 1969).

3. Ibid., 69–70.

4. René A. Spitz, "Hospitalism: An Inquiry Into the Genesis of Psychiatric Conditions in Early Childhood," *Psychoanalytic Study of the Child* 1 (1945): 53–74.

5. Ibid., 70.

6. Mary D. Salter Ainsworth, Mary C. Blehar, Everett Waters, and Sally Wall, *Patterns of Attachment: A Psychological Study of the Strange Situation* (Hillsdale, NJ: Laurence Erlbaum Associates,1978).

7. Thomas Lewis, Fari Amini, and Richard Lannon, *A General Theory of Love* (New York: Vintage, 2001), 74.

8. Daniel J. Siegel, *Mindsight: The New Science of Personal Transformation* (New York: Guilford Press, 1999), xvii, 26–30.

9. Lewis, Amini, and Lannon, *A General Theory of Love*, 74.

10. Ibid., 80.

11. Kerstin Uvnas Moberg, *The Oxytocin Factor: Tapping the Hormone of Calm, Love, and Healing* (Cambridge, MA: Da Capo Press, 2003), 176.

12. Daniel J. Siegel, *Mindsight: The New Science of Personal Transformation* (New York: Bantam, 2010).

13. Richard Maurice Bucke, *Cosmic Consciousness: A Study in the Evolution of the Human Mind* (Cambridge: Cambridge University Press, 2010), 61, original work published 1901.

14. Eben Alexander, *Proof of Heaven: A Neurosurgeon's Journey into the Afterlife* (New York: Simon & Schuster, 2012).

15. Tobin Hart, *The Secret Spiritual World of Children* (Novato, CA: New World, 2003), 57.

16. Dorothy Day, *The Long Loneliness: The Autobiography of Dorothy Day* (San Francisco: Harper & Row, 1981), 286, original work published 1952.

17. Riane Eisler, *The Chalice and the Blade: Our History, Our Future* (New York: Harper & Row, 1988), xix.

18. Ibid., xvii.
19. Ibid., xvii.
20. Martin Luther King Jr., *A Testament of Hope: The Essential Writings and Speeches of Martin Luther King Jr.*, ed. James M. Washington (San Francisco: HarperSanFrancisco, 1991), 253, original work published 1986.
21. Ibid., 254.
22. M. Scott Peck, *The Different Drum: Community-Making and Peace* (New York: Touchstone, 1988), 17.
23. St. Augustine, *Confessions*, trans. R. S. Pine-Coffin (New York: Penguin Books, 1961), 39.

11: The True

1. Thomas Gilby, ed. *St. Thomas Aquinas Philosophical Texts* (New York: Oxford University Press, 1967).
2. Merton M. Sealts, *Emerson on the Scholar* (Columbia: University of Missouri Press, 1992), 257.
3. Paul B. Baltes and Jacqui Smith. "Toward a Psychology of Wisdom and Its Ontogenesis," in *Wisdom: Its Nature, Origins, and Development*, ed. Robert J. Sternberg (New York: Cambridge University Press, 1990), 87–120.
4. Abraham Joshua Heschel, *God in Search of Man: A Philosophy of Judaism* (New York: Octagon Books, 1972), 78, original work published 1955.
5. Robert J. Sternberg, ed. *Wisdom: Its Nature, Origins, and Development* (New York: Cambridge University Press, 1990).
6. Heschel, *God in Search of Man*, 78.
7. Umberto Eco, *The Name of the Rose*, trans. William Weaver (London: Picador, 1984), 492.
8. Morris Berman, *Wandering God: A Study in Nomadic Spirituality* (Albany: State University of New York Press, 2000), 148.
9. Oldenberg Hermann Palmer, trans., *The Qur'an.* (Delhi: Motilal Banarsidass, 1965).
10. Gershom Scholem, *Zohar: The Book of Splendor* (New York: Schocken Books, 1995) 79, original work published 1949, 79.
11. Nathaniel Needle, "The Six Paramitas: Outline for a Buddhist Education," *Encounter: Education for Meaning and Social Justice* 12, no. 1 (1999): 9–21.
12. Don E. Marietta, *Introduction to Ancient Philosophy* (Armonk, NY: ME Sharpe Inc, 1998), 82.

12: Possibility

1. Walter J. Freeman, "The Physiology of Perception," *Scientific American* 264, no. 2 (1991); 78–85.

2. Roger Bannister, *The Four-Minute Mile* (Guilford, CT: Lyons Press 2004), original work published 1955.

3. Ibid.

4. Jerome Groopman, *The Anatomy of Hope: How People Prevail in the Face of Illness* (New York: Random House, 2003).

5. Curt P. Richter, "The Phenomenon of Unexplained Sudden Death in Animals and Man," *Psychosomatic Medicine* 19 (1957): 191–198.

6. Richard J. Finneran and George Mills Harped, eds., *The Collected Works of W. B. Yeats* (New York: Collier Books, 1983), 180–190.

7. Viktor Frankl, *Man's Search for Meaning: An Introduction to Logotherapy* (Boston: Beacon, 1992), 113–114, original work published 1959.

8. Groopman, *Anatomy of Hope*.

9. David Michael Levin, "The Discursive Formation of the Human Body in the History of Medicine," *Journal of Medicine and Philosophy* 15, no. 5 (1990): 515–537.

10. Dante Alighieri, *The Divine Comedy,* trans J. F. Cotter (Washington, DC: Lilian Barber Press, 1988), 13.

11. Friedrich Nietzsche, *Beyond Good and Evil: Prelude to a Philosophy of the Future*, trans. Reginald John Hollingdale (New York: Penguin, 1990), 102, original work published 1886.

13: Guidance

1. Jiddu Krishnamurti, "The Core of the Teachings," Jiddu Krishnamurti Online, http://www.jkrishnamurti.org/about-krishnamurti/the-core-of-the-teachings .php.

2. Fred Kofman, *Conscious Business: How to Build Value Through Values* (Boulder: Sounds True, 2006), 158.

3. Ibid., 159.

4. Ghose Aurobindo, *The Essential Aurobindo*, ed. Robert A. McDermott (Hudson, NY: Lindisfarne, 1987), 149.

5. Meister Eckhart, *Meister Eckhart: The Essential Sermons, Treatises, and Defense* (Mahwah, NJ: Paulist Press, 1981), 240.

6. Ralph Waldo Emerson, "The Oversoul," eds. Joseph Slater and Alfred Riggs Ferguson, vol. 2, *The Collected Works* (Cambridge, MA: Belknap Press of Harvard University Press, 1979), 157–175, original work published 1841.

7. Roberto Assagioli, *The Act of Will* (New York: Penguin Books, 1973), 11.

8. H. Larry Ingle, *First Among Friends: George Fox and the Creation of Quakerism* (New York: Oxford University Press, 1994).

9. William Penn, as cited in Aldous Huxley, *The Perennial Philosophy* (New York: Harper & Row, 1945), 14.

10. Mitchell B. Liester, "Inner Voices: Distinguishing Transcendent and Pathological Characteristics," *Journal of Transpersonal Psychology* 28, no. 1 (1996).

11. Ibid.

12. Tobin Hart, *The Secret Spiritual World of Children*. (Novato, CA: New World Library, 2003), 30.

13. Rupert Sheldrake, *The Presence of the Past: Morphic Resonance and the Habits of Nature* (South Paris, ME: Park Street Press, 1995).

14. Ludwig von Bertalanffy, *General System Theory: Foundations, Development, Applications* (New York: G. Braziller, 1968).

15. Daniel Goleman, *Social Intelligence: The New Science of Human Relationships* (New York: Random House, 2006); Daniel Siegel, *The Developing Mind: How Relationships and the Brain Interact to Shape Who We Are* (New York: Guilford Press, 1999).

16. Michio Kaku, "What Happened Before the Big Bang?" *Astronomy* 24, no. 5 (1996), 34–41.

17. Erwin Schrödinger, *What Is Life? The Physical Aspect of the Living Cell* (Cambridge: Cambridge University Press, 1945), 135.

18. William James, *Principles of Psychology*, vol 1 (Mineola, NY: Dover Publications, 1950), original work published 1890.

14: Clarifying

1. Robert C. Douthit, "Interview with Mattie Stepanek," *Larry King Live,* episode aired February 17, 2003 (Los Angeles: Cable News Network, 2003).

2. Mattie J. Stepanek, *Hope through Heartsongs* (New York: Hyperion, 2002), 49.

3. I Corinthians 13, New International Version.

4. Idries Shah, *The Exploits of the Incomparable Mulla Nasrudin* (London: The Octagon Press, 1966), 9.

5. Plato, *Apology* 38a.

6. Thomas Merton, *What Is Contemplation?* (Springfield, IL: Templegate, 1978), 183, original work published 1948.

7. Peter Fenner, *The Ontology of the Middle Way* (Dordrecht, Holland: Kluwer, 1991).

8. R. A. Johnson, *Owning Your Own Shadow: Understanding the Dark Side of the Psyche* (San Francisco: HarperCollins, 1991), 9.

9. Morris Berman, *Wandering God: A Study in Nomadic Spirituality* (Albany: State University of New York Press, 2000), 8.

10. Georg Wilhelm Friedrich Hegel, *The Logic of Hegel: Translated from the Encyclopaedia of Philosophical Sciences*, 2nd ed., trans. William Wallace (Oxford: University Press, 1904), 149, original work published 1873.

11. Amy Arnsten, "The Biology of Being Frazzled," *Science*, 280, no. 5370 (1998): 1711–1712.

12. Mary Caroline Richards, *Centering in Pottery, Poetry, and the Person, 2nd ed.* (Middleton, CT: Wesleyan University Press, 1989), 35, original work published 1962.

13. Margaret Gee, ed., *Words of Wisdom: Selected Quotes from His Holiness the Dalai Lama* (Kansas City, MO: Andrews McNeel, 2001), 23.

14. Adapted from Judith Brown, *The I in Science: Training to Utilize Subjectivity in Research* (Oslo: Scandinavian University Press, 1996).

15. Ibid.

15: Discerning

1. As cited in David Kelleher, *Get Down Off the Cross (We Need the Wood)* (Central Milton Keynes, UK: AuthorHouse, 2009), 27.

2. Randal Keynes, *Darwin, His Daughter and Human Evolution* (New York: Riverhead, 2001), 3.

3. Edward Robinson, *The Original Vision: A Study of the Religious Experiences of Childhood* (New York: Seabury, 1983), 133, original work published 1977.

4. Robert A. Johnson, *Balancing Heaven and Earth: A Memoir of Visions, Dreams, and Realization* (San Francisco: HarperSanFrancisco, 1998), 80.

5. Ibid., 80.

6. John E. Sarno, *Healing Back Pain: The Mind-Body Connection* (New York: Warner Books, 1991).

7. John of the Cross, *The Poems of Saint John of the Cross*, trans. John Frederick Nims, 3rd ed. (Chicago: University Press, 1979).

8. Richard Rorty, *Philosophy and the Mirror of Nature* (Princeton: Princeton University Press, 1979), 61.

9. Mary Caroline Richards, *Centering in Pottery, Poetry, and the Person*, 2nd ed. (Hanover, NH: Wesleyan University Press, 1989), 7, original work published 1962.

10. Patricia Kennedy Arlin, "Wisdom: The Art of Problem Finding," in *Wisdom: Its Nature, Origins, and Development*, ed. Robert J. Sternberg (New York: Cambridge University Press, 1990), 230–243.

11. David Bohm, "Insight, Knowledge, Science, and Human Values," in *Toward the Recovery of Wholeness: Knowledge, Education, and Human Values*, ed. Douglas Sloan (New York: Teachers College Press, 1981), 25.

12. Ibid., 25.

13. William Shakespeare, *The Complete Works of William Shakespeare*, vol. 6 (New York: Current Literature, 1909), 46, original work published 1602.

14. Pierre Hadot, *Philosophy As a Way of Life: Spiritual Exercises from Socrates to Foucault* (Malden, MA: Blackwell Publishing, 1995), 153.

15. Mary Catherine Bateson, "In Praise of Ambiguity," in *Education, Information, and Transformation: Essays on Learning and Thinking*, ed. Jeffrey Kane (Upper Saddle River, NJ: Prentice Hall, 1999), 133–146.

16. Rainer Maria Rilke, *Letters to a Young Poet*, trans. M. D. Herter Norton (New York: Norton, 1993), 35.

17. Kris Haig, "Discernment: The Art of Choosing God's Will," *Presbyterian Mission Agency,* http://www.pcusa.org/spiritualformation/discernment.pdf.

18. Rachel Livsey and Parker Palmer, *The Courage to Teach: A Guide for Reflection and Renewal*, (San Francisco: Jossey-Bass, 1999), 43–48.

16: Voice

1. Alfred North Whitehead, *The Aims of Education and Other Essays* (New York: The Free Press, 1967), 57, original work published 1929.

2. Joachim-Ernst Berendt, *Nada Brahma: The World Is Sound: Nada Brahma; Music and the Landscape of Consciousness,* trans. Helmut Bredigkeit (Rochester, VT: Destiny 1987).

3. Meister Eckhart, *Meditations with Meister Eckhart*, ed. Matthew Fox (Rochester, VT: Bear & Company, 1983), 74.

4. Ralph Waldo Emerson, *Journals of Ralph Waldo Emerson: 1820–1872*, vol. 3, eds. Edward Waldo Emerson, and Waldo Emerson Forbes (Boston: Houghton Mifflin Company, 1910), 305.

5. Nicholas Black Elk, *Black Elk Speaks: Being the Life Story of a Holy Man of the Oglala Sioux,* as told through John G. Neihardt, 21st century ed. (Lincoln: University of Nebraska Press, 1988), original work published 1932, 173.

6. Viktor Frankl, *Man's Search for Meaning: An Introduction to Logotherapy* (Boston: Beacon Press, 1959).

7. Daniel J. Levitin, *The World in Six Songs: How the Musical Brain Created Human Nature* (New York: Dutton, 2008), 18.

8. M. Wallace, introduction to *Dam-Burst of Dreams: The Writings of Christopher Nolan,* by Christopher Nolan (Athens: Ohio University Press, 1981), vii–xv.

9. John Carey, preface to *Under the Eye of the Clock: The Life Story of Christopher Nolan,* by Christopher Nolan (New York: St. Martin's Press, 1987), ix–xii.

10. Bernadette Nolan, as cited in *Dam-Burst of Dreams*, 2.

11. Nolan, *Dam-Burst of Dreams*, 27.

12. Bernadette Nolan, as cited in Wallace, introduction to *Dam-Burst of Dreams,* vii–xv.

13. Nolan, *Under the Eye of the Clock*, 31.

14. Ibid., 24.

15. Ibid., 27.
16. Ibid.
17. Ibid., 40.
18. Ibid., 57.
19. Johann Wolfgang von Goethe, as cited in Thomas Moore, preface to *The Heal-ing Runes: Tools for the Recovery of Body, Mind, Heart and Soul*, by Ralph H. Blum (New York: St. Martin's Press, 1995), xi–xvi.
20. William Shakespeare, *Hamlet*, in *Works*, vol. 1, ed. Horace Howard Furness, New Variorum ed. (Philadelphia: J. B. Lippincott Company, 1877), 204–207.

17: Will and Willingness

1. Malcolm Gladwell, *Outliers: The Story of Success*, (New York: Little, Brown, 2008), 224.
2. Daniel J. Levitin, *This Is Your Brain on Music: The Science of a Human Obsession* (New York: Dutton, 2006), 197.
3. Michael Howe, *Genius Explained* (Cambridge, MA: Cambridge University Press, 1999), 3.
4. Klaus Voorman and Astrid Kirchherr, *Hamburg Days* (Surrey, UK: Genesis, 1999), 122.
5. Gladwell, *Outliers*, 50.
6. Anne Lamott, *Bird by Bird: Some Instructions on Writing and Life* (New York: Anchor Books, 1995), 42.
7. Ibid., p. 42.
8. Rosamond Evelyn Mary Harding, *An Anatomy of Inspiration* (London: Frank Cass, 1967), 14.
9. Ibid.
10. As cited in Albert Bielschowsky, *The Life of Goethe* (New York: Putnam, 1908), 31.
11. Martin Heidegger, *Being and Time,* trans. John Macquarrie and Edward Robin-son (New York: Harper & Row, 1962), original work published 1927.
12. Albert Einstein, *The World As I See It* (New York: Covici, Friede, 1934), 14–15.
13. Gregg Levoy, *Callings: Finding and Following an Authentic Life* (New York: Three Rivers, 1997), 11.
14. Carolyn Blackmer, *Essays on Spiritual Psychology: Reflections on the Thought of Emanuel Swedenborg*, ed. Stephen Larsen (New York: Swedenborg Foundation, 1991), 17.

18: Originality

1. Tobin Hart, *From Information to Transformation*, rev. ed. (New York: Peter Lang, 2009), 63.

2. Paul Tillich, *Systematic Theology*, vol. 1, *Reason and Revelation: Being And God*(Chicago: University of Chicago Press, 1951).

3. Mary Caroline Richards, *Centering in Pottery, Poetry, and the Person*, 2nd ed. (Middletown, CT: Wesleyan University Press, 1989), 150, original work published 1962.

4. Rumi, in K. Overman-Edmiston, *The Avenue of Eternal Tranquility* (East Perth, Australia: Crumplestone, 2009), 224–225.

5. Martin Buber, *I and Thou*, trans. R. G. Smith (New York: Charles Scribner & Sons, 1958), 11, original work published 1923.

6. Anne Lamott, *Plan B: Further Thoughts on Faith* (New York: Penguin, 2005), 304.

7. William Shakespeare, *Hamlet*, in *Works*, vol. 1, ed. Horace Howard Furness, New Variorum ed. (Philadelphia: J. B. Lippincott Company, 1977), 70.

8. "Rosa Parks: Standing up for Freedom," American Academy of Achievement, last modified April 9, 2012, http://www.achievement.org/autodoc/page/par0bio-1.

9. Marshall B. Rosenberg, *Nonviolent Communication: A Language of Compassion*, (Encinitas, CA: PuddleDancer, 2003).

19: Imagining

1. Albert Einstein and Leopold Infeld, *The Evolution of Physics: The Growth of Ideas from Early Concepts to Relativity and Quanta* (New York: Simon & Schuster, 1938), 92.

2. George Sylvester Viereck, "What Life Means to Einstein: An Interview by George Sylvester Viereck," *Saturday Evening Post*, October 26, 1929.

3. Jonas Salk, *Anatomy of Reality: Merging of Intuition and Reason* (New York: Columbia University Press, 1983), 7.

4. Ibid., 7.

5. Joanne Kathleen Rowling, "The Fringe Benefits of Failure, and the Importance of Imagination," *Harvard Magazine*, (2008), http://harvardmagazine.com /commencement/the-fringe-benefits-failure-the-importance-imagination.

6. Robert J. Sternberg, "The Rainbow Project: Enhancing the SAT through Assessments of Analytical, Practical, and Creative Skills," *Intelligence* 34 (2006): 321–350.

7. Steven Ungerleider, *Mental Training for Peak Performance: Top Athletes Reveal the Mind Exercises They Use to Excel*, rev. ed. (New York: Rodale Press, 2005), original work published 1996.

8. Stephen J. Page, Jerzy P. Szaflarski, James C. Eliassen, Hai Pan, and Steven C. Cramer, "Cortical Plasticity Following Motor Skill Learning During Mental Practice in Stroke," *Neurorehabilitation and Neural Repair* 23, no. 4 (2009): 382–388.

9. James Hillman, *Archetypal Psychology: A Brief Account Together with a Complete Checklist of Works* (Dallas, TX: Spring Publications, 1988).

10. Henry Corbin, *Mundus Imaginalis: Or the Imaginary and the Imaginal*, trans. Ruth Horine (Ipswich, UK: Golgonooza Press, 1972), 1–19.

11. David Bohm, "Insight, Knowledge, Science, and Human Values," in *Toward the Recovery of Wholeness: Knowledge, Education, and Human Values*, ed. Douglas Sloan (New York: Teachers College Press, 1981), 8–30.

12. Evelyn Underhill, *Mysticism: A Study in the Nature and Development of Man's Spiritual Consciousness* (New York: E. P. Dutton, 1961), 75, original work published 1911. Underhill also clarifies the distinction between mystic and artist: "The true mystic is the person in whom such powers transcend the merely artistic and visionary stage, and are exalted to the point of genius: in whom the transcendental consciousness can dominate the normal consciousness," 75.

13. Ibid., 74.

14. Tobin Hart, *The Secret Spiritual World of Children* (Novato, CA: New World Library, 2003).

20: Calling

1. Laura Dove, "Elie Wiesel," Memory Made Manifest: The United States Holocaust Memorial Museum, June 1, 1995 http://xroads.virginia.edu/~cap/holo/eliebio.htm.

2. Agnes de Mille, *Martha: The Life and Work of Martha Graham* (New York: Random House, 1991), 264.

3. James Hillman, *The Soul's Code: In Search of Character and Calling* (New York: Random House, 1996).

4. Eleanor Roosevelt, *You Learn by Living* (New York: Harper and Bros., 1960), 18.

5. Hillman, *The Soul's Code*, 22.

6. "Soraida Salwala: Founder, Friends of the Asian Elephant (FAE) Elephant Hospital," The Eyes of Thailand, 2011, http://www.eyesofthailand.com/story/synopsis/.

7. Barbara Cooney, *Miss Rumphius* (New York: Puffin, 1985), 15, original work published 1982.

8. Karlfried Graf Durkheim, *The Way of Transformation: Daily Life as Spiritual Exercise* (London: Allen & Unwin, 1980).

9. Abraham Maslow, *Toward a Psychology of Being*, 2nd ed. (New York: Van Nostrand Reinhard, 1968), 102.

10. Abraham Maslow, *The Farther Reaches of Human Nature* (New York: Penguin, 1971), 35.

11. Henry David Thoreau, *Walden* (Boston: Houghton Mifflin, 1987), 143, original work published 1854.

12. Joseph Campbell, *The Power of Myth,* with Bill Moyers, ed. Betty S. Flowers (Garden City, NY: Anchor, 1991).

13. John of the Cross, *The Poems of St. John of the Cross,* trans. John Frederick Nims, 3rd ed. (Chicago: University of Chicago Press, 1979).

14. Wendell Berry, *Standing by Words: Essays* (Washington, DC: Shoemaker & Hoard, 2005), 97, original work published 1983.

15. John Gneisenau Neihardt, *Black Elk Speaks: Being the Life Story of a Holy Man of the Oglala Sioux* (Lincoln: University of Nebraska Press, 1988), original work published 1932, 33.

16. Adapted from "U Journaling Practice," Presencing Institute, http://www.presencing .com/tools/u-journaling.

Last Words

1. Jiddu Krishnamurti, "The Core of the Teachings," Jiddu Krishnamurti Online, http://www.jkrishnamurti.org/about-krishnamurti/the-core-of-the-teachings .php.

2. Thomas Merton, Thomas Merton, *Conjectures of a Guilty Bystander* (New York: Random House, 1965), 165.

3. Ibid.